T0271247

Conversations with
John Berryman

Literary Conversations Series
Monika Gehlawat
General Editor

Conversations with John Berryman

Edited by Eric Hoffman

University Press of Mississippi / Jackson

The University Press of Mississippi is the scholarly publishing agency of the Mississippi Institutions of Higher Learning: Alcorn State University, Delta State University, Jackson State University, Mississippi State University, Mississippi University for Women, Mississippi Valley State University, University of Mississippi, and University of Southern Mississippi.

www.upress.state.ms.us

The University Press of Mississippi is a member of the Association of University Presses.

First printing 2021
∞

Library of Congress Cataloging-in-Publication Data

Names: Berryman, John, 1914–1972, interviewee. | Hoffman, Eric R., editor.
Title: Conversations with John Berryman / Edited by Eric Hoffman.
Other titles: Literary conversations series.
Description: Jackson : University Press of Mississippi, 2021. | Series:
    Literary conversations series | Includes bibliographical references and index.
Identifiers: LCCN 2020047417 (print) | LCCN 2020047418 (ebook) |
    ISBN 9781496826343 (hardback) | ISBN 9781496826336 (trade paperback) |
    ISBN 9781496831453 (epub) | ISBN 9781496831460 (epub) | ISBN 9781496831477
    (pdf) | ISBN 9781496831484 (pdf)
Subjects: LCSH: Berryman, John, 1914–1972—Interviews. | Poets, American—
    20th century—Interviews.
Classification: LCC PS3503.E744 Z46 2021 (print) | LCC PS3503.E744 (ebook) |
    DDC 811/.54 [B]—dc23
LC record available at https://lccn.loc.gov/2020047417
LC ebook record available at https://lccn.loc.gov/2020047418

British Library Cataloging-in-Publication Data available

Works by John Berryman

Twenty Poems (1940)

Poems (1942)

The Dispossessed (1948)

Stephen Crane: A Critical Biography (1950)

Homage to Mistress Bradstreet (1953)

His Thought Made Pockets & the Plane Buckt (1958)

Homage to Mistress Bradstreet, and Other Poems (UK, 1959)

The Arts of Reading (1960) (coauthor, with Ralph Ross and Allen Tate)

77 Dream Songs (1964)

Berryman's Sonnets (1967)

Short Poems (1967)

His Toy, His Dream, His Rest (1968)

The Dream Songs (1969)

Love & Fame (1970; rev. UK ed. 1971; rev. US ed. 1972)

Selected Poems 1938–1968 (UK, 1972)

Delusions, Etc. of John Berryman (1972)

Recovery (1973)

The Freedom of the Poet (1976)

Henry's Fate & Other Poems, 1967–1972 (1977)

We Dream of Honour: John Berryman's Letters to His Mother (1988)

Collected Poems 1937–1971 (1989)

Berryman's Shakespeare: Essays, Letters and Other Writings (1999)

Selected Poems (2004)

Poems Selected by Michael Hofmann (UK, 2004)

The Heart Is Strange: New Selected Poems (2014, rev. ed. 2016)

The Selected Letters of John Berryman (2020)

Contents

Introduction

In an important late interview published in the *Harvard Advocate* in 1969, John Berryman (1914–1972) claimed that he "always wanted to be a writer." Though he devoted his life to his art, recognition was hard-won. He was slow to find his voice, yet when he did, he came to be a respected poet. He also went on to become an accomplished short story writer and essayist, and to win many awards. He read, lectured, and taught at several of the world's most distinguished universities, before he became a much-admired professor at the University of Minnesota. He corresponded with some of the finest poets of his generation, some of whom died prematurely. Indeed, Berryman came to believe that "something evil [was] stalking us poets" (quoted in Hamilton 351), and that, burdened by the madness of a suicidal postwar Western civilization, they, the writers and poets, were especially fated to an early, self-destructive end.

Berryman's faults were many, his anxieties nearly all-consuming. He could be hopelessly affected and pretentious, dismissive and egotistical. He was not above vindictive pettiness, and he possessed an extreme competitiveness that bordered on obsession, particularly over the early successes of his literary rivals. Validation of his art depended upon the esteem of both his critics and peers. He often exhibited a rather unfortunate tendency toward histrionics and self-pity. He believed that in order for a poet to be great, that poet must suffer continually. To test this proposition, he engaged in an extramarital affair simply in order to have something to write about, and to determine if, to quote one of his sonnets, "wickedness / is soluble in art." In a late interview he told former student Peter Stitt that "the artist is extremely lucky who is presented with the worst possible ordeal which will not actually kill him [. . .] I hope to be very nearly crucified."

For Berryman, a recovered Catholic, poetry was nothing less than vocation, mission, and way of life. The life of a writer should be all-encompassing; "everything went into his poems," his friend Saul Bellow remarked; "his poems said everything" (quoted in Thomas 78). In a 1957 interview given while he conducted a lecture series in India on behalf of the US State Department,

Berryman argued that civilization will always need poets to "dream their dreams," even if society disregards them. He lamented over the desultory state of poetry in America, where, after his mainstream success in the mid-1960s following the landmark publication of *77 Dream Songs* (1964) and a widely read *Life* magazine profile in 1967, "twenty million people know a lot about me, but nobody ever heard of me." Though he desired recognition, Berryman in the *Life* profile acknowledges its relative unimportance—and how impossible fame was for an American poet in the twentieth century—when he states that the "important thing is that your work is something no one else can do." As he notes of novelist and poet Stephen Crane, Berryman "was a writer and nothing else: a man alone in a room with the English language, trying to get the human feelings right" (Berryman 1950, 4).

However careerist Berryman's biography appears, his poetry defies, while self-consciously commenting upon, convention. His work utilizes a variety of rhetorical styles, often in a single poem, and shifts effortlessly from the lyric to the prosaic. Technique fascinated him from the start; his poetic voice consists of a distinctly "tortured syntax," as several commentators (Harold Bloom, Paul Mariani, Robert Pinsky) have described it, and diction, culled from sources as diverse as sixteenth- and seventeenth-century English and modern European poetry. Still, a tortured syntax does not necessarily indicate or arise from a tortured mind and, despite Berryman's undeserved reputation for impenetrably experimental and self-absorbed verse, he was to the end interested in craftsmanship and its importance in both the structure and meaning of poetry. He writes: "It is hard to measure what has been lost in our prose by the uniform adoption of a straight-on, mechanical word order (reflecting our *thoughtless* speech)" (Berryman 1976, 14).

As with the confessionalist poets—a label coined in a review of Robert Lowell's *Life Studies* (1959) by critic M. L. Rosenthal, who later came to regret its invention—Berryman wrestled with oedipal conflicts, university careerism, alcoholism, and profound anxiety. As several critics have previously pointed out (Philip Coleman, Adam Kirsch), to label Berryman as a confessionalist is to misunderstand his art, as his often wickedly humorous poetry is principally concerned with the self in response to the rapid social, political, sexual, racial, and technological transformations of the twentieth century, and their impact on the psyche and spirit, both individual and collective. The interviews in this volume continually illustrate Berryman's preoccupation with these issues. "The serious poet," Berryman observes, "should seek to explore the 'sources' of these global nightmares and to explore them not just in poetry, but in person. Poetry is a terminal activity, taking place out near the end of things. [. . .] And it aims—never mind either communication or expression—at the reformation of the poet, as prayer does" (Berryman 1976, 312).

Berryman's first collection, *Twenty Poems*, published in 1940 in a New Directions anthology, *Five Young American Poets*, when he was just twenty-six, was not well-received. To Joel Connaroe, one of Berryman's earliest and most astute critics, the poems are "ominous, flat, social, indistinctly allusive, exhausted, and preceded by a stiff essay on the nature of poetry [. . .] flawed by a ponderous, a sententious tone" (Connaroe 27). Berryman's first stand-alone collection, titled *Poems*, appeared in 1942, again published by New Directions, and offers similarly mannered, curiously empty imitations of William Butler Yeats. These early poems exhibit considerable self-consciousness, and an almost single-minded attempt at the mastery of established forms, which, ironically, only serve to emphasize their decided lack of originality.

The years 1947 to 1953, however, proved to be transformative for Berryman. During this productive seven-year period, he managed to complete a series of sonnets (published as *Berryman's Sonnets* in 1967), published a major collection *The Dispossessed* (1948), a critical biography of Stephen Crane (1950), and his most important essays—on Ezra Pound, Walt Whitman, and Isaac Babel—that provide glimpses into the development of his new poetics. Most crucially, he began (1948) and finished (1953) his breakthrough long poem *Homage to Mistress Bradstreet*, and he established a productive publishing relationship with Farrar, Straus and Giroux (Robert Giroux was a classmate of his at Columbia University) that would last to the end of his life. To some extent this prolificity resulted from extensive psychoanalysis; Berryman was encouraged to undergo therapy by his then-wife Eileen Simpson. Freudianism was then in vogue, and psychoanalysis later became an inexhaustible source of material for his poetry.

Energized by his breakthroughs in therapy, Berryman decided to augment his Crane biography with a psychoanalytical reading of his subject's life. Both Berryman and Crane suffered from the early death of a father, an overbearing yet doting mother, suicidal tendencies, and several unsuccessful attempts at playwriting, correspondences that Berryman believed might allow him to empathize with Crane. He and Crane also shared common thematic concerns: central to Crane's writing, Berryman maintained, was the emotion of panic, a kind of anxiety that derives from what Berryman describes as "an earlier, general terror" (Berryman 1950, 305), that resulted from some early, unspoken trauma. Berryman's emphasis on the psychological context of Crane's work is hampered by the inherent limitations of 1940s psychoanalytical methodology. Furthermore, Berryman's relative inexperience with this methodology at times handicaps the biography and proves to be more distraction than revelation.

The combined stresses of Berryman's work on Crane, a planned critical edition of William Shakespeare's *King Lear*, and a tumultuous, six-month-long affair with a married woman named Chris Haynes, culminated in a nervous breakdown. As a result, his alcoholism worsened. The sonnet sequence, with its theme of a love affair with a cruel woman approximating the common trope of sixteenth-century English sonnet sequences, was composed after the affair ended and only published in its entirety nearly twenty years after its completion. Berryman's sonnets involve an odd mixture of slang and colloquialisms, a heightened, "poetical" rhetoric that disguises what are for the most part conventional poems of unrequited love and self-pity. His twenty-year suppression of the poems may have resulted in part from their then somewhat provocative themes and at times overt scatology. However, given their eventual appearance, one suspects that the real reason for their suppression was largely personal as opposed to artistic, as both he and Chris were still married and she had a child.

In 1948, Berryman made an initial attempt—two stanzas worth—at his *Homage to Mistress Bradstreet*, before he set it aside to turn his attention to preparation of *The Dispossessed*, a collection that merited little critical estimation. The speakers of many of Berryman's early poems address a specifically postwar exhaustion and anxiety of the 1950s atomic age, yet here Berryman was gradually relieved of his anxiety of influence and fears of his potential failure to achieve an original, authentic poetic voice. For though *The Dispossessed* is largely a disciplined, lifeless collection, lacking the sheer imaginative breadth, humor, audaciousness, experimentalism, psychological depth, and originality of his later work, the volume does include several of his most accomplished early poems, most notably "Winter Landscape" and "The Ball Poem," as well as the "Nervous Songs," which introduce the eighteen-line-long lyric comprised of three six-line stanzas Berryman used for the Dream Songs,[1] modeled after the Petrarchan sonnet and suggested by Yeats's *Last Poems*. If, as a young poet, Yeats saved Berryman from what he describes as the "then-crushing influences of Ezra Pound and T. S. Eliot" (Berryman 1976, 324), then it seems appropriate that Berryman's maturation retains a residue of his master's influence. Apart from a few of the newer poems, this was a volume that looked back, rather than forward, for, with the as-yet-unpublished sonnets and the first few stanzas of *Homage*, Berryman had already acquired his mature voice, one that finally liberated him from the burdensome influence of Yeats.

Despite an auspicious start, the Crane study had left Berryman emotionally, physically, and psychologically drained. As a result, he seemed resigned to set aside his poem about Anne Bradstreet. He instead turned his attention back to scholarship and to his research into Shakespeare, unresolved since his abandonment of the *King Lear* project four years earlier. Berryman nevertheless managed to complete a significant amount of research on Shakespeare, principally on the subject of authorship, and in 1954 at Harvard delivered an astonishing thirty-four lectures that covered twenty-two of the plays. Berryman proved himself to be a captivating, electrifying speaker, and finally began to receive the recognition he so long desired.

Frustrated by the seemingly insurmountable immensity of that "multiform & encyclopedic bastard" Shakespeare (Berryman 2020, 257), and after he read a typescript of Bellow's Bildungsroman *The Adventures of Augie March*, and Tolstoy's *Anna Karenina*, whose eponymous heroine he regarded as the finest-ever literary portrait of a woman, Berryman, with the help of a Guggenheim fellowship, once again turned his attention to his long-deferred Bradstreet poem. By early 1953, in a flurry of activity and creativity, Berryman completed the poem that had long eluded him. Bellow's brave jettisoning of narrative restrictions in *Augie March* encouraged Berryman to do the same, and to simultaneously rid his poetry of the equally slavish imitations of W. H. Auden and W. B. Yeats.

Composed in a style distinct from Bradstreet's formal, seventeenth-century-style verse, *Homage to Mistress Bradstreet* is a historically and biographically dense poem, though Berryman plays fast and loose with historical accuracy, courageously inventing incidents where it suits the narrative or is emotionally resonant. The poem, essentially an "autobiographical monologue" (Kaspar Aldrich 161), is stylistically eccentric and highly allusive, most notably in its use of archaisms, neologisms, inversions, esoteric language, and awkward phrasing and diction that alternates between King James biblical and colloquial speech. Bradstreet is depicted as a barren woman, disfigured by smallpox at an early age, and trapped in a loveless marriage. She addresses an unnamed confessor and, midway through the poem, this confessor, a twentieth-century man, responds to Bradstreet and professes his love for her. She at first responds, and the two voices alternate, before Bradstreet, a proper Christian and colonist, rejects his advances. The poem concludes with Bradstreet's visceral account of a hard-won pregnancy and childbirth, a renewed declaration of love for her husband and their eventual shared domestic bliss, her slow decline and delirium, and eventual death in 1672 from rheumatism and pulmonary edema. "The poem laid itself out in a series of rebellions," Berryman writes in his essay "One Answer to a Question: Changes" (included below), and it is Bradstreet's rebelliousness that initially drew him to her. As poet, Bradstreet refused to assume the "appropriate" role assigned to her by Puritan society. "I had her rebel first against the new environment," Berryman explains, "and above all against her barrenness (which in fact lasted for years), then against her marriage (which in fact seems to have been brilliantly happy), and finally against her continuing life of illness, loss, and age." Berryman's life involved similar rebellions, most importantly his initial rejection of his Catholic upbringing as a result of his anger toward God following his father's apparent suicide, the constant turmoil of his lifelong devotion/resistance toward an overbearing mother, his rejection of early poetic models, and the composition of his finest work, *The Dream Songs*, as a rebellion against what a poem—and long poem—can mean and be. He planned an "elaborate" essay on the subject "called 'The Care & Feeding of Long Poems,'" which, like so many of his intended projects, remained unwritten (Berryman 2020, 476).

Berryman's close reading of Pound's *The Cantos*, prompted by a volume of Pound's selected poems to be published by New Directions, along with the more crucial example of Whitman's *Song of Myself*, provided Berryman with the principal inspirations for *The Dream Songs*, which like Pound and Whitman's long poems, depends largely on the personality of its author for its structure and content. Moreover, the individual Songs borrow much of their stylistic bravado from French poet Tristan Corbière's late-nineteenth-century poems—at the time of the Songs' initial composition recently translated into English (1954, 1958)—and approximates their style (em dashes, ellipses), tone, sense, and language, with abrupt shifts from the formal to the colloquial. Like Corbière's poetry, the Songs are alternately contemplative, comic, quizzical, irreverent, ironic, sarcastic, and tragic. (Berryman dedicated his collection *Love & Fame* [1970] to the memory of Corbière.)

In addition to their method of composition, the Dream Songs represent another departure for Berryman in that, like the sonnets and *Bradstreet* before them, they enact a conscious break with T. S. Eliot's modernist notion of the impersonality of the poet, an effort at detachment and objectivity. These poems also mark a transformative moment in modern poetry from impersonal events to—particularly in Bradstreet—personal history, both historical and contemporary, viewed through the lens of the psychology of the fragmented self. As Berryman observes, "I set up the Dream Songs to be hostile to every visible tendency in both American and English poetry—in so far as the English have any poetry nowadays" (quoted in Haffenden

1980, 6). Because they are "dreams"—a fact Berryman was always careful to emphasize, though a more accurate description might be Lowell's "not real dreams but a walking hallucination" (quoted in Kostelanetz 112)—the Songs are not strictly logical.

Berryman's self-analytical Dream Songs, instigated by two as-yet unpublished prose efforts started in 1954, *Journal of Self-Analysis* and the dream transcriptions that make up a manuscript entitled *St. Pancras Braser* (St. Pancras, a martyr, died at age fourteen; a braser is a strap used to protect an archer's arm), capture the psychological zeitgeist of mid-century America. The Songs' occasionally multiple—and at times competitive—speakers, ever-shifting pronouns, voices, dialects, tenses, neologisms, archaisms, colloquialisms, inversions, and ellipses suggest the psychic fragmentation of a borderline personality. Oedipal factors—a father's suicide when he was a young boy and his subsequent love/hate relationship with an imperious mother—left significant psychic wounds that Berryman seemed distinctly unable to cauterize, and contributed to insecurities and emotional instabilities that fueled his achievements and simultaneously provided him with the nervous energy, desperation, incompleteness, and lack of fulfillment and resolution that formed the core drama of his Dream Songs. Like Hamlet's, the memory of Berryman's father haunted him, and his father's presence, as numerous critics have noted, either implicitly or explicitly informs some of his greatest poems. Berryman was in fact so traumatized by the circumstances of his father's suicide that he lost his unquestioned faith in God, and with it his innocence ("That mad drive wiped out my childhood," he grieves in one of his final Dream Songs); as a result, belief in God and a childlike innocence remained inextricably connected in Berryman's adult psyche, as did the concept of God as absent father.

Berryman argues in his *Harvard Advocate* interview that *The Dream Songs*, though difficult to summarize given its somewhat open structure, does in fact have "a plot [. . .] Its plot is the personality of Henry as he moves on in the world." The Songs document his character Henry's eccentricities. If he is not Berryman then he is someone conspicuously similar to him, a thinly veiled alter ego: Henry is a talented, intellectual, nervously disposed, alcoholic, womanizing professor of English who, amidst his constant breakdowns and self-created emergencies, leads an otherwise quiet, comfortable middle-class 1950s–1960s suburban life, one of family life, work, travels, social gatherings, and obligations both professional and personal that seem to underline the speaker's desperation to find value or escape, and who obsessively composes elegies for fellow poets

(Delmore Schwartz, Theodore Roethke, Robert Frost, Randall Jarrell, Yvor Winters, Sylvia Plath, Louis MacNeice, William Carlos Williams), or for himself. Henry has suffered an undisclosed "loss," meant to obscure auto-biographical elements in much the same way that Berryman suppressed the sonnets, or disguised his affair in *Homage*.

The Dream Songs are comical, serious, tendentious, morbid, and opaque. Their coherence derives from Henry's persona and his persistent pre-occupation with emotional extremity. The central conceit of the ini-tial three books of Songs, published in 1964 as *77 Dream Songs*, is that of the relationship between Henry and his unnamed interlocutor, who re-fers to Henry by a number of different monikers, a relationship that de-rives from both biblical and cultural influences. The Songs, Berryman explains, are "essentially about an imaginary character (not the poet, not me) named Henry, a white American in early middle age sometimes de-picted in blackface, who has suffered an irreversible loss and talks about himself sometimes in the first person, sometimes in the third, sometimes even in the second. He has a friend, never named, who addresses him as Mr. Bones and variants thereof" (Berryman 1968, vi). The personal pronouns are Henry's (Berryman's persona), who is also the poem's third-person sub-ject; Henry also addresses himself in the second and third person. His in-terlocutor, who speaks to Henry in a pseudo-black dialect, is once referred to as "cagey John," though generally remains nameless. This anonymous interlocutor acts as both Henry's confessor and enemy, a kind of solitary Greek chorus; the sobriquet "Mr. Bones" is inspired by one of two com-mon minstrel stage names, Mr. Tambo and Mr. Bones, the "endmen," or underdogs, the targets of the interlocutor's attacks, whose names are de-rived from two minstrel instruments, the tambourine and bones. The end-men conceal their intelligence with buffoonish behavior, and much of the humor in this routine results from their witty response to the interlocu-tor's attacks. In a sense, Henry, in his state of perpetual collapse, is a fre-quent object of comic ridicule, most often self-inflicted. In this self-persecution Henry is also identified with the interlocutor. The ambiguity of pronouns, Berryman discovered, allows the poet to be "both left out and put in."

Many of Berryman's early Songs were composed at the height of the civil rights era, and his use of minstrelsy as a literary device, superficially regres-sive and racially insensitive, is in fact quite transgressive. Berryman does not pull any punches in the Songs; he recognizes the obvious inauthentic-ity, theatricality, and artificiality of minstrelsy, and in fact foregrounds its absurdity when set against the very tangible realities of the tragedies of human experience. Rather, blackface minstrelsy's tradition of mockery, and its tragic subtext of slavery, complements the various misfortunes that provide both the impetus and the basic framework for the Songs. Berryman draws on minstrelsy's tendency to mock or make light of human misery in order to ruminate on the extent to which all of humanity is victim, subject to historical circumstance. His use of minstrelsy aligns Berryman's Henry with persecuted races in order to give voice to the existential condition of man as one of exploitation and dehumanization, and of grief remedied by comedy.

Berryman's fascination with jazz and blues music, and his desire to transgress both high and low culture, perhaps explains his use of music, specifically popular American music, as a contrapuntal theme. This transgression is illustrated by the epigraphs for *77 Dream Songs*: "I am their musick," "Thou drewest near in the day," and "Go in, Brack Man, De Day's Yo' Own." The first two epigraphs are derived from the King James translation of Lamentations, while the third is from a minstrel lyric derived from Carl Wittke's seminal history of minstrelsy, *Tambo and Bones: A History of the Minstrel Stage*. As scholar Daniel Smith-Christopher has observed, blues music, of which minstrel music is a bastardization, is the African American equivalent to Hebraic laments both personal and communal (557). Thus, these epigraphs suggest the biblical theme of an oppressed people whose persecution becomes a source of strength, cohesion, and preservation, a theme also reflected in Berryman's self-conscious—and deeply ironic and subversive—use of minstrelsy.

In 1968, Berryman published *His Toy, His Dream, His Rest*, a substantial collection of an additional 308 Dream Songs. The earlier poems collected here reprise the experimentalism, ambiguity, and opacity of the songs from the first volume, yet as Berryman's fame increased, the need for a disguise became less and less necessary. As a result, the latter Songs are surprisingly straightforward, both in form and content, and are nakedly autobiographical, leaving behind a speaker who is transparently Berryman, and at times more interested in the vicissitudes of his newfound fame, something he both desires and despises, than with his own morality and mortality.

Berryman continued to write Dream Songs until the end of his life, though he left many of them unpublished. He instead began to compose poetry in a style that, like the later Dream Songs, did not rely on guises, a series of nearly transparent short poems that relate his experiences as an unknown young poet (up to 1940) and as an accomplished man of letters (after

1969). These new poems saw print in the collection *Love & Fame* (1970, rev. ed. 1971), and map Berryman's early desire for celebrity, a desire gradually replaced with wisdom and resignation. The collection concludes with poems of social, ethical, political, and especially religious concerns, part of a late career turn toward unambiguously religious-themed projects, including a projected *Life of Christ* left unfinished at the time of his death. The poems in *Love & Fame* alternately offer explicitly sexual reminisces of a lustful youth to lyrics that lovingly describe his friends and companions of adulthood, and concludes with "Eleven Addresses to the Lord," a series of repentant hymns of devotion, awe, and humility, occasioned by Berryman's experiences while in treatment for alcoholism throughout 1969, and composed by a broken and aging man, alone with his torments. That same year, Berryman began the Bildungsroman (in critic Roger Forseth's view [189]) *Recovery*, inspired by Berryman's repeated hospitalizations and subsequent experiences with Alcoholics Anonymous.

In late 1970 to early 1971, Berryman wrote a series of short religious poems, culminating in a profoundly meditative religious sequence, "Opus Dei," which illustrates his struggle with the God whose reality he perhaps unconvincingly accepted in the earlier "Eleven Addresses of the Lord." "Opus Dei" and other stray or otherwise unpublished poems, most of them composed between January and April 1971, were eventually published in two posthumous collections, *Delusions, Etc.* (1972), which Berryman prepared for publication, and *Henry's Fate & Other Poems* (1977), which he did not; the latter is comprised mostly of Dream Songs written after 1968, intended to replace certain older Songs for a revised collected edition that Berryman never completed. Yet the uneven *Delusions, Etc.* still contains some of Berryman's finest poems, and reveals his continued development as an artist. These are poems that, for the most part, display a master at work. As Eve Cobain evocatively observes, with *Delusions, Etc.*, "Berryman was retreating deeper into the world of fantasy and remembrance—expressing all the hallmarks of a terminal imagination" (263).

After a yearlong sobriety, Berryman, perhaps as a result of the primarily venomous reviews of *Love & Fame*, began to drink again. This combined with double doses of an antipsychotic and anticonvulsant medication prescribed prior to his relapse, likely worsened his health, both physical and mental. Moreover, he feared that his lectures would eventually suffer from this inevitable mental and physical decline; that students would drop his course, and that the university would dismiss him, leaving his family destitute. As ever, the specter of his father loomed large. He was wracked with guilt over his neglect of his wife and children. (After he divorced Eileen in 1956, Berryman remarried twice, to Ann Levine and then Kate Donahue. With Levine he had one son, Paul, born in 1957, whom he rarely saw, and with Donahue, two daughters, Martha, born in 1963 and named after his mother, and Sarah Rebecca, born in 1971.) There was a sense, too, that, in spite of his many accomplishments—and they are significant—his "life's work" as he describes them in *Recovery*, remained "invisible (so far) achievements, like an iceberg" (Berryman 1973, 164) in part because of his drinking. Instead of pride, he felt shame. His religious leap of faith must have seemed to him an eleventh-hour act of desperation.

In the days that led up to his suicide, Berryman contemplated his poor health and the apparent hopelessness of his situation. Not drugs, alcohol, treatment, family, friends, or even God could relieve him of his guilt and sense of a life wasted. Two days before his death, he left his house carrying a long-bladed Spanish knife. He contemplated slitting his wrists before leaping from the Washington Street Bridge a few blocks from his home in Minneapolis—a bridge he crossed frequently—to spare his family the trauma of discovering his body. Instead, he purchased a bottle of alcohol and returned home to compose a final poem in which he imagined climbing over the railing of a bridge. The next night, he wrote his long-suffering wife Kate a note on the back of an envelope, which he quickly discarded. The note, which wasn't discovered until the morning after his death, read: "O my love Kate, you did all you could. I'm unemployable and a nuisance. Forget me. Remarry. Be happy." On the morning of January 7, 1972, John Berryman leapt from a height of one hundred feet from the Washington Street Bridge to an icy riverbank below. He died instantly. According to one eyewitness at the scene, before he leapt, he waved. Connaroe observes, pityingly, tragically, that "this unhappy man, who spent his life lamenting the suicide that left him fatherless at age eleven . . . [left] behind a young wife and two daughters, aged eight and one" (1).

To this day, Berryman is regarded as a second-tier poet, even when the scope is limited to the mid-twentieth century. Several critics have offered their theories as to why he is so stubbornly overlooked—though critical works, theses, and the return to print of his books (most recently on the centennial of his birth [2014]) continue to appear occasionally—yet it is difficult to account for Berryman's ongoing literary neglect. Certainly, political correctness has claimed its share of victims, and Berryman, with his use of the blackface minstrel tradition in *The Dream Songs*, and the quality of his work often eclipsed by the context of his crippling alcoholism, presently appears to number among the fallen. This present volume, which collects all of the interviews, is a humble attempt at rectifying what continues to be a scholarly oversight. It is this editor's hope that this collected volume of interviews will offer a more nuanced, conciliatory view of Berryman, in all his complexity, and help to place him within a more forgiving context wherein his faults and the more uncomfortable aspects of his poetry are not at best excuses or at worst offenses, but rather, an encouragement for us to face our collective demons rather than turn away from them or bury them under a veneer of appropriateness and inclusivity.

At the time of his death, Berryman was in the preparation stages of several different projects. Many of them were left incomplete. Of the thousands of pages of unpublished correspondence, diaries, and journals—some, like *St. Pancras Braser*, of crucial importance to the understanding of the published work—only two volumes of letters and two volumes of prose thus far have been published. Perhaps someday more resourceful scholars will curate Berryman's yet-to-be published material, an abundance of drafts and fragments, dream journals, and previously unseen poems that currently reside in the Special Collections department at the University of Minnesota and deserve immediate discovery. There have been recent, encouraging developments: Philip Coleman edited, with Philip McGowan, *"After Thirty Falls": New Essays on John Berryman,* and with Peter Campion, *Centenary Essays,* drawn from proceedings of two conferences (in 2014 in Dublin and Minneapolis) organized to celebrate the centenary of John Berryman's birth. The industrious Coleman has also authored the seminal study *John Berryman's Public Vision* (2014), which argues for a reexamination of Berryman as a socially minded as opposed to self-absorbed poet. Together with scholar Calista McRae, Coleman recently published a generous selection of Berryman's correspondence (2020), which evidences Berryman's impassioned desire for genuine dialogue with others, even when that dialogue is often limited in scope to an analysis of his own work.

Despite Berryman's willingness, in both published and unpublished work, to expose the deepest recesses of his psyche, however thinly veiled in his poetry's adoptive personae, in interviews published in local newspapers or university publications, Berryman conveys a curiously old-fashioned reticence, a kind of politeness in mixed company, as if he did not wish to air the same dirty laundry in public conversation that he was all too eager to confess in poetry not beholden to the same demands for the decorum he apparently believed to be a prerequisite of newspaper articles.

"I teach and I write. I'm not copy," Berryman told journalist Phyllis Meras in a brief article from May 1963, published in the women's section of the *Providence Journal.* At the time of this interview, copy is largely what

Berryman was, at least in the eyes of the press. Literary journals, apart from a few notable exceptions, had not yet decided to give him the attention and space for a serious conversation. Among the reasons for Berryman's dislike of the format is that, unlike writing or lecturing, there is usually no opportunity for preparation, and, more importantly, for an interview to be successful, its subject must perform in such a way that they provide entertainment value for the reader. "Interviews are no great problem because you don't feel put in the position of an entertainer," he tells interviewer Martin Berg. "But often you are." Even so, Berryman routinely submitted to the interview format, though he was rarely pleased with the result. "I've given hundreds [of interviews]," he complains to interviewer Elizabeth Nussbaum, "few were successful."

Given his conversational prowess, it is remarkable that Berryman wasn't interviewed more often, particularly after he received the Pulitzer Prize, though in subsequent years the number of serious interviews increased dramatically. Prior to 1965, Berryman sat down for only a handful, many of them brief. Indeed, most of his pre-Pulitzer interviews are short newspaper items (the "copy" to which Berryman refers) that include brief sound bites from him, human interest stories in local newspapers—primarily Minneapolis—occasionally printed in the "women's page" sections common in periodicals at that time. Perhaps Berryman intimidated his potential interviewers, or fear of exposure of his alcoholism, or an unspoken reticence on his part, prevented him from accepting invitations. "I stand ashamed of myself," he writes, "I stick up like Coriolanus with my scars / for mob inspection." A deliberately withheld intimacy in his early conversations possibly results in part from a similar urge toward self-censorship. Publicly, Berryman believed that he must act the part of the respectable scholar, and not the maladjusted degenerate he considered himself to be in private.

Due in part to changing social mores, and his professional security as a tenured professor, in the mid-1960s Berryman's approach to the format evolved as his interviews changed from brief "copy" in newspaper articles, with their restrictions on length and content, to the more accommodating medium of literary journals, which allowed for lengthier and more in-depth conversations. In these interviews, Berryman can be alternately guarded and uninhibited, gregarious and reserved, receptive and dismissive, modest and immodest, philosophical and glib, trenchant and obscure, sometimes all at once. He is either eloquent or inarticulate about his poetic inspiration and technique. Yet generally speaking, much like his poetry, over time he became less concerned with the formalities of the interview format and as a result, less circumspect in his responses. Most often, regardless of his dislike of interviews, Berryman remained a sensitive and responsive subject, all too willing to offer candid responses to questions posed to him, as genuinely fascinated and perplexed by the artistic process as his audience. "I used to be very hard to interview," he explains to Berg, "but lately, I've relaxed." Berryman occasionally befriended his interviewers (William Heyen, Peter Stitt) or was interviewed by friends (Bob Lundegaard), and it is notable that these interviews rank among Berryman's finest. Indeed, the somewhat withdrawn, aspiring, professorial Berryman of the early interviews and the increasingly eccentric, outspoken, and candid version in later ones are in themselves carefully cultivated personae: the scholar as modern poet, the poet as modern scholar.

In the conversations, personality pieces, profiles, and local interest items collected here,[2] the newswomen and newsmen attempt to unravel Berryman, as both he and his interlocutors struggle to find value in poetry in a fallen world, and to question the intelligence and good decision making of those who choose to write poetry. Stitt notes that Berryman, in granting these late interviews, succumbed to the dangers of fame late in his own career. "He loved to be treated as a celebrity," Stitt observes, and as a result he "gave indiscreet interviews to large-circulation magazines, even wrote a series of poems (in *Love & Fame*) that seem more nearly addressed to a popular than a serious audience."

Whatever his reservations, ultimately Berryman *did* grant interviews, and not simply because he believed that it brought him love or fame. His most penetrative discussions took place after his 1967 interview in *Life* magazine, the highest-profile he ever gave, and even that exposure, on the heels of his Pulitzer win, still left him jealous of the celebrity his peers (Dylan Thomas, Robert Lowell, or Sylvia Plath) achieved. Yet Berryman, with the exception of a handful of essays or in comments interspersed in critical writings on others' work generally not given over to public expression of his methods or speculations that concern the sources, inspirations, or materials for his poetry, nevertheless felt compelled to discuss these very subjects with interrogators both amateur and professional.

The interviews and conversations contained herein capture some of the contours of what Lowell describes as "This great Pierrot's universe [. . .] more tearful and funny than we can easily bear" (111). They bring us nearer to Berryman's peculiar sorrows and joys, of a life given over to a prayerful dedication to his craft—a life lived, as Berryman says of Beethoven "at the mercy of his art"—and a lifelong attempt at the reformation of a poet out near the end of things.

Acknowledgments

Grateful acknowledgment is extended to Jennifer Claybourne, Erin George, Kathryn Hujda, and Erik Moore at the University of Minnesota Special Archives; Kristen Chinery and Alison Stankfrauff at the Walter Reuther Library of Labor and Urban Affairs at Wayne State University; for permissions provided by Charlie Weaver at *Minnesota Daily*, Vicky Mitchell at BBC Commercial Rights and Business Affairs, the trustees of the *Harvard Advocate* (Susan Morrison, James Atlas, and Daniel Max), Kate Donahue, William Heyen, Al and Anne Alvarez, Robert B. Shaw, John Plotz, Richard Kostelanetz, Bruce Jackson, and to John Stitt for permission to use his late father Peter Stitt's interview with Berryman. Dominick Grace and Joe Pava helped to source hard-to-find interviews, Anthony Rudolf assisted in facilitating the acquisition of rights to the Alvarez BBC2 interview. Philip Coleman and Grace and Sarah Gleason assisted in proofreading and copyediting. Finally, thanks to my editor Katie Keene at the University Press of Mississippi, for her enthusiasm and support for this project.

A Note on the Text

I have attempted to remain faithful to the source material, for the most part preserving the individual authors' and sources' peculiarities and idiosyncrasies; however, any errors or omissions, typographical or otherwise, have been silently corrected. For reasons of cost, substantial quotations beyond fair use or reproductions in their entirety of poems referenced in the interviews have been omitted and are replaced with bracketed references to the primary material. Readers may refer to *Collected Poems 1937–1971* and *The Dream Songs*, for the excised material.

EH

Notes

1. At times, it is difficult to parse whether an interviewer or Berryman is referring to the Dream Songs as a series of individual poems or *The Dream Songs* as an individual work, as they can generally be regarded as both. In this volume, where it is apparent that the speaker is referring the work in its entirety, or their publication in 1969 in a single volume, italics are utilized.

2. This collection includes all of Berryman's extant published interviews, except for three not included due to prohibitive republication costs: two short pieces from the *Minnesota Daily* (1965, 1967) and a brief profile from 1970 by journalist Charles Hammer, "Poet Indifferent to Anonymity" from the *Kansas City Star*.

Works Cited and Consulted

Arpin, Gary Q. *The Poetry of John Berryman*. Port Washington, NY: Kennikat Press, 1978.

Berryman, John. *Berryman's Shakespeare*. John Haffenden, ed. New York: Farrar, Straus and Giroux, 1999.

Berryman, John. *Collected Poems 1937–1971*. Charles Thornbury, ed. New York: Farrar, Straus and Giroux, 1991.

Berryman, John. *The Freedom of the Poet*. Robert Giroux, ed. New York: Farrar, Straus and Giroux, 1976.

Berryman, John. *His Toy, His Dream, His Rest*. New York Farrar, Straus and Giroux, 1968.

Berryman, John. *Recovery*. New York: Farrar, Straus and Giroux, 1973.

Berryman, John. *The Selected Letters of John Berryman*. Philip Coleman and Calista McRae, eds. Cambridge: Harvard University Press, 2020.

Berryman, John. *Stephen Crane: A Critical Biography*. New York: William Sloane, 1950; rev. ed. New York: Farrar, Straus and Giroux, 1962.

Berryman, John. *We Dream of Honour: John Berryman's Letters to His Mother*. Richard Kelly, ed. New York: W. W. Norton & Co., 1988.

Cobain, Eve. "'He begot us an enigma': Berryman's Beethoven," in *John Berryman: Centenary Essays*. Philip Coleman and Peter Campion, eds. New York: Peter Lang Publishers, 2017, 251–66.

Clendenning, John. "Rescue in Berryman's *Crane*," in *Recovering Berryman: Essays on a Poet*. Richard J. Kelly, and Alan Lathrop, eds. Ann Arbor: University of Michigan Press, 1993, 179–88.

Coleman, Philip. *John Berryman's Public Vision: Relocating the scene of disorder*. Dublin: University College Dublin Press, 2014.

Connaroe, Joel. *John Berryman: An Introduction to the Poetry*. New York: Columbia University Press, 1977.

Forseth, Roger. "Spirits and Spirituality: The Art of *Recovery*," in *Alcoholite at the Altar: The Writer and Addiction: The Writings of Roger Forsyth*. Grace Forseth and Dave Lull, eds. New York: Cassandra Communications, 2018, 185–202.

Haffenden, John. *John Berryman: A Critical Commentary*. London: Palgrave Macmillan, 1980.

Haffenden, John. *The Life of John Berryman*. London: Ark, 1982.

Hamilton, Ian. *Robert Lowell: A Biography*. New York: Random House, 1982.

Johnsen, Carol, director. *I Don't Think I Will Sing Anymore Just Now—John Berryman: A Retrospective*. Film. The University of Minnesota, 1974.

Kaspar Aldrich, Elizabeth, "Berryman Saved from Drowning," in *John Berryman (Bloom's Modern Critical Views)*, Harold Bloom, ed. New York: Chelsea House Publications, 1989, 149–63.

Kirsch, Adam. *The Wounded Surgeon: Confession and Transformation in Six American Poets*. New York: W. W. Norton & Co., 2005.

Kostelanetz, Richard. *The New Poetries and Some Old*. Carbondale, IL: Southern Illinois University Press, 1991.

Linebarger, J. M. *John Berryman (Twayne's United States Authors Series)*. New York: Twayne Publishers, 1974.

Lowell, Robert. "For John Berryman, 1914–1972." in *Collected Prose*. London: Faber & Faber, 1987, 104–18.

Mancini, Joseph. *The Berryman Gestalt: Therapeutic Strategies in the Poetry of John Berryman*. New York: Garland, 1987.

Mariani, Paul. *Dream Song: The Life of John Berryman*. New York: Paragon House, 1989.

Meyers, Jeffrey. *Manic Power: Robert Lowell and His Circle*. New York: Arbor House, 1987.

Smith-Christopher, Daniel L. "Biblical Lamentations and Singing the Blues," in *The Oxford Handbook of Biblical Narrative*. Danna Nolan Fewell, ed. New York: Oxford University Press, 2016, 550–59.

Stitt, Peter. "John Berryman: His Teaching, His Scholarship, His Poetry," in *Recovering Berryman: Essays on a Poet*, Richard J. Kelly, and Alan Lathrop, eds. Ann Arbor: University of Michigan Press, 1993, 43–56.

Stitt, Peter. "John Berryman's Criticism and His Poetry." *John Berryman Studies* 3, no. 3 (Summer 1977): 4–16.

Thomas, Harry, ed. *Berryman's Understanding: Reflections on the Poetry of John Berryman*. Boston, MA: Northeastern University Press, 1988.

Thornbury, Charles. "A Reckoning with Ghostly Voices," in *Recovering Berryman: Essays on a Poet*, Richard J. Kelly, and Alan Lathrop, eds. Ann Arbor: University of Michigan Press, 1993, 77–111.

Thornbury, Charles. "Introduction," in John Berryman, *Collected Poems 1937–1971*, xvii–lix.

Chronology

1914   Born John Allyn Smith Jr. on October 25 to John Allyn Smith, a banker, and his wife, schoolteacher Martha Smith (née Little) in McAlester, Oklahoma. Over the next decade the family will live in towns throughout Oklahoma, including Anadarko, Lamar, Sasakwa, and Wagoner.

1919   Robert Jefferson Smith, Berryman's younger brother, born September 1.

1921   Family moves to Anadarko, Oklahoma, in January, after father takes new position as bank vice president. John attends West Grade School.

1925   Family moves to Tampa, Florida, with Martha's mother, Martha May Little, where John's parents and grandmother co-own and operate the Orange Blossom Restaurant. John and Bob are left behind in Anadarko, where they attend boarding school at St. Joseph's Academy. In December, the boys move to Florida.

1926   Father purchases Florida real estate just before the speculative Florida real estate crash. As a result, family is forced to sell the restaurant. Parents separate in April, and Martha takes John and Robert to live in an apartment in Clearwater, Florida. Martha files for divorce on June 19, accusing John Smith of adultery. Father allegedly commits suicide just below John's bedroom window by self-inflicted gunshot wound to the chest. John Angus McAlpin Berryman, owner of the Clearwater apartment where Martha and sons are living, files for divorce from his wife. Martha moves family to New York City where she and Berryman are married on September 8. John's name is changed to John Allyn McAlpin Berryman. Begins attending P.S. 69 in Jackson Heights.

1928   Writes science fiction novel, a work of juvenilia. Family moves to Great Neck, Long Island.

1928–32   Attends South Kent School, a private Episcopal boarding school in Connecticut.

1929   Market crashes; stepfather, a stockbroker, is unemployed. Martha begins work as a secretary.

1931   Family moves to Manhattan. Stepfather finds sporadic employment. John attempts suicide for the first time.

1932   Graduates from South Kent and begins attending Columbia College in New York City. Mark Van Doren, professor of English, encourages John's literary career.

1934   Writes first poems, four sonnets on the occasion of his mother's birthday.

1935   First poems and professional reviews in the *Columbia Review*, edited by classmate (and later publisher) Robert Giroux, and anthology *Columbia Poetry*. Awarded the first of many poetry prizes. Poem "Note on E. A. Robinson" in *The Nation*. Meets Allen Tate.

1936   Poems and essay "The Ritual of W. B. Yeats" in the *Columbia Review*. Poems in *Columbia Poetry*. Meets R. P. Blackmur. Graduates Phi Beta Kappa from Columbia with a BA in English and a minor in Philosophy. Receives Euretta J. Kellett scholarship for two years of study overseas at Clare College, Cambridge, England. Engaged to Jean Bennet. Writes first play, *The Architect*, unfinished.

1937   Meets Yeats, Auden, and Dylan Thomas. Writes one-act play *Cleopatra: A Meditation*. Travels to Germany and France. Engaged to Beryl Eeman. Awarded the Charles Oldham Shakespeare Prize.

1938   Poems published in the *Southern Review*. Moves back to New York City and is unable to find employment. Beryl joins him in New York City. Meets Bhain Campbell. Martha begins work in advertising. Begins play, *Dictator*.

1939   Made poetry editor of *The Nation*. Meets Delmore Schwartz. Stepfather and mother are separated. Begins teaching at Wayne State University in Detroit, Michigan, where he lives with Campbell and his wife. Diagnosed with *petit mal* seizures following a confrontation with his mother, later determined to be a type of epilepsy, a misdiagnosis.

1940   Teaches at Harvard University. First collection, *Twenty Poems*, in New Directions anthology *Five Young American Poets*. Bhain Campbell dies prematurely from cancer. Ends position as poetry editor for the *Nation*.

1941   On New Year's Day, meets Eileen Mulligan. Receives 4-F classification from United States Selective Service and is exempt from military service.

1942   Collection *Poems* published by New Directions, as part of their "Poet of the Month" series. Ends engagement to Beryl. Marries Eileen on October 24.

1943   Teaches English and Latin at Iona School, a preparatory school in New Rochelle, New York, for three weeks; resigns after Blackmur finds him a position as English instructor at Princeton University.

1944   Lectures at Briarcliff College, New York. Receives a Rockefeller Foundation fellowship for 1944–45 research for a new scholarly edition of *King Lear*, never completed. Meets Robert Lowell.

1945   Short stories "The Lovers" and "The Imaginary Jew" in the *Kenyon Review*. Receives *Kenyon Review*–Doubleday Doran prize for "The Imaginary Jew."

1946   Teaches creative writing at Princeton.

1947   Affair with Chris begins in May. Composes a series of sonnets about the affair in which Chris is renamed "Lise"; they remain unpublished for two decades. Meets T. S. Eliot. Start of psychoanalysis at the suggestion of Eileen.

1948   Named resident fellow in creative writing, Princeton. Collection *The Dispossessed* published. Visits Ezra Pound at St. Elizabeths Hospital in Washington, DC. Meets Saul Bellow. Begins *Homage to Mistress Bradstreet*, which is set aside until 1952, and the unfinished long poem *The Black Book*.

1949   Receives the Shelley Memorial Award from the Poetry Society of America for *The Dispossessed* and is awarded Princeton's Alfred Hodder fellowship for 1950–51. Writes additional sections of *The Black Book* and works on the Crane book, now a critical biography. Defends Pound's Bollingen Prize for *The Pisan Cantos*.

1950   Essay, "The Poetry of Ezra Pound," originally intended as an introduction to the New Directions *Selected Poems of Ezra Pound*, published in *Partisan Review*. *Stephen Crane: A Critical Biography* receives the American Academy Award, National Institute of Arts and Letters Award, and the Levinson Prize from *Poetry*. Meets Randall Jarrell. Lectures at the University of Washington in Seattle to fill in for Theodore Roethke after Roethke suffers a nervous breakdown.

1951   Lectures at Princeton on Shakespeare. Composes unfinished play, *Mirabeau*.

1952   Elliston Lecturer on Poetry at the University of Cincinnati. Provides afterword to reprint of Theodore Dreiser's *The Titan* and the introduction to a reprint of M. G. Lewis's *The Monk*. Awarded

Guggenheim fellowship for his poetry and Shakespeare research and contracts with Viking to produce a critical study on Shakespeare, which he never finishes. Publishes "Sonnet 25" in *Poetry*. Starts work again on *Homage to Mistress Bradstreet*. Writes short story "Our Sins Are More Than We Can Bear," which remains unpublished until 1973.

1953   Completes *Homage to Mistress Bradstreet*. With Eileen travels to Europe; they separate upon their return. Meets Theodore Roethke and Louis MacNeice. Moves to New York City. *Homage* published in *Partisan Review*. Dylan Thomas dies at St. Vincent's Hospital on November 9.

1954   In spring, lectures on poetry at the University of Iowa Writers Workshop in Iowa City. Teaches course on Shakespeare at Harvard in summer months. Fired during fall term at the University of Iowa for public intoxication. Allen Tate secures him a position at the University of Minnesota in Minneapolis. Begins dream analysis, the unpublished *St. Pancras Braser.*

1955   Lectures in humanities at the University of Minnesota. Continues research on Shakespeare. Writes earliest Dream Songs.

1956   Contracts with Farrar, Straus for *Shakespeare's Friend*, never completed. *Homage to Mistress Bradstreet* published as single volume by Farrar, Straus and Cudahy; nominated for Pulitzer. Receives Rockefeller fellowship from the *Partisan Review*. Translates Paul Claudel's *Le Cremin de la Croix*. Divorces Eileen on December 19; marries Elizabeth Ann Levine the following week.

1957   *Homage* awarded Harriet Monroe Poetry Prize from the University of Chicago. Son Paul born March 5. Named tenured associate professor of interdisciplinary studies at the University of Minnesota. Travels to India on behalf of the State Department's United States Information Service to present a series of lectures on literature at various Indian universities. Visits Japan. Family reunited in Europe; travels in Italy and Spain.

1958   Chapbook *His Thought Made Pockets & the Plane Buckt*. Begins a handbook on Shakespeare, never completed. Hospitalized for alcoholism at Regent Hospital in New York City. He and Ann separate. University of Minnesota faculty board closes Department of Interdisciplinary Studies.

1959   UK publication of *Homage to Mistress Bradstreet and Other Poems*; this edition collects *Homage* along with selected earlier poems. Translation of *Le Cremin de la Croix* performed by the Minneapolis Symphony Orchestra. Undergoes treatment for alcoholism. Divorced from Ann April 28. Spends two weeks lecturing at the University of Utah. First Dream Songs published.

1960 Lectures at the University of California, Berkeley. Writes introduction to reprint of Thomas Nashe's *The Unfortunate Traveler*. Awarded Creative Arts Award from Brandeis University. Coauthors *The Arts of Reading*, a textbook collaboration with Ralph Ross and Allen Tate.

1961 Meets Kathleen ("Kate") Donahue. Summer teaches at Indiana School of Letters. Marries Kate September 1. Memoir "Thursday Out."

1962 Lectures at Bread Loaf, Middlebury, Vermont, in summer. Writer-in-residence at Brown University, Providence, Rhode Island, for fall 1962 and spring 1963 semesters. Daughter Martha born December 1.

1963 Receives Ingram Merrill Foundation Award. Travels to Washington, DC, and participates in the National Poetry Festival.

1964 Composes "Formal Elegy," a poem commemorating the death of John F. Kennedy. Publication of *77 Dream Songs*. Receives Russell Loines Award from the National Institute of Arts and Letters. Purchases home on Arthur Avenue in Minneapolis.

1965 Wins the Pulitzer Prize for *77 Dream Songs*.

1966 Awarded a Guggenheim fellowship to assist in completion of *The Dream Songs*. Moves to Dublin for academic year 1966–67. Travels throughout Europe. Attends Poetry International Festival in Spoleto, Italy.

1967 Attends the tenth anniversary of the Festival of Two Worlds in Spoleto. Returns to the US. Composes additional sonnets for sonnet sequence, published as *Berryman's Sonnets*. *Short Poems*, collecting early poems, *The Dispossessed*, and "Formal Elegy," published. Awarded the Academy of American Poets and National Endowment for the Arts Award for his contribution to American letters. Hospitalized for alcoholism.

1968 *His Toy, His Dream, His Rest* published.

1969 Receives the National Book Award and Bollingen Prize for *His Toy, His Dream, His Rest*. *The Dream Songs* published, collecting *77 Dream Songs* and *His Toy, His Dream, His Rest* together in one volume. Named Regent's Professor of Humanities. Hospitalized for alcoholism.

1970   Begins writing poems that make up *Love & Fame* in February. Recommences work on the Shakespeare biography. In May, undergoes alcoholic rehabilitation and experiences religious conversion. Travels with family to Mexico. Joins Alcoholics Anonymous. US version of *Love & Fame* released.

1971   Starts novel *Recovery* and long poem, *The Children*. Works on *Life of Christ*. Drake University in Iowa awards Berryman an honorary doctorate. Daughter Sarah Rebecca is born June 13. Berryman receives senior fellowship from the National Endowment for the Humanities to continue his work on a biography of Shakespeare. Begins work on selecting prose pieces for a collected volume of prose. A second, revised edition of *Love & Fame* is published in the United Kingdom. Submits manuscript for *Selected Poems* to UK publisher Faber and Faber, and new collection, *Delusions, Etc. of John Berryman*, to Farrar, Straus and Giroux.

1972   Dies January 7. Faber and Faber *Selected Poems* and *Delusions, Etc. of John Berryman* published posthumously.

1973   Unfinished novel *Recovery* published, with an introduction by Saul Bellow. Short story "Our Sins Are More Than We Can Bear" in the *Twin Cities Express*.

1975   Short story "Wash Far Away" in *American Review*.

1976   Selected prose volume *The Freedom of the Poet*, edited by Robert Giroux.

1977   *Henry's Fate & Other Poems (1967–1972)*, a selection made by John Haffenden of poems left uncollected or unpublished at the time of his death.

1988   *We Dream of Honour: John Berryman's Letters to His Mother*, edited by Richard Kelly.

1989   *Collected Poems 1937–1971* (1989), edited by Charles Thornbury.

1999   Various writings on Shakespeare collected as *Berryman's Shakespeare: Essays, Letters and Other Writings* (1999), edited by John Haffenden.

2004   Two *Selected Poems* are published, one for the Library of America series, edited by Kevin Young, and the other for the Faber and Faber Poet to Poet series, edited by Michael Hofmann.

2014   *The Heart Is Strange: New Selected Poems* (rev. ed. 2016), edited by Daniel Swift, published in recognition of the one hundredth anniversary of the poet's birth.

2020   *The Selected Letters of John Berryman*, edited by Philip Coleman and Calista McRae.

Conversations with
John Berryman

Poet, Editor, Teacher—Looks Forward to Own Book

Jane Stedman / 1939

From the *Detroit Collegian*, October 23, 1939, 2. Reprinted by permission.

[Berryman's first extant interview, published in the *Detroit Collegian*, a Wayne State University faculty newspaper, was occasioned by Berryman having secured a teaching position at Wayne State at the recommendation of Berryman's classmate and friend Bhain Campbell. Campbell, who died the following year of cancer, taught freshman English at Wayne, and persuaded the department chair to hire Berryman to replace him. Essentially at the start of his career, Berryman, then editor of *The Nation*, was still ambivalent about his having to teach, and viewed it as a way of making ends meet, an avocation as opposed to a calling.—Ed.]

Mr. John Berryman of the English department has, for the past five months, been pursuing two new methods in his editing of poetry used for the weekly political magazine *The Nation*. He received his appointment as poetry editor last summer, three months before he joined Wayne's faculty.

An example of the way he solicits material is seen in the collection of seven poems that appeared in *The Nation* September 30. Not one of them, he says, would have been submitted of the author's own accord. All were selections that he had requested. Among others is a poem "Of Gramatan's Transaction" by Bhain Campbell, another member of Wayne's faculty.

The second innovation Mr. Berryman has made is in the presentation. Formerly poems were scattered through the magazine with no unity whatsoever. This, Berryman believes, keeps the reader from noticing them. So he has initiated the idea of grouping poetry in a sort of miniature anthology.

What type of poetry does the editor see most of? In this case, political verse, since *The Nation* is primarily a political magazine. He finds little of the surrealistic snatches that gave so many people consternation a while ago. "The revolution in poetry has really been over for about twenty years," he says.

Most poems are in conventional forms, with the addition of some free verse. "We have readers say that our poetry is too conservative, and others who call it too radical," observed Berryman.

Aside from his recently assumed editorial duties, Mr. Berryman has published his own verse, listing among periodicals in which his poems have appeared such magazines as *Southern Review, Kenyon Review, Partisan Review, New Direction, Republic,* and *The Nation.*

In addition, various English magazines have used his work. He plans to bring out a book either next spring or fall since several publishers have requested him to let them have a manuscript.

The State of American Writing, 1948: Seven Questions

John Berryman / 1948

From *Partisan Review* 15, no. 8 (August 1948): 855–60. © The Estate of John Berryman, used with permission.

Note published at head of *Partisan Review* article: We are publishing below some of the replies to a questionnaire submitted to a group of American writers. [The writers other than Berryman included R. P. Blackmur, Robert Gorham Davis, Leslie A. Fiedler, Clement Greenberg, John Crowe Ransom, Wallace Stevens, Lionel Trilling, and H. L. Mencken. —Ed.] The questions follow:

1. What in your opinion are the new literary tendencies, or figures, if any, that have emerged in the forties? How does the literary atmosphere of this decade compare with that of the thirties? In what way, too, does the present period differ from the first postwar period? Can the differences between the two postwar periods be defined in relation to the European situation?
2. Do you think that American middlebrow culture has grown more powerful in this decade? In what relation does this middlebrow tendency stand to serious writing—does it threaten or bolster it?
3. What is the meaning of the literary revivals (James, Forster, Fitzgerald, etc.) that have taken place as of late? Is this a publishing phenomenon or is it an organic literary interest in the sense that the rediscovered writers of the past are in some way truly expressive of current literary needs?
4. Is the general opinion that, unlike the twenties, this is not a period of experiment in language and form? If that is true, what significance can be attached to this fact? Does present writing base itself on the earlier experimentation, in the sense that it has creatively assimilated it, or can it be said that the earlier experimentation came to a dead end?

5. In the twenties most writers were freelancers, whereas now many make their living by teaching in universities. Has this change affected the tone and mood of literature in our time? Can it with justice be said that American writing has grown more academic since the twenties?

6. In recent decades serious literary criticism has shown a special bent for the analysis and interpretation of poetry. What is the significance of this concentration at a time when poetry itself has had an ever-diminishing audience? Would literature benefit from a critical concern, equally intense, with other genres of writing? In our time, when the fate of culture as a whole is called into question, does the basic meaning of the literary effort stand in need of reexamination?

7. What is the effect on American writing of the growing tension between Soviet Communism and the democratic countries? How are cultural interests affected by this struggle and do you think a writer should involve himself in it (as writer? a person?) to the point of commitment?

John Berryman responds:

The questions are interesting, and I take them all, with one or two prefatory remarks. The forties are, of course, not over yet, and are not comparable anyway, as a "postwar" period, with the twenties; in relation to the end of open warfare, 1948 is only 1921—to say nothing of the sluggish influence of what is called the "cold war." If therefore we do not see flashing about us yet the novelists we would like to set against Hemingway, Faulkner, Fitzgerald, we needn't weep with chagrin. Since the story has in general to be very gloomy, it is worth remembering also an inevitable lag; a number of the poems, for instance, with which Eliot raised hell in the twenties, were written by 1910. And the country is a big one, no one can know what is happening everywhere. With these qualifications, and without argument, a few opinions:

1, 2, 4, 5

It has been a bad decade so far. If the twenties were Eliot's decade, and the thirties Auden's, this has been simply the decade of Survival. Wider military operations, their prolongation, their involvement of civilians, above all the preceding and accompanying genocide, distinguish wholly this war from the last. Everybody lost years, and many seem to have lost their nerve. There is a political, perhaps a moral, paralysis. The one movement of interest has been foreign, existentialism, and shows little artistic effect in America. The chief cultural phenomenon of the decade here has probably been the intellectuals' desertion of Marxism. What they have replaced it with, I cannot discover; nihilism is more articulate and impressive than in any other period of which I have knowledge.

In parenthesis, I would remark what seems to me to be a widespread, violent condition of *bad conscience*. Under the patent name of "guilt" we are familiar with this, but then, of course, everybody is "guilty" of everything, and that is that. Bad conscience is more serious. Few men of reflection can be satisfied now with their actions and attitudes during the recent war. Well, we put that aside: the Enemy was clear, and moreover what happened (producing what is happening now) would have happened anyway, "It was done for us"—your modern intellectual is astonishingly fatalistic. This is the view generally taken, with a gain in uneasiness, of the use of the atomic bomb. But few men of reflection can be satisfied with their actions and attitudes *now*. Well, again the Enemy is clear (Stalin for Hitler), what is happening cannot be influenced by us, and so on. That is, men of reflection are reconciled, in their degree, to their past and to their present. The trouble is the future: what they—or what *They* for them—are going to be doing in the months and years and days to come. This is the trouble. In order to be reconciled to *this*, one would have to learn to be reconciled beforehand to an atrocious crime one might well soon commit without having the slightest wish to commit it; and that, I suppose, is out of the question. So that men who can think and are moral must stand ready night and day to the others of blind evil. What has created this is an usurpation which is not complete: usurpation of individual decision, which yet leaves the individual nominally free—and of course actually free if he happens to be a hero. But literary men are seldom heroes, and heroes of this sort, at present, as soon as they announce themselves, cease anyway to be literary men. It is not a state of mind, this readiness, favorable to writing.

Literary prostitutes and milksops feel it less acutely, and they are thriving. *Of course* American middlebrow culture has grown powerful in this decade. *Of course* American writing has grown increasingly academic since the twenties. But my terms were extravagant—I have nothing against prostitutes, not knowing any, and professors, many of whom are very manly indeed, drink whiskey not milk. No doubt the meretricious in upper-middle-class popular writing (as it apes serious writing), and the spineless in professorial imitations of serious writing, may invite these old-fashioned epithets. But all I intended was an instant's emotion, sign of a conflict that really must be held to exist between serious writers and these other groups.

Whether anything can be done about it or not, it is necessary to recognize the conflict.

It is necessary because it is sometimes difficult. Although Authority is one of the two or three points at which literary criticism is just now feeblest, we see in the public, even in its most attentive section, a pathetic over-reliance upon what it conceives to be "authority"—the eagerness for guideposts of a badly educated and swamped-with-writing audience. Among the most influential of these is mere contiguity: what writing is published where. But good writing may be published anywhere at present, and trash may, in a degree of confusion not yet reached in the thirties and not approached earlier. Several things have produced this state of affairs: the death or decline of magazines useful ten years ago, absence of serious new magazines, inadequate hospitality to new talent by the best continuing magazines, and their inability (until recently they were all very poor) to retain or to print all the work of some of their best contributors as these became well known. The sudden avidity of some high-paying popular magazines, however, for serious writing or what will look as much like it as possible, is what counts most. In the thirties we saw Hemingway in *Esquire*. But he was world-famous. Now they get writers earlier, indeed they try to get them at once, and a brave new talent may be corrupt in the fashion magazines before it can vote. These things are confusing to the young, and not to the young only. Then there is the matter of temptation—which would be merely every writer's own business, if talent were not in truth what is sometimes called, a "gift," for which one has somehow to be responsible, as best one can.

The alternative to journalism, for most American writers, is teaching, and the dangers from it are similarly complicated. They range from pure slump to pure irritation. To write is hard and takes the whole mind and wants one's whole time; a university is the perfect place not to write. The irritation is seldom mentioned in print, but matters. Many professors of English cherish (I can't imagine why) unsatisfied literary ambitions—just as most writers do. And then they think writers queer and arrogant, and many writers are. Trouble from all this. And a teacher's audience is always there, and is *so* responsive. Repetition of books and courses numbs. For poets and fiction writers, as for critics, it might be claimed that teaching is valuable because in a seat of learning one keeps on learning. I have no faith in this claim. Writers of any sort certainly ought to know more than they do and as much as possible, but the writers I know outside universities read more, on the whole, more that counts, than those inside. I have no faith in the claim even for critics; and it is not widely enough understood that literary criticism is an activity which bears no necessary relation whatever to good teaching. But the energy used by good teaching is very much the energy required for writing. Finally, the substantial repetition of *experience* involved in teaching, after two or three years, constitutes, for a fiction writer at any rate, the most unsatisfactory life conceivable short of imprisonment. Something can certainly be said for a writer's teaching, but something has, by Blackmur, Stegner, and others: teaching is but one way of keeping alive.

The effects of these difficulties are very clear in American writing of the decade, especially of course in recent criticism, which is almost as interesting as fourteen classrooms in one building, all carefully constructed, all empty. It is specially unfortunate, because criticism has in front of it just now a delicate task, namely the exploration of the matter broached in Question 4. The nature of experiment in writing wants restating, and the return-to-form in poetry during the last ten years wants general study. Now the inevitable bias, in an academic criticism, against "experiment" and in favor of "form," is wretched equipment for this task. In poetry, too, the process of steadying has been assisted—not to its gain—by wide academic instruction in the hands of writers, and the whole transitional period which I think is now coming to an end, perhaps hastened. But I can't enter on these things here.

3. The revivals are "an annoying relief" (as Erich Kahler described to me the telephone strike).[1] It is good to see the authors come to fame and familiarity, and it is galling to see them battened on, praised for a hundred qualities they don't possess, mis-selected, made catch-cries. James was inevitable! Forster and Fitzgerald are being overrated. The question apparently wants me to say that these novelists are being revived mainly because we have no fiction of our own; so I will; but it's obvious. There have been single novels, but the one new writer who looks now to give us book after book that will not disappointment, and in fact to grow, is Jean Stafford. The amazing cults, as of Kafka and Kierkegaard, are more interesting to me than the revivals. It is the advance of middlebrow culture that has made all these possible, and I read in *Life* that *Don Giovanni* is—oh, just great, great.

6. In the first place, it is not clear that poetry *has* benefited from the intense concentration upon it of modern criticism. There are things that you cannot see with a microscope, for instance you cannot see the sun, and some critics specially devoted to the microscope have therefore argued that the sun does not exist. There are poets who believe whatever they are told, and so the sun disappeared from certain tracts of American verse. One or two extraordinary things, like Robert Lowell's poetry, were helped into

existence by some of this criticism, and undoubtedly the general conscience of literate poets improved, but at certain costs.

In the second place, there is something frightening in the notion of a criticism "equally intense" being turned on work much less able to bear it in general than poetry—dialogues, say, travel books, and so on. Could not the criticism be simply more thoughtful, perhaps more learned, perhaps more penetrating, capable of making larger connections? On the other hand, there can be no doubt that the criticism of drama and fiction has something to learn from the criticism of poetry. It has also something to learn—if it liked—from Shakespearean criticism. And criticism of every kind has everything to learn from the science of the mind as that has developed from Freud forward.

To the last part of this question: Yes.

7. "The effect of the tension is" depressing. "Cultural interests are affected" adversely. "The writer should" do any damned thing he can think of to keep on writing, writing well.

Note

1. In April 1947, the National Federation of Telephone Workers (NFTW), representing some 340,000 telephone operators throughout the United States, the majority of them women, went on strike, demanding wage increases, pensions, job definitions, and other issues.

Read a Book of Verse at Least Once a Year, Lecturer Urges

Charles Ludwig / 1952

From the *Cincinnati Times-Star*, 1952, 4.

[Berryman granted a single interview during his stay in Cincinnati, a period of formidable self-discovery and artistic growth. The piece focuses on more prosaic details that concern his position at the University of Cincinnati, and some rather perfunctory remarks about his series of Shakespeare lectures, which were by all accounts well-attended and well-received. It does, however, provide a curmudgeonly Berryman the opportunity to express his views on the decline in culture since the Elizabethan era.—Ed.]

"Everybody should read at least one book of verse a year," was the advice offered Tuesday by John Berryman, youthful poet, critic, and author, who has arrived at the University of Cincinnati. He will fill, during the second semester, the lectureship in poetry founded at UC by the late George Elliston, poet and news writer who for many years was on the *Times-Star* staff.

Berryman, who comes from Princeton, New Jersey, has been Oldham Shakespeare scholar at Cambridge University, England, and a Rockefeller research fellow. He is the author of *Dispossessed*, a volume of poems, and the biography, *Stephen Crane*.

"The intelligent young man of the year 1600 would be found interested in the poetry of Shakespeare and Ben Jonson," said Berryman. "It is an oversimplification to say this was because his mind was not distracted by radio, television, film stars, automobiles, world wars, and political anxieties."

Though Shakespeare started poor, he achieved a fine income beside his immortality—his income was probably the equivalent of what forty thousand dollars a year would be now. Few poets today make a living from their poetry—most of them teach, some do other work. The fine poet, Wallace

Stevens, is vice president of a large insurance company; William Carlos Williams is a practicing physician.

"The Victorian poets often sold fifty thousand copies of a work but probably not two American books of poetry a year reach sales of five thousand.

"Quality of our American poets has improved. The impetus of the nineteenth-century fame of Longfellow, Bryant, Whittier, and [James Russell] Lowell has died out and they have no standing abroad. Far better are many of our modern poets such as T. S. Eliot, Frost, Robinson, Ezra Pound, and John Crowe Ransom now in Ohio at Kenyon College. Of our old names Walt Whitman stands out, and Emerson, Poe, and Emily Dickinson will live."

Berryman will reside with his wife at 250 Greendale Avenue. He will conduct a course in Shakespeare at a poetry workshop at UC and give two series of free public lectures in McMicken Hall. One on "Shakespeare" will start at 4 p.m. Wednesday, the other on "Modern Poets" will start February 21.

Homage to Mr. Berryman

Dorothy Strudwick / 1956

From *Minnesota Daily*, November 5, 1956, 6, 16. Reprinted by permission.

[The first of nine Minnesota-based newspaper articles that featured interviews with Berryman—of which all but two, the slightest, are included in this volume—appeared in late 1956, several years after he was hired as professor at the University of Minnesota. Dorothy Strudwick, his interviewer, in a short column nevertheless manages to derive some memorable commentary from Berryman, then enjoying a personal and professional recuperation afforded by his employment at the university, his new relationship with Ann (then pregnant; the couple was married and Paul was born the following month), and most importantly his artistic naissance in the wake of the October 1 publication of his acclaimed Bradstreet poem.—Ed.]

"A man's gifts," Ibsen once rebuked a great friend of his, "are not a privilege, but a duty."

This observation is reflected today by the works of John Berryman, lecturer in the humanities program of the Department of Interdisciplinary Studies, who has been lauded for his recently published poem, *Homage to Mistress Bradstreet.*

"The appearance of this work has been acclaimed by literary critics throughout the nation," explains Russell M. Cooper, assistant dean of general studies. "Already it has been cited as one of the outstanding poems of our generation."

Writer Conrad Aiken has called *Homage to Mistress Bradstreet* "one of the finest poems ever written by an American, a classic right on the doorstep." John Holmes, *New York Times* critic has said, "the poem is a dense whole, masterly in construction, a book made to stand as a landmark in American poetry and withstand much reading."

The epic poem, published in a fifty-seven-page book released October 1, is one poet's look at another. Anne Bradstreet was the first American woman to write poetry.

A well-educated English girl, Anne Dudley married Simon Bradstreet and came to the New World in 1630. Her husband is remembered as a governor of the Massachusetts Colony.

"I have always been interested in American history," Berryman says, "especially the rough times."

The first settlers who arrived with Governor Winthrop knew "rough times," and the total effect of the hardships, sacrifices, sorrow, and rebellion is pictured vividly in sharp concise diction which distinguishes Mr. Berryman's verse. As a contrast, Mrs. Bradstreet's poetry today is judged dull and didactic. She was strongly influenced by Du Bartas, a French Huguenot poet, and the Englishman Francis Quarles.

Later, Anne Bradstreet turned to personal subjects which display a more modern flavor—prose and poetry dedicated to her husband and children and on her house which had burned to the ground.

"I had no special reason for selecting Anne Bradstreet as my subject," Berryman explains, "except that she was the first poet of this country and that her great effort to create, to exercise her intellect is to be greatly admired. She lived in a society which frowned on a woman's interest going beyond the home, where harsh circumstances made survival of prime importance."

In the poem, by process of imagination, Berryman has placed Anne in rebellion against youthful virtue, an arranged marriage, inability to produce a child for many years, the confinement of household duties, and finally, against God's will on her death-bed. These rebellions are followed by submissions, illustrating both her brave and miserable moments.

Thus *Homage to Mistress Bradstreet* stands not only as a tribute to American heritage, but it is also the sharp portrait of a remarkable woman who was inspired to make an earlier contribution to literature.

Like all true scholars (Berryman by choice is a Shakespearean scholar), he expresses "gratitude for the wealth of knowledge and literature that men have bequeathed to future generations," and he points out how inspiring this knowledge can be to students who are striving to make their own contribution.

At forty-two, Berryman's own contributions have been the result of years of concentrated effort, some sacrifices, and often "going without sleep."

In 1945, he was awarded first prize (Kenyon-Doubleday) for his story, "Imaginary Jew." He won the Shelley Memorial award in 1949 and a year later an American Academy Award. *The Dispossessed*, a collection of poems, came out in 1948; *Stephen Crane*, a critical biography, in 1950. He has been contributor to *Five Young American Poets*, 1940, *Best American Short Stories*, 1946, *A Little Treasury of American Prose*, and to literary criticism and professional publications.

Through all the praise of his works, Berryman retains a boy-like modesty. Dean Cooper has said, "In many ways, Berryman is self-effacing and modest. He does not mention the 'rave' notices on his book, although in other ways he is quite an outgoing person."

Although Berryman claims Oklahoma as his birthplace, for many years he lived in the East before coming to Minneapolis two years ago. In the East he lectured on creative writing at Princeton, Harvard, and Wayne Universities.

"I prefer writing poetry to prose," Berryman confesses. "Given a temperament directed that way and practice, poetry is often the easier medium for expression of thought."

Yet he has proved that he can express himself as easily in prose as in poetry, and his future plans include work in both fields. He is currently working on three books of poetry and four of prose.

"I have no interest in what I have done in the past," he reports, "the creative work to be done is my greatest pleasure."

Berryman does not rest on his laurels.

Around the Town

Ralph Mendonca / 1957

From the *Indian Express Sunday Standard*, August 4, 1957, n.p.

[In "The State of American Writing, 1948," Berryman laments the need for writers to teach as it generally saps their energies and limits them to reading only what is required for the curriculum. A decade later, in an interview for a New Delhi–based newspaper—conducted during his lecture tour of India on behalf of the US State Department—Berryman seems to have reconciled himself to his scholarly avocation. Here he argues that in fact writers make better teachers than career educators, primarily due to their relative "experience" and "wider reading," and their tendency, as creative and intellectually curious individuals, to not lapse into monotony, but instead to be constantly learning and exploring. Certainly this change in perspective can in part be accounted for by Berryman's increased age, or perhaps also by his refinement of his skill as educator, and his new position at the University of Minnesota teaching a variety of humanities courses as opposed to strictly literature.—Ed.]

Is the modern highly organized and highly industrialized civilization tending to make the poet increasingly "rara avis"? Will our epics, as some predict, be written in the future by our scientists? And will we have to decipher mathematical formulas to find our poetry?

John Berryman, one of America's leading poets, admits that poets today are like hothouse plants. Finding themselves uneasy, uncomfortable in a hostile world, a civilization which had enthroned values different from those they cherished, they were forced to climb up into their ivory towers.

That means that the poet who has always been an erratic phenomenon, is considered as even more so today. There was a time, explains Berryman, when there used to be a gentleman's agreement between the poets and the readers. And according to that agreement, the poet had to satisfy certain expectations on the part of the readers. But those poets, who faithfully carried out that agreement had to pay the price for their popularity.

Longfellow, for instance, earned a thousand dollars for a poem. But, according to Berryman, he ultimately became a victim of his audience and his poetry suffered. The modern poet, wiser perhaps from the experience of his predecessors, has disowned that agreement.

Berryman admits that a poet cannot operate in a vacuum. But the modern poet, he says, is no longer concerned about the size of his audience. "What is permanent is what matters to him more." He seeks not the values that are in vogue, but desires those that have the "quality of permanence."

Will this rift between the public and private values go on widening and will the great public cease to bother about the values the poet has discovered "within himself"? It is true that the modern poet is not much concerned about his audience, says Berryman, but he expects the audience to come up to him and see what he is doing and try to know what he has to say.

But he seems confident that poets and poetry will go on, because "every age and every civilization need their crystal-gazers, someone to dream their dreams."

Revolt

As a young man—he is, incidentally, only forty-two—Berryman resented the highly organized life, revolted against the society in which he lived, and consequently longed to live in Europe.

After graduating from Columbia University in literature and philosophy Berryman went to England and joined Cambridge in an attempt to drink deep of an ancient culture in an ancient land, the land of his forefathers.

But as far as the values of society at large were concerned, Berryman did not find England very different from America. And so at the end of two years he was "wild to get back home." France, usually regarded as the Mecca by other artists, also never appealed to him much. One thing he missed terribly in France was hearing his language spoken.

And as he moved on to other countries on the continent, it gradually became evident to him that if he was to settle down in any of them, it was necessary to build up "a whole new series of associations," and that at the end of it he would "still remain a stranger."

Unlike most poets, Berryman began by writing prose. At twelve, he wrote a novel about life on planet Neptune. But his first literary effort to be published was a poem when he was nineteen. And unusual for a poet, and certainly very unusual for a young man, although Berryman continued to write poetry while in England, he decided he would not send his poems anywhere for publication.

"Considering how greedy one is when young to publish everything one produces," Berryman recalled when I met him in Bombay last week, "that seems quite a wise decision."

Berryman, who also writes short stories, biographies, and literary criticism, says that he would have liked to live by his pen. "I tried and failed," he confesses. Poetry, he says, "cannot be a full-time profession, because you cannot write poetry all the time." Besides, poets being essentially lazy, it is good that they be forced to take up some other profession.

And so to fill in time between dreams and to supplement the income he earned through his pen, Berryman began to teach.

Teaching

By now he has taught in about ten American universities, and he has come to like teaching. "Writing is an isolated profession," he explains, "and teaching and travelling provide the much-needed contact with the people." He has also come to feel that most writers make good teachers.

One reason for it, according to him, is that most writers have more experience and wider reading than most other career teachers. Another is that since most writers record their words and thoughts, they naturally avoid repeating themselves, they are "against what is monotonous."

Berryman has come to India on a two-month tour sponsored by the American government. His business here is naturally to talk about American literature, and being a poet that naturally involves a lot of poetry reading.

He learned poetry reading from one who was considered a master. He befriended Dylan Thomas when he was in England, and he not only admired his poetry, but "he was also the most brilliant reader of poems I have ever heard."

Berryman has been doing poetry reading for the last ten years, but he is still reluctant to read his own poems.

When he reads, he explains, he sometimes dons the "singing robes" and sometimes only a "sweat shirt." That is because a poem can be read in different ways, and every time emphasis is placed on different lines, which means highlighting a part of it and not presenting the poem as a whole. And therefore, he feels that reading one of his poems alone would mean betraying it.

John Berryman on Today's Literature

Phyllis Meras / 1963

From the *Providence Sunday Journal*, May 26, 1963, W-20. Reprinted by permission.

[Berryman biographer Paul Mariani provides the scene for this brief interview: On his way out to see a doctor, Berryman, having greeted interviewer Phyllis Meras at the door, at first made a rude attempt at cutting short the interview. Once Meras got him talking about the distinct lack of worthwhile American literature, however, he relented, and spoke with Meras at some length about the writers he most admired (Mariani 394).—Ed.]

Poet, critic, teacher, John Berryman is a loose-jointed, bespectacled man nearing fifty who pretends to an air of vagueness and diffidence. But an underlying energy and enthusiasm belie it.

At the start of a recent interview at Brown University, where he has been visiting professor this year, he tugged at his bow tie and explained that he had very little to say, and a doctor's appointment in half an hour. "I teach and I write," he said, "I'm not copy."

All the same, an hour and a half later, doctor's appointment forgotten, Berryman was still pulling his green, yellow, and purple tie, and talking.

He is author of *Homage to Mistress Bradstreet* (1956), which has been called one of the half dozen best American long poems of this century. Anne Bradstreet was America's first woman poet, turning out a respectable body of verse despite the cruel hardships of Puritan Massachusetts frontier life. Berryman's poem derives its powerful cutting edge from the granitic realism of Puritan courage at its most tenacious and God-fearing.

But Berryman, Oklahoma-born with the University of Minnesota as his present home base, talked less of poets in the interview than of the dearth of "anything good in the literary magazine field" in this country.

"I read *Time* magazine for science and crime but certainly not for literature. I'm not all that patriotic but I feel it's kind of a national injury that the book reviews in our magazines and newspaper supplements are so tedious and the short stories that are published are so unbelievably boring. The two best literary magazines are both published in London. They're *Encounter* and the *Times Literary Supplement.*"

Despite the feebleness of American critical publications at present, he believes that American literature—and poetry in particular—is proving very influential abroad.

"I had a State Department fellowship a while ago to set up degree programs in American studies overseas. I was in western India one time and I found a seminar being given on one of my long poems. American poetry has had an immense, indescribable influence abroad. Rilke and Lorca have exerted a formidable influence in the United States, but except for them, everything is going the other way—though, admittedly, our top has been lifted off slightly in the last year or so."

"We lost Hemingway and Faulkner conked out and then Frost quit. That's a very heavy loss all at one time. I'm not being parochial or nationalistic, but it's hard to find anyone anywhere with the reputation those men had.

"It's too bad Frost never had the Nobel Prize, but the trouble was he didn't translate well—even his comments when they were translated sounded silly. One of the people who went to Russia with him,[1] for example, admitted that by the time you got what he was saying into Russian, the punch was all gone. All of the independence and hard-headedness disappeared in translation, yet he was as shrewd and as cruel as a Medici."

Berryman indicated that the only American critic of stature today is Edmund Wilson. As for novelists and short story writers he mentioned Saul Bellow, Terry Southern, Walter Clemens, and James Powers.

"Mailer's gone to pieces, but we've got some amazing women, too—Flannery O'Connor. One trouble with most women writers, though, is that they're too personal. Beckett looks at the human mind with darkness and it's jagged and ghastly the way that things don't happen in his plays. But the way, Rebecca West, for example, looks at things they become so vicious and cruel I can hardly read her. Of course, though, I'm generalizing about women, and I will say it's not that way at all with Flannery O'Connor."

He remarked that although he was a teacher of creative writing, he was sorry to see a lot of his students in creative writing courses.

"I probably shouldn't say this—and I think the department at Brown is one of the best in the country—but people who want to write shouldn't be in creative writing courses. If they really want to write, they'll write anyway. They should be studying history or language or mathematics."

As for his own writing, Berryman is currently at work on a long poem, *The Dream Song*.

"It's been in the works for eight years. I have an anti-hero in it who's a character the world gives a hard time to. About forty-five sections of it have already been published in various places, but it's still hopelessly unfinished even though it fills a whole suitcase. When I was in Calcutta I had to buy it a new suitcase."

Berryman also has three books on Shakespeare in various stages of development. One is a critical biography; the second is based on discoveries about Shakespeare he made while on a Guggenheim Foundation fellowship in 1953. The third is a critical edition of *King Lear*.

Note

1. In the summer of 1962, just prior to the Cuban Missile Crisis, Robert Frost, together with Stewart L. Udall, secretary of the interior in the John F. Kennedy Administration and a close friend of Frost's, traveled to Moscow at Kennedy's behest to act as an emissary of peace and in the hopes of securing a private meeting with Soviet Premiere Nikita Khrushchev, which they eventually did. "A great nation makes great poetry, and great poetry makes a great nation," Frost is quoted as saying to Khrushchev during their brief yet poignant meeting. Udall later speculated that Khrushchev's willingness to meet with them was to ascertain what might be Kennedy's potential reaction to Soviet build-up of missiles in Cuba. Udall was later enlisted to convey a "secret message" from Khrushchev to Kennedy, that of Khrushchev's intent to "do nothing to 'heat up' the Berlin crisis until after the November elections." Stewart L. Udall, "Robert Frost's Last Adventure," *New York Times*, June 11, 1972.

Song of a Poet: John Berryman

Bob Lundegaard / 1965

From *Minneapolis Tribune*, June 27, 1965, 1E–2E. Reprinted by permission.

[Apart from some rather brief comments for appreciative newspaper articles in spring 1965, in the wake of receiving the Pulitzer Prize for *77 Dream Songs*, the most substantial interview—and, at 1,700 words in length, the longest to date—was given to a friend of Berryman's, the Minneapolis-based journalist Bob Lundegaard. Perhaps due to the air of comradeship, Berryman comes across as relatively good-natured, and Lundegaard manages to cover a variety of different subjects: Berryman talks of his method of composition, of late night calls to friends to read them the latest Dream Songs, of his childhood and early career, and his Shakespeare researches.—Ed.]

The telephone may ring anytime, interrupting dinner or shattering sleep. The person who answers it may live in New York, California, or Minneapolis, but he is probably a poet and certainly a friend of John Berryman, University of Minnesota humanities professor and the owner of the rich growl at the other end of the line.

For the phone call is John Berryman's way of announcing the arrival of a new poem, probably an addition to the *77 Dream Songs* that won him the Pulitzer Prize for poetry last month.

"Writing poetry is a funny business," he said last week, collapsing into his favorite faded green armchair in the living room of his southeast Minneapolis home. "Something happens in your mind, and it happens extremely fast, namely in three or four hours. I write out a song" (neatly in pencil on whatever comes to hand—the back of an envelope, a scrap of paper) "and then I go back to bed. Meanwhile, I figure that this is the most marvelous song ever written by anybody in the entire world, and I ring up all my friends in various parts of the country and read it to them. People like Allen Tate,

Robert Lowell, Robert Fitzgerald, Ralph Ross, my chairman, and Philip Siegelman and his wife.

"They never have any suggestions to make. They all think it's marvelous also.

"Then an awful thing happens. One, I lose all interest in that song—namely, I figure it's no good. Secondly, I stamp up and down and I feel very bad, because I can't any more use it as a weapon against gentility."

There follows a period of examining the poem objectively—of revising it, and re-revising it, perhaps back near its original feeling. "You wipe out the defects that you have inserted," Berryman explained. "Frequently what you first think of it is indelicate, but it's original, and you have to do the best you can with it. THAT'S IT."

The shout with which he had ended the sentence is characteristic of Berryman's dramatic approach to conversation. He is not only a poet, teacher, and scholar ("I masquerade as a writer. Actually I'm a scholar"), but, in his humanities lectures at the University of Minnesota and in his informal talk, he is also an actor.

His pauses are not used groping for the right word but for effect. He will ingratiatingly anticipate his anecdotes with a "this will amuse you" or "I'll tell you a wonderful story," all the while gesturing dramatically or, especially when he reads his poems, nodding his head vigorously before a crucial line.

He will even, to show his opinion of Indian university teachers, bark like a dog: "The professor was standing in front of his class—now get this—not talking to his students, but *barking* at them. It was really scary. 'ARF, ARF,' he would say, 'A is A, B is B, ARF, ARF.'"

He has been delighting, stimulating, provoking—and teaching—Minnesota students for ten years now, a time he calls "spectacularly pleasing and agreeable." Judging by the reaction of most students, the feeling is mutual. "I teach hard," he says, "very hard." But he adds, "I like my kids. I like them good."

The Oklahoma-born Berryman's roots are here ("My grandfather was one of the people who settled this city, and my father was born in St. Paul"), but his coming here to teach, he says, had nothing to do with his ancestors.

"I came here because Allen Tate was here, and I was fed up with the place I was at, which was Iowa, and I didn't know quite where to go. New York? Various places? So I rang up Allen, that good man, and I said, 'Allen, what shall I do? Where shall I go?' and he said, 'Come here.' So I came here. Just one friend. That's all you need. One friend."

Among the other companions he has acquired in his sojourn here are his third wife, Kate, who is, at twenty-five, exactly half Berryman's age, and their two-and-a-half-year-old daughter, Martha, alias "Twissy-Pits."

Kate was the closest friend of a former student of Berryman's who went to California in 1960. Berryman telephoned her to ask about the student and, as Kate puts it, "We talked over the phone for about three weeks without meeting, then we decided we'd get together and have lunch, and we're still having lunch." She was at the time a student at the College of St. Catherine in St. Paul.

Berryman also had a Catholic childhood ("a very bad parochial school in Oklahoma") that was marked by a trauma: "My father killed himself when I was eleven, and I've never been the same since. I have a funny feeling that a father's death is the most important fact in a life. At last the cover is removed. You understand me?

"I'll give you two instances," he says, briskly assuming his professorial role. "Freud in his correspondence with [Wilhelm] Fliess, while he was working on the dream analysis business said, 'My father has just died and I cannot bear all this flooding of memoranda. I can't handle it. The OLD ONE'S DEATH HAS CAST ME ASTRAY.' And he went on to write the fundamental work of psychoanalysis. That's one way of looking at it.

"Another way of looking at it: A. E. Housman, the poet and classical scholar? He wrote all his important poems, the ones in *Shropshire Lad*, directly after his father's death. And never wrote anything else. Individual poems, but no other spate."

Berryman's artistic output in the year following his father's death was less spectacular: "It was a science fiction novel with a hero named E-Loro-a' Ala. I called it *Trip to Neptune*. It was never published, except by a girl named Helen Justice, who was eight feet tall and deeply in love with me. She took the manuscript and bound it in two volumes with brown paper.

"As a matter of fact, I came very late to poetry. Very. Like nineteen? Now by nineteen most people's lives are established, but not in my case. You know what the teaching of poetry is like. Sir Walter Scott? Leigh Hunt? And others? Well, I developed a hatred for poetry which did me very well for years. Did me VERY well. But at last it wore me out."

New Directions published his first poems when he was twenty-eight. His reputation grew with a critical biography of Stephen Crane and *Homage to Mistress Bradstreet*, published in 1956 and called by Edmund Wilson "the most distinguished long poem by an American since *The Waste Land*."

After writing it, he recalls, "I resolved with all my heart and soul never to write another long poem. I wrote a song about a couple named Henry and Mabel. They were names my wife and I gave to each other because they were the most boring names we could think of. So I started a poem, since killed, about Henry and Mabel. It was about my father. Henry was not me, but he bears some resemblance to me. And I've been at the poem for ten years."

It is not easy to say what the Dream Songs are about. Henry is in most of them, but, according to Berryman, "he talks about himself not only in the first person, but also in the third person and in the second person. And that's not simple. But my whole self-respect is based on my administration of pronouns. I understand the pronoun better than any other writer. However it's troublesome for the receiving brain of the good-natured, helpless reader."

Like most modern poets, Berryman has been carrying on a protracted lovers' quarrel with those readers.

"Everyone says I'm obscure," he bristles. "So was Keats. So was Wordsworth. But some people don't seem to find me so difficult. My work is regarded as experimental, obscure, weird, and new, but actually it is not. The rhyme scheme of the Dream Songs comes from the Italians and Milton. In fact, I regard myself as a highly traditional artist."

As evidence, his favorite poet is Shakespeare, and he divides his published criticism in three categories: fiction, poetry, and Shakespeare. "I learned an immense amount from Shakespeare," Berryman observed. "How to be brief. How to be, or try to be, gorgeous. You know, lyric grandeur. But the main thing I learned from him is that you put people together and in action and see what happens.

"That's what I did in Dream Songs with Henry and his friend, Mr. Bones. Some friend! More like Job's Comforter. The point is to have a maximum amount of activity and see what happens."

He has been working, off and on for years, on four books about Shakespeare—a four-hundred-page critical biography, a critical edition of *King Lear* ("There is no satisfactory critical edition of *King Lear*, and I thought we might as well have one") and two studies of Shakespeare's sources. "Needless to say, I don't expect to do all these things. It's just a plan."

If they are done, it will be in his second-floor "Shakespeare Room," which lies directly above his living-room chair. On its floor are piled, ten-deep, about thirty stacks of books on Shakespeare. There are only two non-Shakespearian touches. One is a bulletin board near the desk with pictures of such friends as Mayor Arthur Naftalin, Lowell, the late Theodore Roethke, and an "anti-picture" of poet Kenneth Rexroth, whom Berryman loathes.

The other is an *Oxford Dictionary* standing upright on the floor. Its cover crumbles at the touch and it only goes up to Thu, but it is one of the Berryman's proudest possessions.

He is more detached about the Pulitzer award. Not the five hundred dollars, which comes in handy, but the lofty language of the certificate. "I attended Columbia College," he recollects, "and received a big diploma, written entirely in Latin. Then I went to the University of Cambridge and they gave me a little thing written in English."

As for the money, Berryman invoked another favorite author, Stephen Crane, who once said, "My charity begins in my right pants pocket."

One Answer to a Question: Changes

John Berryman / 1965

Published in *Shenandoah*, August 17, 1965, 67–76, reprinted in *Poets and Poetry*, edited by Howard Nemerov, 94–103, and in *The Freedom of the Poet*, 323–31. © The Estate of John Berryman. Reprinted by permission.

[Berryman's essay-length response to a questionnaire poet Howard Nemerov submitted to a number of poets, while not strictly a "conversation" is collected here as it provides one of Berryman's few prose statements concerning his poetics, and for its revealing insight into his inspirations, themes, and methods, topics of similar importance in his more classically "conversational"—in other words relatively unprepared, off-the-cuff, and interrogatory—interviews which make up the remainder of this present text.—Ed.]

This slight exploration of some of my opinions about my work as a poet, you may wish to bear in mind, is the statement of a man nearing fifty, and I am less impressed than I used to be by the universal notion of a continuity of individual personality—which will bring me in a moment to the first and most interesting of the four questions proposed by Howard Nemerov. It is a queer assignment. I've complied with similar requests before, but never without fundamental misgivings. For one thing, one forgets, one even deliberately forgets in order to get on with new work, and so may seriously misrepresent the artist-that-was twenty years ago. For another, there are trade secrets. At the same time that one works partly to open fresh avenues for other writers (though one would not dream of admitting it), one has secrets, like any craftsman, and I figure that anyone who deserves to know them deserves to find them out for himself. So I do not plan to give anything away.

The question was this: "Do you see your work as having essentially changed in character or style since you began?"

I would reply: *of course.* I began work in verse-making as a burning, trivial disciple of the great Irish poet William Butler Yeats, and I hope I have moved off from there. One is obsessed at different times by different things and by different ways of putting them. Naturally there are catches in the question. What does "essentially" mean? What is "character"? What is "style"? Still the question, if semantically murky, is practically clear, and I will respond to it with some personal history.

When I said just now "work in verse-making," I was leaving out some months of proto-apprenticeship during which I was so inexperienced that I didn't imitate *anybody*. Then came Yeats, whom I didn't so much wish to resemble as to *be*, and for several fumbling years I wrote in what it is convenient to call "period style," the Anglo-American style of the 1930s, with no voice of my own, learning chiefly from middle and later Yeats and from the brilliant young Englishman W. H. Auden. Yeats somehow saved me from the then-crushing influences of Ezra Pound and T. S. Eliot—luckily, as I now feel—but he could not teach me to sound like myself (whatever that was) or tell me what to write about. The first poem, perhaps, where those dramatic-to-me things happened was (is) called "Winter Landscape." It is mounted in five five-line stanzas, unrhymed, all one sentence. (I admit there is a colon near the middle of the third stanza.) ["Winter Landscape"' reproduced in its entirety; see *Collected Poems 1937–1971*, p.3] This does not sound, I would say, like either Yeats or Auden—or Rilke or Lorca or Corbière or any of my other passions of those remote days. It derives its individuality, if I am right, from a peculiar steadiness of somber tone (of which I'll say more presently) and from its peculiar relation to its materials—drawn, of course, from Brueghel's famous painting. The poem is sometimes quoted and readers seem to take it for either a verbal *equivalent* to the picture or (like Auden's fine Breughel poem, "Museé des Beaux Arts," written later) an *interpretation* of it. Both views I would call wrong, though the first is that adopted in a comparative essay on picture and poem recently published by two aestheticians at the University of Notre Dame.[1] After a competent study, buttressed by the relevant scholarship, of Brueghel's painting, they proceed to the poem—where, there being no relevant scholarship, they seem less at ease—and so to the relation between the two. Some of the points made are real, I believe. To quote the two with which they begin: they say the poem's "elaborative sequence urged on by the sweeping carry-over lines"—they mean run-on—"within the stanza or between stanzas—preserves the same order of presentation and the same grouping of elements as the Brueghel composition . . . Purposively restricting himself to a diction as sober, direct, and matter-of-fact as the painter's treatment of scene and objects, Berryman so composes with it that he achieves an insistent and animated pattern of strong poetic effect." And so on, to the end of the article, where the "disclosed affinities" of the two works are found testifying to the "secret friendship" of the arts. Nowhere is anything said as to what the poem is *about*, nor is any interest expressed in that little topic; the relation between the works is left obscure except for the investigation of affinities. An investigation of *differences* would have taken them further.

Very briefly, the poem's extreme sobriety would seem to represent a reaction, first, against Yeats's gorgeous and seductive rhetoric and, second, against the hysterical political atmosphere of the period. It dates from 1938–39 and was written in New York following two years' residence in England, during recurrent crises, with extended visits to France and Germany, especially one of the Nazi strongholds, Heidelberg. So far as I can make out, it is a war poem, of an unusual negative kind. The common title of the picture is *Hunters in the Snow* and of course the poet knows this. But he pretends not to, and calls their spears (twice) "poles," the resultant governing emotion being a certain stubborn incredulity—as the hunters are loosed while the peaceful nationals plunge again into war. This is not the subject of Breughel's painting at all, and the interpretation of *the event of the poem* proves that the picture has merely provided necessary material from a tranquil world for what is necessary to be said—but which the poet refuses to say—about a violent world.

You may wonder whether I dislike aestheticians. I do.

Very different from the discovery made in "Winter Landscape," if the foregoing account seems acceptable—namely, that a poem's force may be pivoted on a missing or misrepresented element in an agreed-on or imposed design—was a discovery made in another short piece several years later. (It also is twenty-five lines long, unrhymed, but, I think, much more fluid.) ["The Ball Poem" reproduced in its entirety; see *Collected Poems 1937–1971*, p. 11] The discovery here was that a commitment of identity can be "reserved," so to speak, with an ambiguous pronoun. The poet himself is both left out and put in; the boy does and does not become him and we are confronted with a process which is at once a process of life and a process of art. A pronoun may seem a small matter, but she matters, he matters, it matters, they matter. Without this invention (if it is one—Rimbaud's "*Je est un autre*" may have pointed my way, I have no idea now) I could not have written either of the two long poems that constitute the bulk of my work so far. If I were making a grandiose claim, I might pretend to know more about the administration of pronouns than any other poet writing in English or American. You will have noticed that I have said nothing about my agonies and joys, my wives and children, my liking for my country, my dislike of Communist theory and practice, etc., but have been technical. Art is technical, too.

So far I have been speaking of short poems and youth, when enthusiasms and hostilities, of an artistic kind, I mean, play a bigger role in inspiration than perhaps they do later. I do not know, because I see neither enthusiasm nor hostility behind "The Ball Poem." But I was nearly thirty then. I do know that much later, when I finally woke up to the fact that I was involved in a long poem, one of my first thoughts was: Narrative! let's have narrative, and at least one dominant personality, and no fragmentation! In short, let us have something spectacularly NOT *The Waste Land*, the best long poem of the age. So maybe hostility keeps on going.

What had happened was that I had made up the first stanza of a poem to be called *Homage to Mistress Bradstreet* and the first three lines of the second stanza, and there, for almost five years, I stuck. Here is the passage: [*Homage to Mistress Bradstreet* section 1 and section 2 lines 1–3 reproduced; see *Collected Poems 1937–1971*, p.133] The dramatic mode, hovering behind the two meditative lyrics I've quoted, has here surely come more into the open; and also here I had overcome at once two of the paralyzing obstacles that haunt the path of the very few modern poets in English who have attempted ambitious sizable poems: what form to use and what to write about. The eight-line stanza I invented here after a lifetime's study, especially of Yeats's, and in particular the one he adopted from Abraham Cowley for his elegy "In Memory of Major Robert Gregory." Mine breaks not at midpoint but after the short third line; a strange, four-beat line leads to the balancing heroic couplet of lines five and six, after which seven is again short (three feet, like line three) and then the stanza widens into an alexandrine rhyming all the way back to one. I wanted something at once flexible and grave, intense and quiet, able to deal with matter both high and low.

As for the subject: the question put to me about the poem is why I chose to write about this boring high-minded Puritan woman who may have been our first American poet but is not a good one. I agree, naturally, and say that I did not choose her—somehow she chose me—one point of connection, at any rate, being the almost insuperable difficulty of writing high verse at all in a land that cared and cares so little for it. I was concerned with her though, almost from the beginning, as a woman, not much as a poetess. For four-and-a-half years, then, I accumulated materials and sketched, fleshing out the target or vehicle, still under the impression that seven or eight stanzas would see it done. There are fifty-seven. My stupidity is traceable partly to an astuteness that made me as afraid as the next man of the ferocious commitment involved in a long poem and partly to the fact that although I had my form and subject, I did not have my theme yet. This emerged, and under the triple impetus of events I won't identify, I got the poem off the ground and nearly died following it. The theme is hard to put shortly, but I will try.

An American historian somewhere observes that all colonial settlements are intensely conservative, *except* in the initial break-off point (whether religious, political, legal, or whatever). Trying to do justice to both parts of this obvious truth—which I came upon only after the poem was finished—I concentrated upon the second and the poem laid itself out in a series of rebellions. I had her rebel first against the new environment and above all against her barrenness (which in fact lasted for years), then against her marriage (which in fact seems to have been brilliantly happy), and finally against her continuing life of illness, loss, and age. These are the three large sections of the poem; they are preceded and followed by an exordium and coda, of four stanzas each, spoken by the "I" of the twentieth-century poet, which modulates into her voice, who speaks most of the poem. Such is the plan. Each rebellion, of course, is succeeded by submission, although even in the moment of the poem's supreme triumph—the presentment, too long to quote now, of the birth of her first child—rebellion survives. I don't remember how conceptual all this was with me during the months of composition, but I think it was to a high degree. Turbulence may take you far toward a good short poem, but it is only the first quarter mile in a long one.

Not that the going is ever exactly tranquil. I recall three occasions of special heat, the first being when I realized that the middle of the poem was going to have to be in *dialogue*, a dialogue between the seventeenth-century woman and the twentieth-century poet—a sort of extended witch-seductress and demon-lover bit. The second was a tactical solution of a problem arising out of this: how to make them in some measure physically present to each other. I gave myself one line, when she says "A fading world I dust, with fingers anew." Later on it appears that they kiss, once, and then she says—as women will—"Talk to me." So he does, in an only half-subdued aria-stanza: [*Homage to Mistress Bradstreet* section 31 reproduced, see *Collected Poems 1937–1971*, p. 140] Noting and overconsidering such matters, few critics have seen that it *is* a historical poem, and it was with interest that I found Robert Lowell pronouncing it lately, in the *New York Times Review*, "the most resourceful historical poem in our literature." The third pleasant moment I remember is when one night, hugging myself, I decided that her fierce dogmatic old father was going to die blaspheming, in delirium.

The Bradstreet poem was printed in 1953 (a book here in America in 1956 and in London in 1959) and a year or so later, having again taken leave of my wits, or collected them, I began a second long poem. The first installment, called *77 Dream Songs* (recently published in New York), concerns the turbulence of the modern world, and memory, and wants. Its form comprises eighteen-line sections, three six-line stanzas, each normally (for fee) five, five, three, five, five, three, variously rhymed and not but mostly rhymed with great strictness. The subject is a character named Henry, who also has a Friend who calls him "Mr. Bones." Here is the first section, or Song, where the "I," perhaps of the poet, disappears into Henry's first and third persons (he talks to himself in the second person, too, about himself). [Reproduces "Dream Song 1" in its entirety; see *The Dream Songs*, p. 3]

This is Number One of Book I (the first volume consists of the first three books), and editors and critics for years have been characterizing them as poems, but I do not quite see them as that; I see them as parts—admittedly more independent than parts usually are. Once one has succeeded in any degree with a long poem (votes have been case in favor of, as well as against, *Homage to Mistress Bradstreet*), dread and fascination fight it out to exclude, on the whole, short poems thereafter, or so I have found it. I won't try to explain what I mean by a long poem, but let us suppose (1) a high and prolonged riskiness, (2) the construction of a world rather than the reliance upon one already existent which is available to a small poem, (3) problems of decorum most poets happily do not have to face. I cannot discuss "decorum" here either, but here is a case: [Reproduces "Dream Song 29" in its entirety; see *The Dream Songs*, p. 33]

Whether the diction of that is consistent with blackface talk, hell-spinning puns, coarse jokes, whether the end of it is funny or frightening, or both, I put up to the listener. Neither of the American poets who as reviewers have quoted it admiringly has committed himself; so I won't.

Note

1. Berryman's footnote: If anyone is *truly* curious, this can be found in the University of Texas *Studies in Literature and Language*, v. 3 (Autumn 1963).

My Whiskers Fly: An Interview with John Berryman

Jonathan Sisson / 1966

From the *Ivory Tower*, October 3, 1966, 14–18, 34–35. Reprinted by permission.

[The *Ivory Tower*, now simply the *Tower*, is the University of Minnesota's long-running art and literary magazine. For a time, Berryman's student Peter Stitt was its poetry editor. It is difficult to believe that the journal did not see fit to interview Berryman until over two years after Berryman began to teach at the university, and especially after the Pulitzer award, not least because Berryman was by all accounts a captivating and memorable teacher and a favorite among many university students. One suspects that this may have resulted from his reticence with regards to interviews, or perhaps his desire not to draw his students' attention to his poetry. After he received the Pulitzer, this was obviously a secret he could no longer keep. When poet (and later puppeteer) Jonathan Sisson sat down with Berryman, Berryman had purchased a home on Arthur Avenue and settled hesitatingly into a fragile domesticity. At nearly five thousand words, this interview was his lengthiest to date, and Sisson and Berryman range over both early and recent work, though of primary interest to Sisson are, not surprisingly, Berryman's Dream Songs.—Ed.]

John Berryman, the best American poet, spent Bloomsday 1966 in his house in Prospect Park, cataloguing his many as yet unpublished Dream Songs in preparation for a year in Dublin. I arrived at five o'clock when Mr. Berryman had quit work for the day and was sitting with his feet buried in his manuscripts and letters from various literary notables, primarily English. He had run out of matches, which I supplied, but not scotch, which Mrs. Berryman brought us. Mr. Berryman has a way of holding his cigarette at the base of his fingers, often between the right second and third fingers, so that, with the cigarette in the right corner of his mouth, his index finger stands before his right eye; but his glasses never seem to get smudged. The dog Rufus and the Berrymans' daughter withdrew, leaving several toys comfortably scattered about.

Mr. Berryman has astonished eyebrows and a prominent tongue. His reddish face looks soft; in repose the cheeks are somewhat pouched: his expression is lively only when he speaks. When he turns his profile and one notices the handsome grey and light-brown hair, Mr. Berryman resembles Frederic Dorr Steele's drawings of William Gillette as Sherlock Holmes. It is this contrast—of the hard profile and the vulnerable face head-on—which makes the deep impression. Mr. Berryman's voice, by turns querying and relaxed, also echoes the extreme tension between pain and numbness that is the essence of the Dream Songs, his magnificent, risky long poem. A first section, *77 Dream Songs*, was published in 1964, and the second volume, *His Toy, His Dream, His Rest: 84 Dream Songs*, will be published in about a year. A book of 115 of Berryman's sonnets will probably appear next spring.

Mr. Berryman is perhaps the only poet who can read his own work properly. I hope that sooner or later he will make a recording of his poems, for when he reads them, most of the possible confusion of identity of speaker vanishes.

John Berryman: I've been counting up my Dream Songs, taking piles of manuscripts to pieces and sorting and calendaring them. I've registered, since day before yesterday, 181 of them, besides fragments and programmatic notes. It's a large manuscript, takes up a whole suitcase.

There are two previous registers of songs. One was 126, done in Rhode Island, and then there was a previous one done in Vermont of about 75. But those were in states of the poem well before I published *77 Dream Songs*, which is the first volume of the poem proper, so that those are hopelessly out of date. This new one is strictly up to date except that it only includes finished songs. There's a large body of manuscript which is fragmentary, dealing with beginnings and ends and some middles. I'm taking all that stuff with me. Some of those are much better than some of the finished songs. That is, often after the inspiration has failed, you keep on going out of a sense of duty, and turn up with nothing, so that some of the fragments are much better.

The first volume is in three books and the second volume is in four books: 4, 5, 6, and 7. That volume has to be composed out of whatever I save. I'm a big killer of my own work. I can destroy a song marvelously. All you do is burn it up—very simple—and nobody knows it exists. My work, because of its nature, is a very tricky sort of work: if it doesn't come off, you don't have anything. I'm as different as possible from a poet like Virgil. What he'd do was compose in the morning, and in the afternoon he'd revise and trim, cut. He could be quite sure on getting up in the morning when he was working on the *Georgics* or the *Aeneid* that he'd have thirty or forty lines by the end of the day, all set. But a modern long poem is not like that at all. You have no idea when you get up in the morning what, if anything, you're going to have. Some songs take weeks or even months and others are done in ten minutes. You're at the mercy of the notion of sustained inspiration. Nothing else will do.

Interviewer: Have you published any of them other than the ones in *77 Dream Songs*?

Berryman: Yes, there were four in the *London Times* last fall and three in *The Nation* in New York before that. But otherwise I've just been ignoring requests. So out of roughly 200 to 250, only seven have been printed. I don't print things much anymore, and nobody reads the magazines, and there's no money involved or no prestige, and so, you know—well, why do it except for the anxiety and the begging letters?

Interviewer: How does the form of the three stanzas control you? Do you find that frustrating?

Berryman: Oh no, it's what keeps me alive. The stanzas go five, five, three, five, five, three. They use various rhyme schemes. More and more I'm inclined not to use rhyme at all. But the notion is to preserve an impression of rhyme as the structure, as an end structure, but you don't actually have any. Take a poem which is over-rhymed like Fitzgerald's *Rubáiyát*. That's marvelous. But without the rhymes it wouldn't be anywhere. Of course, in the original Persian manuscript there are no rhymes at all. Or so I'm told; I don't know Persian. So Fitzgerald made up this mad business, really devoted to *aaxa*. Without that he wouldn't have been anywhere at all. That's structure. But in my songs the rhyme business is incidental, and it depends on how things go. Rhyme is a powerful tool.

Interviewer: You couldn't give me an example of this because it's something the reader just gets an impression of?

Berryman: I could give you fifty examples, but I'd rather not. It's a question of what one hears, namely, depending on a good reader, say Miss Plath, who killed herself in London recently. She would have been a good reader. Or Miss Adrienne Rich, who's still alive, in Cambridge, Massachusetts, an excellent reader, one of the best in the United States. It depends on what they hear, whether what you've been trying to do comes off or just is a failure. And of course large numbers of the attempts in a long work are failures. They have to be junked. You just wish you hadn't written them. It's the same thing with the novel. Most novels are no good. Isn't that true? And even good novels are not good for most of their structure. What they depend on is certain capital chapters.

Interviewer: Did you find this happening with *Homage to Mistress Bradstreet*?

Berryman: No, no. The *Bradstreet* poem is an attempt to be perfect.

Interviewer: So that it sustains its—

Berryman: It's intended to be perfect from beginning to end. It's very short. It's only about the length of *The Waste Land*—456 lines. That's all. No, no, I'd been working on that for five years. When I actually sat down to it—I had a Guggenheim—I had a mass of manuscripts that high [gesturing a couple of feet], but I was still under the impression that I could do it in five or six stanzas.

Interviewer: The whole thing?

Berryman: That was my impression. All I actually had was the first stanza and the first three lines of the second stanza. There I stuck, and I stuck there for five years until a series of circumstances got me going. No, all of that is supposed to be excellent. That's as different as possible, that poem.

Novels can't keep up too long, you know. One of the troubles with Saul Bellow as a novelist is that he writes too well really to be a novelist. He makes out as a novelist, but on the whole the way he works doesn't allow for the ups and downs that are ordinary in any work of art, any large work of art, and I'm thinking about his big novels now. He's the best novelist in the country, but he's not a real novelist in that he won't agree with you to sit down and tell a story. Instead, he's always badgering you. Well, most of any given novel is not very good.

So you face that with long poems too. Ezra Pound's *Cantos*, for example. I'm a great admirer of the *Cantos*, but anybody would agree that for long stretches in the poem, canto after canto after canto is similarly unintelligible and boring. That's the problem that he faced when he sat down to do this sort of poem all those years ago. Whereas in a short poem, like *The Waste Land* or my Bradstreet poem, you can try to make everything count. There's one stanza in the Bradstreet poem which I put in after the poem was finished, in order to increase a waiting period.

Interviewer: To mark time?

Berryman: Well, there's a long waiting period before she becomes pregnant in the poem. She was sterile for six years after the marriage, probably owing to the trauma of the crossing and the plantation and so forth. I made that long, but I decided after I'd finished the poem that I hadn't made it quite long enough. So I threw in another stanza which is also supposed to be absolutely first-class in details but fairly low-key for the poem, just to make the reader wait one more stanza. That part of the poem seems to have worked. At least, no critic whose work I've seen has singled it out for dispraise.

Interviewer: Are you doing anything beside the *Dream Songs* now?

Berryman: I have fourteen unpublished books in hand. Just fourteen.

Interviewer: Is *The Black Book* still in progress?

Berryman: I don't plan ever to do that. People ask me about it occasionally and I've never reprinted the parts of *The Black Book* that I've published, but I probably will in my next American book. The subject was—it was more than I could bear. I wrote about eight parts, I guess. It was in the form of a Mass for the Dead. It was designed to have forty-two sections, and was about the Nazi murders of the Jews. But I just found I couldn't take it. The sections published—there were eight of them in *Poetry*—are unrelievedly horrible. I wasn't able at this time—that was about twenty years ago—to find any way of making palatable the monstrosity of the thing which obsessed me. So I think what I'll do in my next book is—we're going to do a *Collected Poems* at some point—is put in those sections of *The Black Book*, but without any explanation or anything else. It was called *The Black Book* because there was a book called the *Black Book of Poland*. Have you ever seen that?

Interviewer: No.

Berryman: It's a diagnostic, an historical survey. Most of the Jews who died in Poland or were Polish, one or the other. My connections with Poland are curious (my long poem, *Homage to Mistress Bradstreet*, was published in Polish), not with the home country but my relations with refugees, Poles in this country. Not personally—I've never met any of the people, but they write me and so on. So I think what I'll do is put those sections of *The Black Book* in the clay, just as separate sections or lyrics or whatever, but let the poem go to hell. I don't think I can do it. I don't feel I want to.

Interviewer: You've done this before, at readings, but could you go over the basic situation of the *Dream Songs*, the character of Henry and his friend, etc.?

Berryman: The basic situation is that of a modern man, early in middle age, pretending to be a Negro, that is to say, a minstrel in blackface, throughout, who has a friend who calls him Mr. Bones. That man is sometimes called Henry and sometimes called other things. His last name is in doubt. He endures and enjoys what is presented to him by contemporary American life. The direction of his fate, which is what you really were asking about, is already handled, but in unpublished stuff, so that I wouldn't want to say anything about it. I would only say that at the end of the first book, *77 Dream Songs*, he disappears from the poem completely, and the whole fourth book, which is unpublished as yet, consists of *opus posthumous* songs, thirteen of them: Opus Posthumous Number One, and then just in case anybody thought I was kidding, Opus Posthumous Number Two, and Three, and so on up to Thirteen. Meanwhile there's a simulacrum of death earlier in the Dream Songs. But Henry is alive and well, in a certain sense, at the end of the seventh book. The work is far from being a comedy although parts of it are funny, but it's not a tragedy either. It's intended as a descriptive.

Interviewer: About the problem of fate, in your biography of Stephen Crane you say that when Crane went West he began to view nature as less a thing to be fought with, or something ganging up on him.

Berryman: More as a neutral.

Interviewer: It offers possibilities and the rest is up to the hero.

Berryman: Working towards "An Open Boat," where nature is indifferent, instead of a hostile, definitely disagreeable force.

Interviewer: How does Henry fit into that, as in the phrase "God's Henry's enemy" or in the song about Henry's crossing ruin's path?

Berryman: "He stared at ruin. Ruin stared straight back."

Interviewer: Yes.

Berryman: There's nothing divine in that song. That's just a naturalistic song, a recital of various things that Henry has had to face over a period of years. In the other song, "God's Henry's enemy," let's make some allowance for rhetoric. His friend criticizes immediately what he says. He says, "Mr. Bones, as I look on the saffron sky, you strikes me as ornery." Meanwhile, Henry has said, "We're in business . . . why, what business must be clear. A cornering." Something like that. Well, obviously we have here a man, at the ends of his wits, who is taking up the Job task of confrontation with the divine with its products.

Two things occur to me. My friend Howard Nemerov in his last book spoke of God's career as being sort of a failure compared with Mozart's. I've loved Mozart's music without reservation all my life, but he's so miraculous that you don't think of him personally as you do about Beethoven. But actually, when you think of it all over—the letters, three volumes of them, translated by Emily Anderson—you see that you're dealing with a saint, not only a genius but an actual saint. His whole life was at the mercy of his art. It was incredible. I'm thinking of that and I'm also thinking about the kind of hysterical states that modern artists go in very much for—an extreme case would be Van Gogh's cutting off his ear—periods of masochism and blasphemy—that kind of business, which in the Dream Songs is temperate and held in control, partly by the form and partly by Henry's friend's criticism.

As for the general fate, in Book Seven I don't know yet how far the divine figure, who has been handled in at least half a dozen songs—one of them begins "Peter's not friendly," an interview just after death—how far the divine figure will figure.

Interviewer: Is there any particular relationship between Crane's use of the name Henry and yours?

Berryman: With whose use?

Interviewer: Stephen Crane's. You mention in your book *Stephen Crane* that many of Crane's characters are named Henry.

Berryman: Ha. I'd forgotten all about that. It's completely accidental. I've had to live with the name eleven years now, and it is borne in on me that there's a comic strip named "Henry" and one of Hemingway's best heroes, Frederic Henry in *A Farewell to Arms*, and as you turn the thing over in your mind there are lots of people named Henry. But no, my Henry has no particular origin at all, except that my second wife and I once agreed that the names Mabel and Henry are the most detestable of all names, whereupon I began affectionately to call her Mabel and she began affectionately to call me Henry. So if the name has an origin, I found myself sort of pitched on it out of this domestic peculiarity a long time ago.

Interviewer: In an article you wrote for *Shenandoah* ["One Answer to a Question: Changes," see above pp. 27–32]—which I guess was a radio broadcast first?

Berryman: I forget.

Interviewer: You mentioned that in your poem "Winter Landscape," which uses Bruegel's painting *Hunters in the Snow* as a point of departure, the poet does not call the spears "spears"; he calls them "poles." And what is not said is what's important. Do the Dream Songs have a similar kind of reticence?

Berryman: Good question. Exactly. There are all kinds of things about the Dream Songs that I wouldn't tell anybody.

Interviewer: Then you're not going to tell me.

Berryman: No, of course. And I would go on to say that the extreme case of this is *Finnegans Wake*. Towards the end of his work on *Finnegans Wake*, Joyce, who had a photographic memory for words, got hold of a list of African dialect words and sifted them through the puns in one big section of *Finnegans Wake*. That is to say, there is at least one big section of *Finnegans Wake* that nobody will ever understand. All clear? There's a lot of secretiveness in modern art. That's an extreme example. This is not so much about polishing their work as hiding it. Let me put it that way. I don't go that far, not at all. But there is a degree of secretiveness. For example, I know who Henry's friend is, but none of the critics have found out yet, but somebody sooner or later will. It's very simple. It's built in, the nature of this friend and the nature of the relationship and so on, but I leave those things to the critics. That's their business. How could they get their PhDs otherwise and pursue their careers?

Interviewer: But in the case of "Winter Landscape," the reader who's familiar with Bruegel's painting—

Berryman: That's everybody.

Interviewer: Yes. So besides the things in the Dream Songs that are private, how about the public things, like knowing that painting, that everybody could understand but might miss? Could you give any hints as to what poetic conventions the reader should not expect, or what sort of cast of mind he should have?

Berryman: Well, I'll tell you. The question is very difficult to answer. My wife went to a reception lately for somebody who was getting married, and she happened to have brought the *77 Dream Songs* and had passed it on to a friend, and the friend lost it in a beauty parlor, of all places. Somebody bothered to steal my book in a beauty parlor. I was rather touched by this. And she, the woman I haven't met, had met somebody and the friend couldn't make head or tail of it, like some of the critics, and she said, "Well, it's very simple. Just read the first one over and over and over until you hear it. Then read the others." Well, that's good advice.

For example, the *Observer* in London wanted some songs of mine, so I sent them a couple, and they said they liked them, but they wouldn't publish them until I had answered various questions about them. One was whether the line "which the cut Alexandrian foresaw" was really about Origen, and I said, "Of course it's about Origen, yes." It's a song about the early Church father Origen. It begins "He yelled at me in Greek": that means Jesus, that is, Christ. And then Origen comes in, and so forth. There are several other poems on the tradition of Christian origins. There's one about St. Mary of

Egypt, and more about St. Peter, and others. But on the other hand you don't need to follow the specific details if you hear the tone of the song in relation to the songs around it. I think. They're not built to be difficult. They're bound to be as clear as possible.

But there are all kinds of things you can't be clear about. *The Waste Land* is a good case. Eliot did everything he could to make his subject obvious. It's to be found in the seduction scene and it's also found in the hyacinth girl passage and then in the Thames daughter's songs—same business all the way through. All the women are one woman and so on. He even explains this in the notes. Nevertheless, lots of people found *The Waste Land* difficult, for reasons which are hard for me to understand. It's not difficult.

Interviewer: In *The Waste Land*, where Eliot switches from person to person—is there any kind of similarity in your switching from "I" to "he" to "Henry" and so on? Is this a different kind of thing that you're doing?

Berryman: I think so. Sort of the opposite. *The Waste Land*, the original poem as Eliot finished it and before Pound took it over and cut it, was about a young man in his thirties, let's say, who was walking and moving around London, the modern world city, hearing and smelling and seeing and experiencing and so forth. That is to say, there was a narrative structure, which Pound cut out. The "I" of *The Waste Land* has to be deduced in sections like the one about the hyacinth girl, whereas in the Dream Songs, the "I" doesn't have to be deduced. The "I" is the entire point! The personality of Henry with his problems, his friends, and his enemies is why the thing came into being.

All the other characters—there are many other characters—those are different voices. They're not Henry's voice. They're always identified by the dash. Always. Well, nearly always. In his review in [the *New York Times*], Lowell took Mr. Bones to be a different character, and in fact he made all kinds of mistakes. He wrote the review hurriedly and I was in hospital and didn't correct him until it was too late to get into print. Well, he's apologized in print, but nobody ever sees the apology. All they see is the original version. But anyway, Henry and Mr. Bones are the same character.

All the other people who speak in the songs are people with voices and personalities and fates of their own, which get into the poem by the instrumentality of the twentieth-century poet, who begins in the opening song, "Huffy Henry," by subordinating his personality, so that by the end of the song it has disappeared. In the last song, Number 161, the end of Book Seven [number 385 in the collected *Dream Songs*—ed.], a thing called "My Heavy Daughter," which was published in London last fall, the poet resumes his personality and speaks, as it were, in his own person, leaving the fate of Henry, which has been discussed elaborately at many points earlier, in doubt—the way, if we now compare a chicken to a buffalo, I'm a chicken and Sophocles is a buffalo: the way in which Sophocles made mysterious the fate of Oedipus in *Oedipus at Colonus*, one of the reasons the play is so difficult to deal with: because Oedipus both dies and does not die, and he is both profane and sacred. I'm using [Mircea] Eliade's terms now. You know the great philosopher of religion at Chicago?

Interviewer: No.

Berryman: Eliade. Absolutely marvelous.

Interviewer: You wrote in the *Shenandoah* article, "If I were making a grandiose claim, I might pretend to know more about the administration of pronouns than any other living poet writing in English or American." Would you like to be grandiose now or let it go at that?

Berryman: No, that's a comic remark. But like most comic remarks—all the best sequences of W. C. Fields are not funny at all. They're enough to break your heart. Well, like most comic remarks, mine is not really comic. What I meant was that most people use pronouns without thinking much about them—I, you, he, she, them—that sort of thing. Whereas it's obvious that the author of the Dream Songs, and also obvious that the author of *Homage to Mistress Bradstreet*, is very keen on pronouns. Namely, they matter to him very much. And he's quite willing to go through a whole sequence—take Terry Southern, who is my favorite younger writer.

Interviewer: Oh?

Berryman: Oh yes. He's excellent, I think. He's willing to go through a whole sequence of extremely detailed fantasy about some absolute jerk until it comes down to the fact where he's writing in the middle of the night to a London racing magazine to explain his disagreement with part of a recent article. This is a full-scale physician; he's the greatest dermatologist in the world. That's his position. But he plays with racing automobiles and with his clinic. He goes and makes like a dermatologist every single day. Well, I like people who are extremely technical. This is why I like Southern so much. All my work's all technical, doesn't lend itself to generalities at all.

Interviewer: Not going to make a movie out of it?

Berryman: Oh no, no. Though I'm very happy to see that—well, Southern works in prose, you see, it's quite different—I'm very happy to know that his work is extremely popular. For example, his book *Candy* is a million seller. Delicious! It's not a very good book, but it's very funny though, extremely funny, and has many merits. It's very close written. It doesn't compare with his best work. This book is *Flash and Filigree*. Have you read that?

JONATHAN SISSON / 1966

Interviewer: No. That was his first book?

Berryman: No, second. But that's the one you should read. *The Magic Christian* you can ignore.

Interviewer: That's what I read first and I wondered what, ah—

Berryman: No, that's not so good. No. I don't know what he's doing now. I've never met him. Do you know him?

Interviewer: No, I don't. The younger writer I would have thought of, especially in connection with pronouns, is J. P. Donleavy.

Berryman: Now, I don't know his work at all. What are his main books?

Interviewer: *The Ginger Man.*

Berryman: I've never read it. Is Donleavy an American?

Interviewer: He's an American but he's now lived in Ireland a long time, I think.

Berryman: No kidding.

Interviewer: Maybe you should look him up next year.

Berryman: You know where he lives? I'd love to see him. Somebody told me *The Ginger Man* is marvelous.

Interviewer: It's brilliant. I would say it's better than his other things, but I haven't been able to finish any of them. Well, maybe he lives on the Isle of Man. I think he lives on an island. I don't really know.

Berryman: Listen, the Isle of Man is a definite thing. You have to either live there or not live there! It's way out! You know, like he either lives in New York or he doesn't. Or Southern California. Don't give me that.

Interviewer: What poets are emerging now who you think will be significant?

Berryman: Very gifted among the people younger than myself are W. D. Snodgrass and Richard Wilbur and W. S. Merwin and Adrienne Rich. Among the prose writers are—I don't know of anybody. I admire various people very much: Edward Hoagland, Walter Clemens. But whether anybody is as good as Southern is I really very much doubt. I don't know. And among younger critics—I take criticism to be a branch of literature; I don't separate it out—the younger critics are really not too interesting, nor are the critics of my generation. Leslie Fiedler and so on mostly seem to have lost their minds recently, and are spending their time and energy on problems that are quite insoluble or not worth solution.

Interviewer: Such as what?

Berryman: Academic. I'm thinking of Steven Marcus, for example, at Columbia, who is an obviously gifted man, but I've never seen anything to prove it.

Interviewer: What direction do you think American poetry will take in the next few years?

Berryman: I couldn't answer the question. Tell you why. Suppose we take two paths, and use Lowell and Roethke as examples of them. Lowell: Latinate, historical, willful in the intellectual sense, unbelievably brainy—that kind of business. Then on the other hand we take Roethke: Teutonic; balladic as against Lowell with his tight, crisp structures; also very learned, Roethke, but learned in plants: flowers, weeds—that kind of business; anti-historical, biologic poet. All clear? Points they have in common: a feeling for human fate, both extremely serious, both absolutely first-class (one now dead to us). Well, that was the situation when this kind of question began to be asked of me in India in 1957, and I set out Ted and Cal, as they're called by their friends, as contrary exemplars. Since then both of their works have been modified and changed, and they're not so obviously opposites as they were nine years ago. But still I would say that the fact of their disagreement among themselves as to what to deal with and how to deal with it and so forth would make mincemeat out of the question of what I think American poetry is. It all depends on who does it.

Interview with John Berryman

Al Alvarez / 1967

Conducted February 1967, aired on BBC2 Television program *New Release*, March 16, 1967. © BBC 1967. Reprinted by permission of BBC, Anne Alvarez, and The Estate of John Berryman.

[In mid-February 1967, two months after Berryman's initial completion of Book VII of *The Dream Songs*, and roughly a week after Kate committed him to St. Brendan's Hospital, Berryman was filmed for a profile segment for the BBC2 television magazine program *New Release*. For this interview, conducted by celebrated British author Al Alvarez, Berryman chose to be interviewed in his temporary residence in Ballsbridge and in Ryan's, his favorite Dublin-area pub, as opposed to London, as initially suggested by the producers (and frowned upon by Berryman in "Dream Song 371: Henry's Guilt"; see *Collected Poems 1937–1971*, p. 393). He didn't want his writing schedule to be interrupted unnecessarily and, despite the exposure and the quality of his questioner Berryman still looked down enough on the format to consider it to be of trivial importance, and an inconvenience.

While clearly inebriated, Berryman on film is something to behold, energetic, eccentric, and oddly charismatic. His recitation of two Dream Songs, though he fudges the lines a bit, are powerful and haunting. It is an enthralling performance, with a decided emphasis on performance. (The interview aired alongside an equally fascinating profile of the eminent British philosopher Bertrand Russell.) Berryman's impressions of the filming at his home are preserved in "Dream Song 298"; see *The Dream Songs*, p. 320.—Ed.]

Announcer: Our second item tonight is about a poet. It is not often that distinguished American poets come over here. The rewards of working on American campuses prevent any brain drain in this direction. But this year John Berryman, thought by some to be, along with Robert Lowell, America's foremost living poet, is living in Dublin, in a little, semi-detached with his wife and child. He's working on the next four books of his *Dream Songs*, to be published, he hopes, later in the year. We went over to Dublin to see Berryman, mostly at his local pub, where he does his writing. The critic Al Alvarez talked to him there.

John Berryman: My feelings about Yeats were quite queer. I didn't want to be *like* Yeats, *I wanted to be Yeats!* But that failed. You can see why that failed! For example, I never wrote *A Vision*, I never wrote "The Tower," I never wrote *Words for Music Perhaps* myself. It's amazing the things I never wrote!

Al Alvarez (narrating): John Berryman. Born 1914 in McAlester, Oklahoma. He is a teacher, scholar, critic. At present he is a professor of humanities at the University of Minnesota. He's also one of the most gifted and original poets now writing. For the last ten years, he has been working on a huge series of interwoven poems called *The Dream Songs*. Seventy-seven of them were published here in 1964. They form a kind of poetic diary of the inner life of a jagged, learned, witty, desperate character called Henry. They follow him as he gets drunk and ill, travels, makes passes, becomes a father, quarrels with God and politicians, reads theology, and thinks about other poets. Henry has a second voice, a straight man who buts in with questions and chilling comments, in a mixture of blues and crude language. Like a nigger minstrel, he's called "Mr. Bones." I suppose he's deaf. There's also a third, unnamed friend who appears from time to time. Each of these songs is written in three, six-line stanzas. Some rhyme, some don't. All are very difficult at first hearing. The syntax is often contorted; the language elliptical. But it's worth the trouble; this is one of the original and important poems of our time. Berryman is spending a year in Dublin, working on books four to six of *The Dream Songs*. Every day he sits in Ryan's Bar at the end of the lane where he lives, working and drinking. That is where we spoke to him.

Berryman: One of the points of *The Dream Songs* is to take an ordinary, early middle-aged American. Let's say a man in his early forties, in blackface, so that we have a convention, and consult and deploy his regular interests. Supernatural, biological, friendly, and yet also take him to his limit. That is to say, again and again—in any rate the first three books of the *Dream Songs*; the later books are quite different—to find out what a man can bear. See? As to pass from me to a great master, Tolstoy in *Anna Karenina*—we were talking about it yesterday; surely one of the greatest novels that the world has ever seen—one of his points was to *torture* Anna Karenina until she couldn't bear it anymore. Vronsky is extremely secondary in the book. Don't you think so?

Alvarez: This is right, yes.

Berryman: So I took Henry in various directions. The directions of despair, lust, of memory, of patriotism, various other things, to take him further than anything in ordinary life can take us. Unless a girl leaves him. That's a special case. We make an exception.

There's a wonderful conversation between them, at the end of that.

Alvarez: Yes, sir.

Berryman: The one that begins: [reads the third stanza of "Dream Song 51"; see *The Dream Songs*, p. 55] It's quite a good passage, don't you think?

Alvarez: Yes, a marvelous passage. But why does the part that represents that represents, as it were, the serious, final answer, the final negative answer, why does that have to be done as a joke? Is that the only way that you can face that?

Berryman: That's a very difficult question. In a book I wrote one time about Stephen Crane—a very serious artist, a major writer, I think, and a fine poet and a pretty good novelist, and a great story writer, one of the greatest story writers the world has ever seen—I said that Crane's irony and grotesquery were forms of response to things *so ghastly* that you cannot respond to them directly. Now I think, something of my feeling—there's no influence from Crane in my work—but I had something like the feeling that that is what I am doing myself. Namely, his friend relieves the tension, relieves the hopeless solitude of Henry faced with the world as it is, and enables Henry—Henry is always in a very bad state when Mr. Bones comes in—the friend is of course the end man, you know, in minstrels, namely, he and Henry are very closely connected. They're part of the same outfit. But on stage, as they are on stage, the scene has to be given to Henry, and his friend only gets in in terms of quite serious disapproval. For example, there's another passage: Henry is getting very excited about a girl, and he says, "There ought to be a law against Henry." And his friend says, "Mr. Bones, there is!" ["Dream Song 4"; see *The Dream Songs*, p. 6] Now that relieves the tension for that song, so that you can move on to the next one!

Poets don't get much fan mail, but I had a lot of mail after I published this song in the United States. I may say that the mail was entirely hostile. [reads "Dream Song 14": see *The Dream Songs*, p. 16]

Alvarez: Let me put this another way, John. If one of the purposes—not one of the purposes, but one of the things you are doing—in *The Dream Songs* is exploring as it were the edge, what is tolerable, and what is not tolerable . . . and in this I think . . .

Berryman: Mostly intolerable.

Alvarez: . . . Yes, mostly intolerable. In that, I think you are doing what tends to be done by, as I say, all the poets that I think of being really serious . . . the final thing that is intolerable is death, isn't it? And is what, for example, possessed Sylvia Plath, except she went farthest on that particular dead end road.

Berryman: "Daddy." "Daddy, you bastard, I'm *through*!" Isn't that a marvelous poem?

Alvarez: Yes, it's a great poem.

Berryman: Don't you think? I called it a great poem myself. An unexpected masterpiece from a dying woman.

Alvarez: But she was—

Berryman: And you know her father died very early. It's all fantasy! She's only dealing with a father *figure*. Or phantom. You know? And it killed her. It killed her. Life is very strange.

Alvarez: But what about Mr. Bones? Isn't Mr. Bones kind of a death figure also, as is—

Berryman: I don't think so. I don't think so. I took Mr. Bones from the language of minstrelsy. And Henry is, in spite of all his troubles, and adventures and so forth, seems to me . . . Henry seems to me a life figure. Namely, after having gone everything . . . and he's dead all through book four. Every song in book four is titled "Opus posthumous." Numbered. Number one. And then "Opus posthumous" number two, just in case anyone thought that I was kidding. And so on up to "Opus posthumous" number thirteen. After which, he has a stretch in hospital; to come back to life must be quite extraordinary. He's not easy on the subject of, you know, Christology, and Christian origins . . . no, no! He has a very heavy religious background, but he doesn't seem to be too friendly to it, because one song begins . . . Henry has just died, one out of many times. He says, "Peter's not friendly" ["Dream Song 55"; see *The Dream Songs*, p. 62]. Just dead. Up for interview. A little like sort of Joyce's remark in *Ulysses*, in the graveyard episode where Mr. Bloom is thinking "Lazarus come forth, and he came fifth and lost the job."[1] The general tone of this song "Peter's not friendly," is a little bit like that. We take the subject very seriously, but we *reject*! How does the song go? It goes: [quotes "Dream Song 55" lines 1, 4–7] . . . and so on. The tone is not reverent.

I hate making remarks about poetry, you know, with a capital "P." But it is one of our most powerful tools for the exploration of human reality. For example: Freud's work. I'm thinking especially of two books: *The Psychopathology of Everyday Life* and *The Interpretation of Dreams* in 1900. Nobody . . . In the first place, everybody *has* to have read those books. In the second place, nobody's feelings about human experience are quite the same after reading those books. Now something like this is true in poetry. For example, Ralph Hodgson, that marvelous man, whom I adore. And so did Eliot. Do you remember his poems about, uh . . . "He has 999 canaries / And round his head, finches and fairies / In jubilant rapture skim."[2] Something about, "ah, Mr. Hodgson, everyone wants to know him."[3] And then Eliot puts himself down. The poem is called "Cuscuscaraway and Mirza Murad Ali Beg"[4] and if you can tell me what that means, I will be instructed.[5]

Alvarez: I cannot.

Berryman: I have never found out what that means. Poetry is one of our most powerful tools for the inquisition, which we have continually to make into our own natures, and into the nature of the world!

Alvarez [narrating]: The theme of the later Dream Songs is death and dying. In the poem to his daughter, the child is growing, the time is autumn, and turkeys are being killed for Thanksgiving dinner. Henry remembers Ralph Hodgson, the Georgian nature poet who died very old. The unspoken theme is that as Henry's daughter grows up, so he descends towards the grave.

[Berryman reads "Dream Song 385"; see *The Dream Songs*, p. 407]

Alvarez: What kind of audience really do you in a real sense do you have?

Berryman: Ah, I have friends! I have about fifteen *real* friends scattered throughout the world, but mostly of course in the United States. That's men. Then I have about fifteen women—often they're wives—who are also readers of mine. Now I'd call thirty readers quite a lot!

Alvarez: Based on that, and it expands from there—

Berryman: It's quite good! I'm impressed! And they write me wonderful letters about anything I publish!

Alvarez: And where—

Berryman: Have you got thirty readers?

Alvarez: I haven't got three readers.

Berryman: Well, then I've been boasting. Thirty is too many. That's a lie. Maybe I have eight. Does that make you feel better?

Alvarez: That makes me feel much better.

Berryman: Okay, eight. But those people are often bright.

Well, eventually, of course, I ended up turning against Yeats, and despised him, yes. And I was helped out of that by two very ephemeral influences. W. H. Auden and Rilke. And then I got rid of them. And by that time I had my own style and was not sounding like anybody.

Alvarez [narrating]: Berryman is preeminently a poet of sleepless, small hours remorse, and a kind of nightmare guilt for crimes of which his waking self knows he's innocent. In Song 29, he's made major poetry out of that "morning after" despair.

[Berryman recites "Dream Song 29."]

Notes

1. The quote is "Come forth Lazarus! And he came fifth and lost the job." From "Hades," the sixth chapter of *Ulysses*.

2. From T.S. Eliot's "Lines to Ralph Hodgson, Esqre." (1936).

3. The lines are "How delightful to meet Mr. Hodgson! / (Everyone wants to know *him*)."

4. The full title is "Lines for Cuscuscaraway and Mirza Murad Ali Beg." Mirza Murad Ali Beg is the author of the historical romance *Lalun the Beragun: or the Battle of Paniput* (1884).

5. Cuscuscarway and Mirza Murad Ali Beg were reportedly the names of Eliot's dog and cat.

Whisky & Ink, Whisky & Ink

Jane Howard / 1967

From *Life* magazine, July 21, 1967, 67–68, 70, 73–76. Reprinted by permission.

[The interview conducted for Berryman's *Life* magazine profile, the largest public exposure Berryman received during his lifetime, took place soon after his April 1967 readings at the American Academy and the Guggenheim Museum in New York City. During this trip, Berryman was briefly hospitalized for alcohol poisoning. In May, he spent four days in Dublin with journalist Jane Howard and photographer Terence Spencer. He took them to Ryan's, to the seaside, and to the ruins of medieval monasteries, where Spencer took several evocative photographs of Berryman carousing with pub dwellers, and interacting with Kate and Twissy. As John Haffenden notes, the profile in *Life* magazine did much to instill in the public's mind the depiction of Berryman as a mad, drunken poet, a Byronesque American university scholar and to associate him autobiographically with his poems (see Haffenden 1982, 346–48). Observes author Jeffrey Meyers: "The eccentric and unkempt Berryman, his eyes wild as his beard, was portrayed in *Life* magazine holding forth in Dublin pubs and making vatic pronouncements amid crumbling stone ruins" (Meyers 1987, 60).—Ed.]

Whisky and ink, whisky and ink. These are the fluids John Berryman needs. He needs them to survive and describe the thing that sets him apart from other men and even from other poets: his uncommonly, almost maddeningly penetrating awareness of the fact of human mortality. All of us pretend we know we are going to die, but his burden is that he is at all times acutely conscious of it, and therefore of the transience of all that he cares about.

His consumption of alcohol is prodigious and so is his writing. "Something can (has) been said for sobriety," he writes in a poem, "but very little." You would no more believe his claim, if you knew him, that he is merely "a heavy social drinker" than you would underrate *Homage to Mistress*

Bradstreet or *77 Dream Songs* or his newest book, *Berryman's Sonnets*. Berryman is beyond doubt a consequential poet, though he has not always been so regarded. As his old friend Robert Lowell said in introducing him at a New York poetry reading not long ago, "It's something to create a sensation when you're over fifty. Most of our friends at age fifty retire into a dignified silence."

In all Berryman's fifty-two years he has never been more conspicuous or less silent, than he is now. He has just finished a year in Ireland on leave from the University of Minnesota, where he is professor in the humanities department. The leave was made possible by a Guggenheim grant, and was interrupted by a ten-day trip back to New York two months ago to collect a five-thousand-dollar award from the Academy of American poets. He is booked for readings long in advance in London, Hartford, New York, and scattered other places. Cults and coteries tend to form in his wake. "He has arrived," as one critic says, "and he knows it."

There is a small danger that all this acclaim will unsettle Berryman. Vanity distresses him in others and is not likely to become one of his own shortcomings. "'i don't matter' and 'I MATTER!' are equally boring," he says. "Never have I known a really vain, arrogant man to transform himself into a decent human being. For myself, it's not *very* nice to be recognized, it's just nice. I'm not an enemy of good news at all, mind you. When news is good, it's fine with me—but me usually expect it to be bad."

Sometimes it is bad. Read through the reviews of his work and you will encounter phrases like "exasperating," "linguistic chaos," "Philistine," "incoherent and turgid," and "a kind of verbal thrombosis: clots of syntax and metaphor and, consequently, areas drained, pallid, inert." Some critics contend that Berryman is scheming to undermine the whole English language, some say his work is shallow. Others don't get it at all and just give up.

Bur read on elsewhere and find John Berryman's poetry described as having "the tension of an instrument tuned almost to the breaking point." Read how his lines can "needle, wheedle, singe, disarm and scarify the reader" with their "dense, brilliantly managed variety," and how he "pursues his insights to the edge of a breakdown and then beyond it, until mania, depression, paranoia and the hallucinations that come in psychosis or are induced by drugs become as urgent and commonplace as Beauty, Truth, Nature and Soul were to the Romantics." This last is the opinion of the British critic A. Alvarez, in whose view Berryman, Lowell, and the late Sylvia Plath constitute the advance guard of a new poetic school he calls Extremism.

Berryman is extreme, all right. Friends describe him as "a bruised, raging and fiendishly intelligent man" whose mission is to explore "the extremes of inner space." He himself says, "Writing is just a man alone in a room with the English language, trying to make it come out right. The important thing is that your work be something no one else could do."

Surely no one else could have written *Homage to Mistress Bradstreet*, which concerns the first poet in colonial America and is filled with cryptic references and ellipses like this: [Reproduces section 3 of *Homage to Mistress Bradstreet*, beginning with "Out of maize & air"; see *Collected Poems 1937–1971*, p. 133]

More distinctive still—without precedent, in fact—is *77 Dream Songs*, to which a companion volume, *His Toy, His Dream, His Rest* (Farrar, Straus & Giroux), will be published next year. (In December a volume called *Short Poems* will also appear.) Attached though Berryman is to both Sigmund Freud and such diverse musicians as Pablo Casals and Bessie Smith, he is patient explaining that his Dream Songs are neither dreams nor songs. They are, he says in a rare moment of self-congratulation, "staggeringly original" episodes about an imaginary character named Henry who, a critic writes, is "a lonely, lecherous, whimsical, unstable academic hipster in the process of growing old, with an extraordinary talent for *becoming* the people and things he likes." Another finds him "the loser in the winner's country, before being strung up by the efficiency expert, or smothered with flowers by the be-in crowd." Sometimes Henry is a black-faced minstrel who speaks and is addressed in Negro dialect Berryman unfashionably calls "coon talk," as in the dream song that goes in part, "We hafta *die* / That is our 'pointed task. Love & die." Sometimes Henry has a friend who calls him Mr. Bones, Sir Bones, or Dr. Bones. Other times he is overwhelmingly alone and vulnerable. "There is a fiendish resemblance between Henry and me," Berryman says. Sometimes Henry isn't the poet, sometimes—as in the first of the *77 Dream Songs*—he is. [Reproduces "Dream Song 1."]

Berryman the man is fully as complex and stylish as Berryman the poet. He has enough personal style, in fact, for any dozen of the rest of us. You never know whether to treat him as an august man of letters or as a prankish little boy, because he is always, simultaneously, both. His wild beard looks like steel wool and spills in a bib down his throat, freeing him from having to wear a necktie. His colleagues at Minnesota, it is said, have to wind his scarf around his throat before he proceeds into the winter cold, because he forgets things like that. He sweats a lot and swears a lot. Sometimes he plunges into silent, private gloom. Sometimes he won't eat. Even the most succulent of steaks grow cold before him, causing his friends to sneak them to their homes in doggie bags.

Then there is his voice. If there's anything he isn't, it's a mumbler. Waiters in restaurants, clerks in stores, and sextons in historic churches he visits are always coming up to ask him *please* to quiet down, because when Berryman is emotionally moved (which is most of the time), HE LOSES CONTROL OF THE VOLUME OF HIS VOICE AND SHOUTS AND ROARS.

This roaring used to embarrass his third wife, Kate, who is twenty-five years his junior, but she has got over it. "I'm not bothered anymore when everyone in a restaurant stares at our table because of John," she says. "I figure they probably don't have all that much to say to each other anyway, and it gives them something to talk about." Kate, whose name at her husband's request has legally been changed from Kathleen, first attracted him eight years ago in Minneapolis. "What did it," he says, "was the spindly, wobbly way she walked in high heels." Kate is now the mother of a beguiling four-year-old named Martha and known to her father as "Twissy."

All three Berrymans have relished their year in Dublin, which the poet chose "because it's right on the edge of Europe, it's crawling with delightful people, and they all speak English." It also contains two special added attractions: shrines redolent of Yeats, Joyce, and Swift—especially Swift—and pubs. Those pubs make New York bars seem like mausoleums. In the pubs Berryman likes best, it is customary for people not to stare with glazed eyes at television sets but to sit facing *each other*, and moreover to sing. They sing not well but together, and on a lively night everyone is asked sooner or later to perform a solo. Berryman, when this happened to him once, obliged with a Bessie Smith blues song, Kate with all she could think of at the moment: "Yankee Doodle." After such a fest, an Irishman told Berryman "I like Robert W. Service's poems best, but I like yours too." Berryman was pleased. "I like people who are *blazing* with self-respect," he says, "and most Irishman are. Not the way people are in New York: there, all eight million of them all scream at the top of their lungs how great they are. Here they're realistic. The man who picks up litter in the park shakes your hand and introduces himself and says, "I'm a laborer, that's what I'm termed as, and I have the lowest job of all."

Berryman responds to Irish whimsy and indulges in it himself. Flying across the Atlantic, he strained to look down out of the airplane window and said, "Think of all the poor fishes we're flying over!" When it was discovered that nobody had remembered to bring forks on a picnic in the country, he announced, "We won't be needing forks, we all have our fingers with us today." The destination of that picnic was Tara, an ancient site where pre-Christian kings of whom Yeats once wrote used to live and die. The thought of this—the association with both Yeats and the kings—moved Berryman, and therefore everyone else around him, nearly to tears. His reactions are contagious; he has a rare gift for communicable literary hero worship. A critic who called him a "shut-in scholar" was all wrong; Berryman would as soon address six hundred people as six, and heaven knows needs no microphone.

"It's a completely extraliterary talent, being able to read aloud," he says. "There's just one thing: I must *love* what I'm reading. When I do read, I think of poor Dylan Thomas and how one time he read, in public, Blake's poem 'The Tyger.' In the audience was some insufferable actor fellow with a stopwatch, who said, 'You had a forty-five-second pause there!' Dylan drew himself up to his full height and said, 'Read it as fast as I *could.*'"

His showmanship has served Berryman well. A sort of academic nomad, he has taught on all kinds of college faculties—Brown, Harvard, California, Wayne State, Princeton, Iowa, Cincinnati—everywhere in the United States in fact but the South, from which "I never even *answer* job offers. I hate the South because they put down Negroes there: it's as simple as that." One critic ventures a guess as to why Berryman identifies quite so much with Negros. "The Negro," he says, "is an expert in survival. He is familiar with death and yet somehow continually picks himself off the very floor, clambers out of the very basement of modern civilization. Supremely a victim, he escapes self-pity through joy in survival. Like the cat, he has nine lives. Henry's search is to learn to be a cat, simply to continue, as coolly as possible, to play it by ear." That is Berryman's search, too, no matter what he is doing.

If you were going to mark a map of the world to show all the places Berryman has ever spent a semester, you would need quite a handful of pins. Where scarcely matters to him. "Of course I'd rather spend a year in Kyoto than in Buffalo," he demurs, "but then a year in *hell* would be better than a year in Buffalo." Apart from that he would as soon be in his stolid wood house in Minneapolis, the tiny, tacky living room of the house he rented in Dublin, or a hotel in Calcutta, a widely maligned city of which he grew enamored when the State Department sent him ten years ago on a two-month tour of India to read his work. Wherever he goes, he has noted, "I always find that the funny thing is that you end up talking not about where you *went* but what you *missed.* We sit there in Connecticut and talk of all the things we didn't see."

Berryman is so unconcerned with his whereabouts that he didn't even mind much during his recent New York visit when he suddenly got desperately sick from what doctors called "exhaustion and malnutrition" and had to go to a hospital. In fact, apart from the nasty business of intravenous feedings, the whole experience filled him with an odd euphoria. He wrote three new Dream Songs and entertained visitors by cheerfully reciting another—written during another recent spell in another hospital—about a new member of his pantheon of heroes, the brave British sailor Sir Francis Chichester. It goes:

Where the waters mingle, Sir, Henry wills you well
& where ice-cliffs overhang your yacht
& where wales wallow under
slide safely toward Plymouth; debark & tell
the listening world your triumph, mention what
pulled you through to our wonder.

I love my doctor, I love too my nurse,
but I am glad to leave them, as now I do.
Too long it's been
Out of this world, away from the whisk, the curse
of Henry's particular life, who has pulled through
too & again makes the scene.

Kings of survival look out with strangeness on
the pleasant all who do not find it hard
& throw out eleven & seven
regularly, apparently. They too will be gathered in
at last long with our majesty, murmured the bard
with half a left foot in heaven.

Berryman resents the fact that in the US, poetry is considered effeminate, and finds it shameful that "no national memory but ours could forget the fact that John Adams and Thomas Jefferson both died on the same day—the fourth of July in 1826." Still, he is unabashedly patriotic. He was born in Oklahoma, to which his parents had separately and by chance migrated from father east, his mother to teach and his father to be a banker. "They married each other," he says, "because they were the only two people for miles around who could read." He and his younger brother were bred there and in Florida, where, in John's twelfth year and right outside his window, his father shot himself in the breast and died. John suffers even today, he says, "from an exaggerated case of what Freud calls 'infantile amnesia.'

"I haven't the slightest interest in my childhood," he claims. Nor is he concerned about most of the rest of his life. "Until about ten years ago, when I suddenly became as hot as a pistol, I was an utter bore." Of the earliest boring years Berryman recalls he aspired briefly to be an archaeologist "because, as I once wrote in a dream song, 'what could be more peaceful, respected and serious than that?'" For years the excitement of poetry eluded him, "because all I was exposed to was 'Abou Ben Adhem, may his tribe increase' and 'Breathes there a man with soul so dead.'" Then, at Columbia, he fell under the considerable spell of his teacher, Mark Van Doren. "You know how kids can read the way adults never do?" Berryman says. "Well, suddenly I wanted to read. I read. It took me three years to work my way through English and American literature and various foreign literatures." He graduated Phi Beta Kappa, spent a summer at Heidelberg, grew his first beard, wore it to Clare College at Cambridge for a fellowship year. During that year he made a prophetic trip to Dublin to pay homage to William Butler Yeats, though his colleague and drinking companion Dylan Thomas, who was not a Yeats admirer, tried to dissuade him.

Still bearded, Berryman returned to New York and applied for a job as an advertising copywriter. He failed to get it—partly because of the beard and partly because he had the innocence to suggest that an insurance company adopt as its symbol the Rock of Gibraltar, unaware that a rival concern had already thought of the idea.

But that was all right. Berryman started teaching because he had to eat—"though," as he says, "when it came to a choice between buying a book and a sandwich, as it often did, I always chose the book." And he started writing, "because I had to and have to. It's what I *do*, the way beavers build dams and presidents make decisions." He published a book of poems called *The Dispossessed*. Because he wasn't and still isn't exclusively a poet, he also wrote *Stephen Crane*, which is regarded as the definitive critical biography of the novelist, and several equally respected articles on Shakespeare.

His brain again began to teem with many more works than his pen may ever glean. Along the line, he started eleven manuscripts that he has yet to finish: a biography of Shakespeare, a critical edition of *King Lear*, "a work of discovery, textual and biographical, called *Shakespeare's Friend*," a book called *Shakespeare's Reading*, three plays, a travel book on India, Spain, and

America, a volume of prose, one called *The Freedom of the Poet*, and a book not of dream songs but of dreams.

Dreams, especially his own, fascinate Berryman. In a recent one he was cast as the Pope, dispatched on a mission of critical importance to Eastern Europe to check up on a malcontent Polish cardinal who had sent him a memo in pencil on lined notebook paper. Berryman, after he had been psychoanalyzed, for years made an elaborate, systematic practice of analyzing his dreams by himself. "It's not something you can do without training," he says, "any more than you can play the piano without practicing scales. One dream I had turned out to have thirty-eight structures—not levels, structures."

His poems reflect his dreams, but not always. "My Heavy Daughter," for example, (never before published), comes from close-at-hand reality. [Reproduces "Dream Song 385"; see *The Dream Songs*, p. 407]

Besides young Martha, Berryman has a ten-year-old son named Paul, by his second wife. He sees Paul seldom but loves him no less. "Kids," he says, "are all we have. We don't go on, we come to a dead stop, so we have to have them. Children and work are the only things that really matter, though conversation with friends goes a long way too. In fact, one month I lived in Berkeley I had a phone bill of $183.

"My wife and I are very fond of kids," he goes on. "Kids make up a sort of social life. We must love our children and teach them. AND TEACH THEM!" He predicts that his own daughter will be "a raving beauty—there's no way out of it, I'm afraid. Maybe they'll be a short, bad stage of pimples when she's around thirteen, but she'll survive that. I want her American-trained until she's twenty-one, and aside from that I just hope she has good judgment in men and has children and is good to them. Would I want her to be a poet? I should say the hell not! Lady poets are mostly spinsters or lesbians, and besides that—though you might not guess it—like all poets they have to work damn hard."

All ladies, poets or otherwise, are an obsession of Berryman's. "I should *know* about women," he says. "I've been married to three of them, and had dozens of affairs. I don't think I'd like to teach at a girls' college, though. I'd go crazy there in a week. To be in *any* room with more than four women makes me feel a little nervous and threatened. And at a girls' school I'd fall in love with my students, which would be troublesome for me and bothersome for Kate."

As might not be guessed by readers of *Berryman's Sonnets*, which tell of one real extramarital affair the poet had "a thousand years ago," their author is now evangelistically opposed to adultery. "You mustn't love a married man," he counsels women. "Not only do you get hurt, but you find yourself capable of actions you would never have thought possible. You behave like a spider." Probably because he is so content with Kate, who he says, "has no faults at all, and yet she's still not boring," he is impatient for the whole world to pair off like characters in the finale of a Gilbert and Sullivan operetta. "It's terrible to give half your life over to someone else," he admits, "but it's worse not to. It's too bad that when you get married, they don't let you say 'I hope so' instead of 'I will,' but it's still important to try. You've *got* to try!"

When Berryman's marriage-broker instincts get the better of him, anyone is fair game: friends, cab drivers, waitresses, stewardesses, students, former students, receptionists in offices, guys who pick up litter in parks. When he comes on some stranger, he says: "And what might your name be, sir or miss? And are you married? Ah! You're not? *Why* not? And how are your prospects? And what's wrong with that man or girl right over there across the room? Up you get! Go to it!"

One of his best poems about the effects of love (though in this case, for shame, the adulterous kind) is a sonnet in the new collection: [Reproduces "Sonnet 23," see *Collected Poems 1937–1971*, p. 82]

John Berryman feels that the best thing about his sonnets, indeed about all his poetry, is his use of pronouns. "If I were sitting around praising myself," he says, "which I'm not, I would claim to understand the pronoun better than any other living writer. Henry, for instance, refers to himself as 'I,' 'he,' and 'you,' so that the various parts of his identity are fluid. They slide, and the reader is made to guess who is talking to whom. Out of this ambiguity arises richness. The reader becomes more aware, is forced to enter into himself." Nor does Berryman apologize for the other idiosyncrasies of his work, which include baby talk, the Negro dialect, and the frequent use of ampersands and abbreviations. "People read with their eyes," he says, "not their ears. I like everything to be as short as possible on the page. Leave out all you can." He writes in longhand, in a handsome if somewhat tremulous italic script. "I don't have Kate type it until it is pretty heavily revised," he says. "The foul and weak spots strike you more when the work is seen in a less fluid form. I rewrite and rewrite and rewrite. As Kipling used to say of his stories, 'I hold them up and let the wind blow through them, and if anything's left, I publish it.'"

Bits of advice like this are imparted with lavish waves of arms that end in graceful fingers yellowed from three packs of cigarettes a day, in gestures less midwestern than Mediterranean. Such talk, so delivered, has won Berryman disciples at every campus where he has ever taught. But he would not be happy if his life were strictly professorial. His passport says "Author," not "Teacher." "Other things being equal," he says, "I don't like academic people very well. They're hard to put up with because there's always tension—they're always griping about tenure and money."

Berryman's own attitude toward money is nonchalant. As long as there's enough to feed, clothe, and shelter him and Kate and Martha and send some off to Paul, he doesn't care about more. Apart from a compulsion to take home a bottle of whisky every night, he has a true intellectual's indifference to material things. "You know how long it takes me to buy a shirt?" he asks. "Two minutes—I just go in and buy the first one I see." He lives, as he writes, with a sense of urgency. "The utter bloody hell with ninety-thousand-dollar insurance policies and educating our children twenty years from now and all that," he says. "We're supposed to do what we have to do RIGHT NOW."

On a good day Berryman feels pretty sanguine about accomplishing the tasks he has set out for himself, and about things in general. "This world works so well!" he says when he feels at his best. "The older I get the more I'm impressed by how brilliantly this thing is administered. I would have cut my throat in 1947 if I hadn't thought then that I was in the grip of something infinitely beyond my own recognition." But there are bad days when he all but weeps as he quotes Henry James: "I too have the imagination of atrocity, and see life as ferocious and sinister." Then comes another plug for old Sir Francis Chichester, at whose feet the poet adds he would like to sit and say, "Sir, you have changed my life"—just as he'd like to say the same thing to Pablo Casals. ("The only thing I regret more than having no sister," Berryman says, "is that I have no gift myself for music.") The Chichester quote that so hit him, of which he says, *"Now you write this down and remember it,"* appeared in the papers just before the sailor set forth on his voyage. It goes: "No important project can be undertaken without fear. I shall be scared stiff most of the time." "Now," says Berryman, "ISN'T THAT ADORABLE?"

Berryman adores the quote because he also shares Chichester's fear. "We have reason to be afraid," he says. "This is a terrible place, but we have to exert our wills. I wake up every morning terrified." Hence the whisky—under whose influence the terror seems somewhat to diminish—and hence, for as long as Berryman keeps up his own rugged fight for survival, the ink and white he writes.

Pulitzer Prize Poet Visiting at Trinity This Week

Florence Berkman / 1967

From the *Hartford Times*, October 11, 1967, 14G

[In the wake of the Pulitzer and the *Life* profile, Berryman began to command hefty fees for readings and lectures, which supplemented his comparatively meager university salary. This brief piece from the now-defunct newspaper the *Hartford Times* was occasioned by a lecture and reading series Berryman gave at Trinity College, a private university located in Hartford. Berryman also read nearby at the Goodwin Theater, introduced by poet William Meredith. While at Trinity, Berryman also read from and commented upon the work of Elizabeth Bishop, Robert Lowell, Theodore Roethke, and Delmore Schwartz. On-stage, he managed to captivate audiences, even those who disapproved of his obvious public intoxication. Off-stage, biographer Paul Mariani notes, Berryman spent most of his time alone in his room, drinking. When the university chairman published an editorial on Berryman in the university newspaper that criticized Berryman for his inebriation, several readers came to Berryman's defense, and accused the chairman of exhibiting a "smug self-righteousness" (see Mariani 432–33).—Ed.]

John Berryman has beautiful hands with long, graceful fingers.

They move incessantly as he talks of the great poets of the past and the present, of the life of the poet in contemporary times.

The fifty-two-year-old winner of a Pulitzer Prize in 1965 (for his book of verse *77 Dream Songs*) is poet-in-residence at Trinity College this week.

A dynamic and vibrant man, he is riding the crest of a newfound fame which was long in coming.

One asks him a question and he says: "Wait, I will tell you a story," and then he will quote from Blake, Plato, T. S. Eliot, or some lesser-known poet whom he admires.

Asked for whom he writes, he replied with a quotation from the German philosopher Hamann. "This is a dialogue between two voices—the Muse and the Poet," he explained. "The Muse says 'Write.' The Poet asks, 'For whom?' The Muse replies, 'For the dead whom thou didst love.' The Poet asks, 'Will they read me?' The Muse replies, 'Ay, for they return as posterity.'"

Pressed further, Berryman said he was so busy he had no time to wonder for whom he was writing, "Except I know I write for my wife, my doctor, my daughter, and my son and for Saul Bellow, the novelist, and for the poets Robert Lowell, Edward Fitzgerald, and William Meredith. A poet has to have time to think," he said.

As he talks he sometimes strokes his beard, which one writer said looks like "steel wool and spills in a bib down his throat, freeing him from having to wear a necktie."

His world is peopled by the great writers, poets, artists and he constantly quotes from their works. So filled is he with admiration for them that his body is aquiver as the words come tumbling from his lips.

"Only one person in five thousand knows what poetry is about and that is a high estimate," he said in an interview at the Austin Arts Center where he will read his poetry in a public lecture tonight and again on Friday.

"Stop a person on a street corner and ask him if he has read a certain poem of Robert Frost and he will answer, 'Who?' and then he may remember that Frost was the poet who participated in the presidential inaugural of John F. Kennedy."

Do poets have a special problem in this affluent, materialistic society in which it is said creative people feel more alienated than in the past?

"It's no different for poets than for other human beings—it is extremely horrible," he said and then added, "there are some happy times."

Happy times for him are when he is at work. "When I get up in the morning I am frightened until I get involved with my poetry."

Berryman, who teaches Greek civilization at the University of Minnesota, does not agree with Shelley that "poets are the unacknowledged legislators of the world."

Berryman and Tate: Poets Extraordinaire

Elizabeth Nussbaum / 1967

From *Minnesota Daily*, November 9, 1967, 7, 10. Reprinted by permission.

[A brief profile on one of the University of Minnesota's most eminent poets, Berryman's section only is reproduced below. Berryman had recently returned from Dublin and completed the laborious process of organizing *His Toy, His Dream, His Rest*, the second volume of Dream Songs. Here Berryman discusses his experiences in Dublin, his high-profile interviews by the BBC and *Life* magazine, and more humdrum topics.—Ed.]

A man with a flowing beard and thick glasses walks down Church Street on a brisk afternoon, engulfed by a swarm of chattering students.

He is John Berryman, Pulitzer Prize–winning poet, and he is discussing Homer and a mélange of other topics with the intent followers he calls "my children."

Berryman, fifty-three, is also a humanities professor, Shakespearean scholar, short story writer, and author of the definitive biography of Stephen Crane—among other things.

Recently returned from a year's sabbatical in Dublin, his lectures and conversation are punctuated with a sprightly selection of stories about his fellow writers, travels, and experiences in academia.

Berryman lives in a comfortable and unassuming house in Prospect Park with his charming, pretty wife Kate and four-year-old daughter. It is there that he spends most of his time, writing, sipping on a drink, and endlessly puffing at Tareytons in a relaxed atmosphere of books and toys.

He is an imposing man physically—half-shut eyes which open wide without warning in an intense stare, the long beard, a reddish complexion, and expressive eyebrows—but he has a way of making student and literary notable alike feel at ease. Enlivening what must be for him a boring interview ("I have given hundreds; few were successful"), he effortlessly and graciously turns the conversation to his own fascinating reminiscences.

At the moment Berryman's fame—although it was probably assured earlier by his highly acclaimed critical work—rests securely on the long poem *Homage to Mistress Bradstreet,* now in its second edition, and *77 Dream Songs.* It was for the latter work that he was awarded the Pulitzer Prize for Poetry.

His Toy, His Dream, His Rest, a volume of 307 Dream Songs which Berryman finished last summer "the day before we flew to London on our way home," will be published in about a year. "It's over three hundred pages long," he explains, "so we want to give the reviewers as long as possible with it."

Berryman also harbors a wealth of unpublished material. "Why should I publish it?" he asks frankly. "I have little need for fame and money at this point. Anyway, somewhere there's an assistant professor waiting to become an associate professor—and here are my manuscripts."

Berryman used Dublin "as a workshop. I had a Guggenheim, you understand, and I could have gone anywhere in the world. But I picked on Ireland because I loved it so much as an undergraduate at Cambridge thirty years ago."

In Dublin Berryman "just wrote; I didn't even read." *Life* magazine and the BBC did stories on him there "and they hired cars to drive us around and take pictures. This hiring cars business became a habit, you know, so we hired one ourselves and did some traveling."

The traveling included a visit to Achill, an Irish promontory ("very rugged, very wild") and a pilgrimage to poet William Butler Yeats's grave ("very simple, very well done"). Berryman gave two poetry readings in London and stopped at Paris and Venice, "which is surely the most marvelous city in the world," on his way to Athens. He and his family spent the summer there and on the Greek islands.

"I'm extremely fond of the modern Greeks," he says, "and I made some very good friends there—café friends, you know. I drank brandy in Greece.

"The Greeks are wonderful; they won't even let you buy an olive, that's how kind they are."

Berryman also spent two hours in Turkey "at 6 a.m. in the morning—life is very strange at 6 a.m. in the morning. I bought a little Turkish doll there for my baby (his daughter Martha) and she is very fond of it."

During the summer Berryman also met Ernest Samuels, a professor at Northwestern University who won the Pulitzer Prize the same year as Berryman for the third volume of "his marvelous biography of Henry Adams.[1]

But the book is damned expensive. I asked Ernest if I could check it out of the library instead of buying it. Do you think he'd mind that?"

Turning to other subjects, Berryman tells of his friendship with the late Welsh poet Dylan Thomas. The two met when Berryman (who was with Thomas when he died in New York in 1953) was a student at Trinity College, Cambridge. The Welshman came to London and asked to see the American. "He had heard of me, for some reason," Berryman explains, "and I had certainly heard of him—oh yes."

Their friendship included pub crawling in London and New York. "We used to play darts a lot at bars," Berryman recalls. "I was much better than Thomas and I beat him all the time. Then he discovered that he was born one day before me, on October 24, 1914. I was born on October 25.[2]

"He thought that was great. From then on, whenever I beat him at darts Thomas would look down at me and say, 'A little more respect there, Berryman, a little more respect.'"

Constantly gesturing with his hands, Berryman casually runs through long lists of friends he has made in the United States and Europe while recounting the inevitable stories about them. One is Minneapolis Mayor Arthur Naftalin, a man he admires greatly.

"Naftalin is one of the best city managers in the United States," Berryman remarks, "and he has no more power than I have. Unless there is a heavy reform in the city charter, we will continue wasting the talents of one of the most able men in American politics.

"You know what that man has?" he asks disdainfully. "He has a big office in City Hall that serves coffee. And there's a big mural on the wall by a teenager. It's that bad."

Berryman says he would like to see Minneapolis adopt a city manager system, "or else I want him (Naftalin) to run for Congress . . . He doesn't seem to like teaching, and he shouldn't go back to the University. I'm very depressed to see him like this. Minneapolis is one of the worst-run cities in the United States.

"Along with Denver, it's relatively free of corruption. But efficiently run? God, no."

Berryman describes politicians as "two types of people: Good Guys and Bad Guys." Mayor John Lindsay of New York, he says, "is obviously a Good Guy. He runs that city like a powerhouse."

Berryman has a curious and delightful way of consciously using bad grammar for emphasis: "I'm very heavy on him" he says of Lindsay. "He's done good."

He thinks New York Governor Nelson Rockefeller is another Good Guy. "He runs that state like a dynamo. Now I don't like Republicans. But these men are Republicans and it doesn't matter. It's tremendous."

Rockefeller is Berryman's choice for president in 1968. If the GOP nominates Rockefeller, he says, "I plant to vote for him twice—once with a black face and once with a white face. I may even go so far as to shave off my beard, and then they'd let me vote for him a third time, don't you think?"

Notes

1. Ernest Samuels, *Henry Adams: The Major Phase* (Harvard University Press, 1964).
2. In fact, Dylan Thomas was born on October 27, 1914.

Berryman Ends Poem of Thirteen Years

Catherine Watson / 1968

From *The Minneapolis Tribune*, May 12, 1968, 1E. Reprinted by permission.

[Another short, local profile piece, Catherine Watson's article, like Elizabeth Nussbaum's, addresses Berryman's completion of *The Dream Songs.*—Ed.]

How does it feel to have finished a poem thirteen years in the writing?

"I'm completely exhausted," poet John Berryman said last week.

He had just sent *His Toy, His Dream, His Rest*, the second volume of "the long poem I've been writing for thirteen years," off to his publisher. The first volume, *77 Dream Songs*, won him a Pulitzer Prize in 1965.

"I've finished the poem fifty times," Berryman said. "I finished it many times in Athens and I finished it many times in Ireland (where the Berrymans were last year) and my wife threatened to leave me if I didn't stop finishing it."

He meant it when he said he's finished it this time—"but I plan to give the galley proofs a hard time," he added.

The two volumes of Dream Songs have taken Berryman's main character, Henry, as far as he will go, the poet said.

Not all the songs about Henry are in the books, Berryman said, but "if there is a third volume, it will not take him further. It will be up to the reader to fit those poems in among the published ones."

The dreams are Henry's dreams, not Berryman's, he said; the songs are not for singing—"their music is verbal."

And Henry?

"Henry is a white American, sometimes in blackface, in early middle age. He has suffered an irreparable loss [comparable to Berryman's own: His father died when the poet was eleven]; he has many adventures; he is a very difficult man.

"The long poem has many characters. Henry has many friends. The main one is Mr. Bones, who is a Job's Comforter to Henry, a Sancho Panza to him."

Berryman, fifty-three, was born and reared in small Oklahoma towns, where he produced his earliest complete work, a novel about a trip to Neptune, written when he was twelve. "Happily the manuscript has been lost," Berryman said.

"I had always intended to be a writer," he said, "but not a writer of verse," since he "detested" poetry as he learned it in school.

But by the time he was nineteen and mostly through with his English and comparative literature studies at Columbia University, he had stopped detesting it and was writing his own.

Berryman came to Minneapolis thirteen years ago because "I detested where I was in Iowa"; because New York seemed remote and because a good friend, poet and critic Allen Tate, was at the University of Minnesota.

Berryman was exhausted then, too. He was working twelve hours a day on a "self-analysis" and had just finished his first long poem, *Homage to Mistress Bradstreet*. Soon after, he began to teach at the university, where he is now a humanities professor.

He says he is coasting now "to the end of the quarter." He plans a few more poetry readings around the country—including Saturday's seminar for city teachers and an 8:30 p.m. (public) lecture that day (both in the Museum of Natural History at the University). But after that, "there will be no more traveling this year."

"I've been asked to translate Sophocles," he said, and started on *Oedipus Rex*, but his plans for the summer are to stay home, at 33 Arthur Avenue SE., with his third wife, Kate, and their five-year-old daughter, Martha. "And to play tennis, swim, and do absolutely nothing," he said.

He noted two other favorite Berryman past-times: "I'm very keen on two kinds of music—blues and jazz; and Mozart, Beethoven, and Schubert.

"And mostly, I like to sit in my rocking chair in the middle of my living room with a glass of bourbon in one hand and a cigarette in the other, rocking and thinking."

An Interview with John Berryman

David McClelland, John Plotz, Robert B. Shaw, and
Thomas Stewart / 1968

Conducted October 27, 1968. Published in *Harvard Advocate* 103, no. 1 (1969): 4–9. Reprinted in *Berryman's Understanding: Reflections on the Poetry of John Berryman*, edited by Harry Thomas (Boston: Northeastern University Press, 1988), 3–17. Robert B. Shaw introduction from *Antaeus*, no. 8 (Winter 1973): 7–19. Reprinted by permission of Trustees of the *Harvard Advocate* and Robert B. Shaw.

Introduction by Robert B. Shaw

This interview first appeared in the Spring 1969 issue of the *Harvard Advocate*, which was devoted entirely to the work of John Berryman. Since at least 1965 the *Advocate* had wanted to publish such an issue. When the editors first approached Berryman on the subject, shortly after the appearance of *77 Dream Songs*, they were gently but firmly put off. Berryman must have felt that a symposium on his career was at that point premature; after the appearance of his *Sonnets* and *His Toy, His Dream, His Rest* he was eager to cooperate. In addition to the interview, he gave us three Dream Songs to print: two of them, "Henry by Night" and "Henry's Understanding," later turned up in *Delusions, Etc.*, while the third, "Apollo 8," has yet to be collected.[1] The Berryman issue also featured essays and shorter tributes in prose or verse by, among others, Conrad Aiken, Elizabeth Bishop, Robert Lowell, and Howard Nemerov.

Berryman arrived in Cambridge late on a Saturday afternoon in October. A taxi let him out on Mt. Auburn Street just as the Dartmouth game was ending and crowds from the stadium had begun to trudge back across the Charles River. I no longer remember which team won, and even on the day itself many people probably forgot amid the usual post-game carousing. A group of us took Berryman first to the Lampoon Castle for several drinks and then, finding the better eating places mobbed, to a rather smoky Greek restaurant where we had some overdone shish kebab. Berryman was in fine spirits; *His Toy, His Dream, His Rest* had just been published and was obviously headed for a National Book Award. He looked on top of things, neat in a bow tie and with his graying beard trimmed back from the Santa Claus proportions it had assumed in Ireland. John Plotz and I escorted him back to his rooms in Quincy House and stayed for several hours, sharing his bourbon, marveling at his capacity and listening to his stories, some of which he told more than once. His anecdotes about fellow writers were funny but without malice; he seemed to see them not as rivals but as colleagues in a worthy cause. As the bottle emptied, he sang snatches of blues and for some reason touched on religion. "You know," he said, "I've often considered going to Confession, but the list of my sins is so long by now that I wouldn't get out of there for a week." He said this laughingly but with an undercurrent of seriousness that I remembered in reading his later "Eleven Addresses to the Lord." Some readers were taken by surprise by these quirky penitential psalms; but they might have remembered that *The Dream Songs* is on one important level a theological poem.

The interview the next day went smoothly, on the whole. Another bottle had replaced the one we'd killed the night before. Plotz and I were more the worse for wear than Berryman. He was as voluble as we had hoped, and suffered patiently our fumblings with recording and photographic equipment. Throughout, he was affable to the young men and courtly to the women.

The publication of *His Toy, His Dream, His Rest* was celebrated in New York on October 25, 1968; the following day, Mr. Berryman arrived in Boston to speak with the *Advocate* and to read at Brandeis University. On Sunday, the twenty-seventh, David McClelland, John Plotz, Robert B. Shaw, and Thomas Stewart visited Mr. Berryman in the guest suite of Quincy House at Harvard, armed with tape recorder and phonograph. After listening to Bob Dylan and Robert Johnson for several minutes, we got down to cases.

Interviewer: Could you talk about where you were born and where you came from and how you started writing poetry?

Berryman: Yes, I can do that very quickly. I was born in Oklahoma; my father was a banker and my mother was a schoolteacher; they were the only people who could read and write for hundreds of miles around and they were living in the same boarding house, so they got married; so I arrived. Son number one. Then we moved to Florida, and my father killed himself.

Interviewer: How old were you then?

Berryman: Then we moved to Gloucester, Massachusetts, and then New York and I was in school for some years on Long Island, in Jackson Heights, P.S. 69, that was the number of the school. Then I went to a Connecticut prep school—South Kent; I was there for four years, but got very bored in South Kent, so they gave me college boards a year early, so I skipped sixth form. I went from the fifth straight into Columbia. Then I was at Columbia for four years—or rather three and a half years since I got thrown out.

Interviewer: What was that about?

Berryman: Well, I wasn't going to class and things like that, you know, and I flunked a course, lost my scholarship. Then I went back in. By this time the administration knew me very well. I used to get notes from the Dean saying, "Dean [Herbert E.] Hawkes would like you to call on him at your earliest convenience." I used to say to myself, "That's damn white of the Dean. I must drop in on him." Until, Plotz, one day a message arrived, saying, "If you are not in the Dean's office by eleven o'clock you are suspended."

Interviewer: And you went?

Berryman: I went—and he suspended me.

Interviewer: How did you get from there to Cambridge?

Berryman: Well, during my last couple of years, I was a good boy. I toed the line and was a decent character. So they gave me everything—even made me Phi Beta Kappa. And they gave me their main travelling fellowship; and then I was two years at Cambridge, and then I came back to New York and lived in New York for a year. Then I taught at Harvard for three years, then I taught at Princeton off and on for ten years, and now I'm at Minnesota, where I'm not very often, but I sometimes go there: I bought a house.

Interviewer: When did you first start writing?

Berryman: I was very late in developing—very late in developing. I was about nineteen when I wrote four sonnets for my mother's birthday—and they were about the worst sonnets that the world has ever seen, but I thought they were quite good, and my mother thought they were terrific. I have always had a very close relationship with my mother—that's very bad for me I'm told.

Interviewer: Did studying under Mark Van Doren at Columbia have an influence?

Berryman: Oh yes. I always wanted to be a writer—I wrote a science fiction novel when I was twelve; the chief character was called E-Coro-'aka. But a poet? I never imagined that. All I knew about poetry then was, "Abou Ben Adhem, may his tribe increase, / Awoke one night from a dream of peace" and "Breathes there the man with soul so dead / Who never to himself has said, / This is my own, my native land"[2]—junk like that. Who wants to write that? So I never imagined being a poet, until I reviewed Mark Van Doren's book, *A Winter Diary*, which appeared after about seven years of silence, because he was having trouble getting a publisher. I became friends with him and I called him "Sir"—a habit I had picked up at prep school, when we had to call not only the maters, but the sixth formers "Sir." So I called "Sir"; so he said, "If you call me 'sir' once more I'll kick you in the ass." I was very touched by this, so I didn't call him "sir" anymore.

Interviewer: What other poets did you especially enjoy and feel influenced by?

Berryman: Yeats. Yeats was my master. I went through a long period of hating Yeats, but now I regard him as extremely good. And Auden. I had to get free of both Yeats and Auden.

Interviewer: Why do you call *The Dream Songs* one poem rather than a group of poems in the same form?

Berryman: Ah—it's personality—it's Henry. He thought up all these things over all the years. The reason I call it one poem is the result of my strong disagreement with Eliot's line—the impersonality of poetry, an idea which he got partly from Keats (a letter) and partly from Goethe (again a letter). I'm very much against that; it seems to me on the contrary that poetry comes out of personality. For example, Keats—I'm thinking of "La Belle Dame Sans Merci," I'm thinking of that; and I'm thinking of Hopkins—any one of the sonnets. So I don't buy this business about the eighteenth century being impersonal, either. Now Jonson's best poem in my opinion is about a factor in his household—I forget the name of it—and it's a beautiful poem, and it's extremely personal.

Interviewer: What is the relationship between *77 Dream Songs* and *His Toy, His Dream, His Rest*?

Berryman: Well, *77 Dream Songs* is just the first three books.

Interviewer: Do you see a gap between the two volumes?

Berryman: No, I don't see a gap; it's a continuous relationship. Except, there's this: at the end of the first volume, *77 Dream Songs*, Henry goes into orbit. He was "making ready to move on." Well, I was already ahead of him.

Interviewer: I noticed that Henry's state of death, Book IV, corresponded to the epic convention of placing a descent into the underworld in the center of the narrative; was there any consideration of that in structuring the poem?

Berryman: I don't think so. *Opus Posthumous* is just a recovery from the end of Book Three in the first volume of Dream Songs. The placement of the poems in *The Dream Songs* is purely personal.

Interviewer: Is there any ulterior structure to *The Dream Songs*?

Berryman: Ah—you mean, somebody can get to be an associate professor or an assistant professor by finding it out? Mr. Plotz, there is none. *Il n'y en a pas!* There's not a trace of it. Some of the Songs are in alphabetical order; but, mostly, they just belong to areas of hope and fear that Henry is going through at a given time. That's how I worked them out.

Interviewer: In the last volume you said the poem's ultimate structure is according to Henry's nature.

Berryman: Now, that's right.

Interviewer: So, in fact, the book has no plot?

Berryman: Those are fighting words. It has a plot. Its plot is the personality of Henry as he moves on in the world. Henry gains ten years. At one time his age is given as forty-one, "Free, black, and forty-one" ["Dream Song 40"], and at a later point he's fifty-one. So the poem spans a large area, you see that.

Interviewer: You admire Stephen Crane, we know, and many of his characters are named "Henry"; is this the origin of the name?

Berryman: Oh no—that's all just accident and junk. I'll tell you how the name Henry came into being. One time my second wife and I were walking down an avenue in Minneapolis and we decided on the worst names that you could think of for men and women. We decided on Mabel for women, and Henry for men. So from then on, in the most cozy and adorable way, she was Mabel and I was Henry; and that's how Henry came into being.

Interviewer: What is the relationship between you and Henry?

Berryman: I think I'll leave that one to the critics. Henry does not resemble me, and I resemble Henry; but on the other hand I am not Henry. You know, I pay income tax; Henry pays no income tax. And bats come over and they stall in my hair—and fuck them, I'm not Henry; Henry doesn't have any bats.

Interviewer: Would you talk about Henry in terms of heroism, as the hero of a poem?

Berryman: Well, he's very brave, Henry, in that he keeps on living after other people have dropped dead. But he's a hopeless coward with regard to his actual death. That never comes out in the poem, but he is afraid of death. I tried to make it clear in the epigraphs from Sir Francis Chichester and [Charles George] Gordon.[3]

Interviewer: Why is Henry called "Mr. Bones"?

Berryman: There's a minstrel show thing of Mr. Bones and the interlocutor. There's a wonderful remark, which I mean to use as an epigraph, but I never got around to it. "We were all end-men," Plotz—that's what it says— "We were all end-men."

Interviewer: Who said that?

Berryman: One of the great minstrels. Isn't that adorable? "We were all end-men, and interlocutors." I wanted someone for Henry to talk to, so I took up another minstrel, the interlocutor, and made him a friend of my friend Henry. He is never named; I know his name, but the critics haven't caught on yet. Sooner or later some assistant professor will become an associate professor by learning the name of Henry's friend.

Interviewer: What about the influence of blues and minstrel shows on *The Dream Songs*?

Berryman: Heavy. I have been interested in the language of the blues and Negro dialects all my life, always been. Especially Bessie. I picked all of it up from records, although while I was at Columbia, the Apollo on 125th Street used to have blues singers. It was a completely coony house, and I used to go there sometimes; but mostly from records. For example, I never heard Bessie herself—she died.

Interviewer: You listened primarily to Bessie Smith. Who else?

Berryman: Victoria Spivey and Teddy Grace. [*Sings.*]

> He went away and never said goodbye.
> I could read his letters but I sure can't read his mind.
> I thought he's lovin me but he was leavin all the time.
> Now I know that my true love was blind.

I found out that wasn't Victoria Spivey; it was Teddy Grace. As for others, oh, I could go down the line.

Interviewer: Why did you choose to employ the Negro dialect in *The Dream Songs*?

Berryman: Well, that's a tough question. I'll tell you. I wrote a story once called "The Imaginary Jew." I was in Union Square in New York, waiting to see my girl, and I was taken for a Jew (I had a beard at the time). There was a tough Irishman who wanted to beat me up, and I got into the conversation, and I couldn't convince them that I wasn't a Jew. Well, the Negro business—the blackface—is related to that. That is, I feel extremely lucky to be white, let me put it that way, so that I don't have that problem. Friends of mine—Ralph Ellison, for example, in my opinion one of the best writers in the country—he has the problem. He's black, and he and Fanny, wherever they go, they are black.

Interviewer: I'm taking Chaucer from [Bartlett Jere] Whiting now—

Berryman: Is he still teaching? How splendid!

Interviewer: He is talking about Chaucer's use of dialect. Trying to give an example in modern English to show how drastic the mixture of dialects was in Chaucer, he said it was as if a poet writing today would have a line ending in the word "wile," slightly archaic, and rhyme it with "honey-chile." I thought—wait, I know someone who would do that.

Berryman: Well, it does attract me.

Interviewer: When you were going through all the Dream Songs you'd written, how many did you discard?

Berryman: I killed about fifty in Greece. I wrote about a hundred in Dublin, and I killed about fifty in Greece. I killed a lot of songs in Ireland, too.

Interviewer: About your other long poems—did you revise the sonnets extensively between the time when they were written and when they were first published?

Berryman: No, I didn't. All I did was fix up identifiable symbols—namely, I didn't want *her* to be identified, so I changed the name of the place, and street names, and I changed her name. I'd used her name a lot, and it was very difficult, because sometimes there were rhymes. So I had to change her name into a name that would rhyme. That's about all I did.

Interviewer: A question about the sources of *Mistress Bradstreet*. Your interest in American history seems relatively unusual for a contemporary American poet. Have you always been preoccupied with early American figures?

Berryman: Well, yes—because my people have been here a long time. I have a great-great grandmother who's Canadian, but otherwise all my people have been here since the Revolution—that's a long time. About the Bradstreet poem: I don't like her work, but I loved her—I sort of fell in love with her; and wrote about her, putting myself into it. It took me two years to get over the Bradstreet poem (it took me five years to write it, and two to get over it) and I don't think I incorporated any of it into the Dream Songs—I don't think so.

Interviewer: Had you ever thought that you would write a poem that long before you got into it?

Berryman: No, as a matter of fact, I didn't know, because I was very wrong about the Bradstreet poem—I thought I could do it in fifty lines, but when it worked out it came to 450.

Interviewer: Do you feel that narrative is becoming increasingly the province of poets?

Berryman: No, actually I don't—history teaches me that most of my colleagues, my friends, poets, can't write narrative poems. They just can't do it—and some of them have tried. Lowell tried it in *Mills of the Kavanaghs*—and that's a bad failure. And other people have tried; and I remember one afternoon with William Carlos Williams—my wife was waiting and the taxi was waiting—with Flossie, his wife, at the table, and Bill took me upstairs and said he was descended from Emily Dickinson,[4] and I said that was wonderful, William, I didn't know that. And then he said he was also descended from Shelley, and he opened a trunk and took out the documents to show me. Now, writing poems is scary and very few people will be found who can do it.

Interviewer: Do you find that, since you've been writing long poems for such a long time, you don't feel like writing short ones?

Berryman: I don't write short ones—no, I don't. You're right.

Interviewer: Except when the occasion comes up, like the Kennedy assassination.

Berryman: Ah, that's a very special kind of poem. When Kennedy died, I was living at the Chelsea in New York, at the hotel; I'm not much of a TV fan at all, but I got a set immediately and they brought it in and for four days, like everybody else in the United States, I was watching TV, about all the murders and so forth, and I did write one poem about his death—it's called "Formal Elegy"—and one reviewer in the *Times Literary Supplement* said, "Mr. Berryman, whose recent poems are all an attack on organized poetry, has a new poem now, the title of which is deeply ironic. It is called 'Formal Elegy.'" The title isn't wrong, it's right.

Interviewer: What do you see as the present relationship between politics and poetry in terms of your own work?

Berryman: Oh, I don't think I can answer that question, but I'll try. Robert Bly makes a living out of the war, and I'm against this. He uses my name in different cities; and he finally rang me up once and asked me to read in a given city at a given time, and I told him to go fuck himself. And he said, "Do you mean you're not willing to read against the war?" And I said, "No." And he said, "Well, I'm appalled!" and hung up. I'm completely against the war—I hate everything about it. But I don't believe in works of art being used as examples. I would like to write political poems, but aside from "Formal Elegy," I've never been moved to do so, because my favorites in the current campaign were [Eugene] McCarthy and Rockefeller; I would love to have had a chance to vote between either one of them, but they both got bombed and the shit was poured on them. The current candidates—the existing candidates—don't seem to me interesting; they seem to me extremely boring and troublesome and I wish they weren't there. I agree with you—I feel like laughing when I think of these candidates. [Hubert H.] Humphrey—my God—Humphrey who's repudiated every position that he ever took, you know. And Nixon, who has never held any position, is going to win, and be our next president; we're going to have to say "President Nixon."

Interviewer: Please!

Berryman: I'm sorry, John, that's what we're going to have to say now.

Interviewer: A formal question about the unit in *The Dream Songs* of three stanzas—did you have any idea of this particular length from earlier poems, specifically "The Nervous Songs," which have a similar structure?

Berryman: Yes, well, the stanza is complicated. It goes five, five, three, five, five, three; five, five, three, five, five, three; five, five, three, five, five, three—that's the business—and it's variously rhymed, and often it has no rhyme at all, but it sounds as if it rhymed. That I got from Yeats—three six-line stanzas. His songs don't really resemble mine, but I did get that from him. It's rather like an extended, three-part sonnet. You know, the Italians have it much better than we—when I was writing sonnets, years ago, I was troubled by the fact that their sonnets were much better than ours because they could get more into it. They had eleven syllables per line, instead of ten. But you add it up, you see, and it comes to more. I made up the Bradstreet stanza in 1948—it's a splendid stanza, it breaks in three-five, not four-four—and my new poem has a completely different stanza; it's a seven line-stanza and it's about Mo-Tzu—and I invented it in 1948 also—and since then I've been reading Chinese philosophy and art and history and so on. Let me see if I can remember the stanza—it goes like this: [Recites first stanza of "The Scholars at the Orchid Pavilion"; see *Collected Poems 1937–1971*, p. 246] Isn't that beautiful? It's a poem about Heaven. It's called "Scholars at the Orchid Pavilion." A single poem—which I still feel I can do in about fifty lines, but it may work out to be a whole book.

Interviewer: Isn't this "Scholars at the Orchid Pavilion" mainly what you're working on now?

Berryman: No, I'm translating Sophocles, with a back-up by a classical scholar at the University of Cincinnati. I do the translation, and then I show it to him. It's in verse. But to mount on one of those sentences—it's scary, because you can see the period way down at the end of the third line, or the sixth line. You have to get up on top of that sentence and ride it down.

Interviewer: Which do you find harder, Chinese or Greek?

Berryman: Chinese—much harder. Greek has an alphabet. Chinese doesn't have any alphabet—it's every goddamn *word*—you have to learn each individual word. It's scary.

Interviewer: Could you talk to me about how—physically—you write your poems? Do you do several drafts, start with a line, a page, or several drafts, just write them out? What is the process?

Berryman: Well, you feel uneasy, and you get going with a pencil or a pen, and rhymes emerge, sentences emerge. [Recites the first five lines of "Dream Song 31"; see *The Dream Songs*, p. 35] You know what a parnel is? It's the mistress of a priest. [Continues with the remainder of the poem.] Now what happened? Something began to boil around in my mind.

Interviewer: When you say you start out with an uneasiness in beginning to write—do you ever worry about the uneasiness that instigates the sitting down to write going away? Is this something that you can turn on when you want to?

Berryman: No, you can't, no, it depends on accidents. I took my new wife to see Scollay Square several years ago . . . and Scollay Square—everything was removed—all the nightclubs, everything was gone—it was a goddam government project. But I took my wife there to see Scollay Square and later I was moved to write about it but I didn't feel friendly to the idea, so I did not write about it, so I have never written about it.

Interviewer: You have two poems, I think—at least two—about Charles Whitman on the Texas tower. Why is it that that appeals to you so much?

Berryman: Well, the guy had a complete armory with him, do you know that? It's unbelievable. And even *Time* magazine (which I hate and which I read every week, cover to cover; every Tuesday afternoon I have a big war with *Time* magazine) they did a cover story on him called "The Madman on the Tower," and it was very moving to me. Anyway the word Whitman is very ambiguous in our time.

Interviewer: Do you revise your work at all?

Berryman: Oh, heavily, very heavy. Mostly they're unrecognizable by the time I'm finished with them. Although many of them I don't revise at all.

Interviewer: How do you see your role as a teacher in relation to your poetry?

Berryman: There's no connection. Teaching keeps my relations with my bank going. Otherwise they would be very stuffy with me. I teach my kids, heavy. I'm giving two courses. The University of Minnesota loves me dearly, so I only teach two courses, each one for an hour and a half. One course is in the American character, seen mostly from abroad. I use De Tocqueville, and D. H. Lawrence, and various other foreign characters, and then I zero in on *The Scarlet Letter* and *Moby-Dick* and so on. The other course is about the meaning of life, and I use the high religions—Christianity and Buddhism—and then I use other books.

Interviewer: Which poets living and writing now do you particularly admire?

Berryman: Well, I'm very keen on Auden, and very keen on Robert Lowell, and I'm very keen on Ezra Pound. I would think they were the three best poets working in our language. I couldn't choose between them or among them.

Interviewer: How did you view generally the state of American poetry today? Are you encouraged by the quality of work being printed?

Berryman: Oh I don't know. It's all a matter of what any individual is doing.

Interviewer: What do you think of the Beats, Ginsberg especially?

Berryman: Ginsberg I like very much—I love him. He doesn't shake your hand, he comes and kisses you—and that's extreme. But I like him very good. I don't like his work very much, but in general he's an excellent operator.

Interviewer: What about women poets?

Berryman: Well, among the women poets Miss Moore is obviously the best. But very close to her is Miss Bishop—very close.

Interviewer: What about Louise Bogan?

Berryman: Oh, no—Louise Bogan I read out; she blows through a different realm of existence.

Interviewer: How do you feel British poetry compares with that of America?

Berryman: Well, Edwin Muir is dead, and Auden is still alive. I regard him as a British, not an American poet . . . I'll tell you a story about Auden. He came over here and pretended to be an American for some years, and he was elected to the National Institute of Arts and Letters, which I'm a member of, too. They were having a fantastic conversation about uniforms. And Auden got up and said, "We in England feel . . . ," but then he suddenly remembered that it was the *American* Institute of Arts and Letters!

Interviewer: What do you think of Basil Bunting's verse?

Berryman: My God—Basil Bunting? The only connection I can make here is from Yvor Winters. Yvor Winters once published a letter in *Hound and Horn* saying, "Mr. Bunting seems to offer me some kind of challenge. I will be happy to meet him at his own weapons—prose or verse; Marquess of Queensberry rules; my weight is 180." That's all I know about Basil Bunting. And I don't think he took up the challenge, either.

Interviewer: You said yesterday that to be a poet you had to sacrifice everything. Can you amplify on that, and tell why and how you first decided to make the sacrifice and be a poet?

Berryman: Well, being a poet is a funny kind of jazz. It doesn't get you anything. It doesn't get you any money, or not much, and it doesn't get you any prestige, or not much. It's just something you *do*.

Interviewer: Why?

Berryman: That's a tough question. I'll tell you a real answer. I'm taking your question seriously. This comes from Hamann, quoted by Kierkegaard. There are two voices, and the first voice says, "Write!" and the second voice says, "For whom?" I think that's marvelous; he doesn't question the imperative, you see that. And the first voice says, "For the dead whom thou didst love"; again the second voice doesn't question it; instead it says, "Will they read me?" And the first voice says, "Aye, for they return as posterity." Isn't that good?

Notes

1. "Apollo 8" was eventually collected in *Henry's Fate & Other Poems*, p. 36.

2. The first is from the poem "About Ben Adhem" by Leigh Hunt, and the second, from Sir Walter Scott's "Lay of the Last Minstrel, Canto VI."

3. No interesting project can be embarked on without fear. I shall be scared to death half the time.—Sir Francis Chichester in Sydney.

For my part I am always frightened, and very much so. I fear the future of all engagements.—Gordon in Khartoum

4. By coincidence, Williams's grandmother was named Emily Dickinson Wellcome, no relation to the poet.

Poetry Was Once Nonsense to Berryman

Anonymous / 1969

From *Minneapolis Tribune*, January 6, 1969, 22. Reprinted by permission.

[A brief personality piece published in recognition of Berryman's having been awarded the prestigious Bollingen Prize for *His Toy, His Dream, His Rest.*—Ed.]

At nineteen, poet John Berryman called poetry "the most ridiculous nonsense I ever heard." Now at fifty-four he has added the 1968 Bollingen Poetry Prize to his 1965 Pulitzer Prize and is clearly recognized as a leading American poet.

The University of Minnesota faculty member was named Sunday as a winner of the biennially awarded Bollingen Prize, given by Yale University and considered by many to be the top US award for poets.

Berryman shares the award with Karl Shapiro, a faculty member at the University of California at Davis. The two will divide the award's five-thousand-dollar prize.

The award was granted for Berryman's latest book, called *His Toy, His Dream, His Rest.* This is the second volume about a character named Henry, who also appears in an earlier book, *77 Dream Songs*, which won a Pulitzer Prize in 1965.

Berryman takes a relaxed view of his new honor. "I don't need the money, you know," he said, and noted that he had received other awards before.

He expects to write about Henry again, but his immediate plans are to continue teaching at the University while he writes a book about Heaven, tentatively titled *Scholars at the Orchid Pavilion.*

He also is working on translations of two Greek plays, though he concedes he is "essentially Greekless." He hopes to produce poetic versions of

Sophocles's *Oedipus, the King* and *Oedipus at Colonus,* in the indefinite future.

Berryman holds bachelor's degrees from Columbia University and Cambridge University in England. Until Columbia, he says, the only poetry he had seen was "the cheapest kind of romantic nonsense," but since then he has written constantly.

"I write when it occurs to me to write, and that is almost every day," he says. "I don't take vacations."

A member of the Minnesota faculty since 1954, Berryman this semester is teaching a course on Christian origins in the Humanities Department. "I don't get along with the English Department," he said.

"I don't read very much, though I try to read my friends, like Saul Bellow," Berryman said. Among modern poets he reads, Berryman listed Robert Lowell and Robert Fitzgerald. He also tries to read Chinese, Japanese, Portuguese, and other foreign poetry.

Berryman described himself as "fed up" with politics, and called the Vietnam war "the crummiest war ever."

Berryman has traveled the academic circuit extensively but says he expects to stay at the University of Minnesota, except for an occasional lecture trip or visiting professorship. He lives now at 33 Arthur Avenue SE. with his wife Kate, son Paul,[1] eleven, daughter Martha, six, and an overweight "useless" dog named Rufus, three.

He will give a reading of his works Wednesday at 2:15 p.m. in the main ballroom of the Coffman Student Union at the University.

Note

1. Certainly the anonymous author is mistaken, as Paul lived with his mother.

Conversation with Berryman

Richard Kostelanetz / 1969

Conducted March 1969. Originally published in the *Massachusetts Review* 11, no. 2
(Winter 1970): 340–47; revised version in *The New Poetries and Some Old* (Southern Illinois
University Press, 1991), 99–114. Reprinted by permission.

[Richard Kostalenetz's profile on Berryman was occasioned by Berryman's
receipt of the 1969 National Book Award for *His Toy, His Dream, His Rest.*
Two versions of this profile are extant: the first was published in the *Massachusetts Review* in late 1969; Kostelanetz then revised the interview for
publication in a 1991 collection of essays and other prose works. At Kosta-
lanetz's request, the latter version is reproduced below. Proceeding chrono-
logically, Kostelanetz and Berryman discuss his life and career, providing
Berryman an opportunity to reflect on his artistic development and his life
as scholar and poet.—Ed.]

*He [the poet] must be able to telescope image and symbol, if necessary, without
relying on the obvious connectives: to speak in a kind of psychic shorthand when
his protagonist is under great stress. He must be able to shift his rhythms rapidly,
the "tension." He works intuitively, and the final form of his poem must be imagi-
natively right.*
—Theodore Roethke, "Open Letter" (1950)

John Berryman greeted me at the door of his modest but comfortable, detached, three-story Minneapolis house, situated atop a steep (and, in snow,
treacherous) incline from Arthur Avenue. A few blocks away is the University of Minnesota where he is professor of humanities. It was lunchtime;
and in the course of taking my coat Berryman invited me to join him for
some Gluckenheimer, a blend mostly of bourbon, he said, and a raid of the
refrigerator. The occasion for my coming was his winning the National Book
Award for *His Toy, His Dream, His Rest* (1968), his second collection of the

Dream Songs he had been publishing over the past decade. Several other major honors had also recently come his way—a Bollingen Prize in poetry (shared with Karl Shapiro), five thousand dollars from the Academy of American Poets Fellowship, ten thousand dollars from the newly established National Endowment for the Arts, and the republication of his earlier works. For this year at least he stands at the top of his field.

We quickly settled down into two comfortable living room chairs, before a window looking out into a street that even at the end of March was filled with snow. Relaxing each other by swapping gossip about mutual friends, I won his confidence for intimate talk by bringing regards from a girlfriend of seventeen years before. I got the impression that though the poet was a local celebrity whose name and face regularly appeared in the city newspapers, his life in Minneapolis was isolated. The telephone rang only twice in my eight hours there, once with an apology for the wrong number, while those he identified as his "closest friends here" were busy cultural officials—the chairman of his department, the director of the Walker Art Center, and the Minneapolis mayor (who once taught political science at the university). "I have a dreadful tendency when drinking to make long-distance phone calls," he confessed at one point, "but I haven't made one in months." Berryman also admitted that he had not left his house in several days; and after describing all the socializing prior and posterior to his poetry readings around the country, he rationalized, "Doing that once a week doesn't leave you with much need for a social life." On the day we met he was particularly peeved by a slick magazine's long-distance telephone request for "What ought the first astronaut to say on the moon?" "I said, 'I'm working on my lecture,' and hung up. Isn't that incredible? It's beneath contempt."

Berryman is shorter than his pictures suggest—perhaps five feet, ten inches, slight of build, though rounded in the tummy; in demeanor, both dapper and dowdy. His hair is fleecy and light brown, more thinning than balding; and the color of his full, but neatly trimmed beard runs from reddish brown under his nose to gray on his cheeks. Dressed that day in a white, button-down shirt, open at the neck, gray slacks, and black slippers, he walked gingerly, with motions that might be graceful, were they not so halting. Continually recrossing his legs, he swings his loose foot back and forth in a steady rhythm. His blue eyes look at you through fairly thick eyeglasses, and in his long-fingered, pale, visibly shaking hand is either a cigarette, a pencil, or a glass. The furniture is nondescript American; and beside him in the living room were several piles of books which he is currently reading, an ash tray, a pack of Tareytons, some unanswered letters, and a couple vials of pills. Rufus, a black, chubby mongrel with a brown-splotched face, walked in and out. When I first arrived, Berryman was quite lucid, though rambling; but as the afternoon wore on and all the drink got to his tongue, his conversation became more erratic, his tone more oracular, his attitude more peremptory, and his diction more slurred. There was ample evidence of his reputation for causing, if not cultivating, tension in those around him.

I opened by asking to what extent Berryman the poet resembled "Henry," the character who dominates the Dream Songs. "Henry, eh? He is a very good friend of mine. I feel extremely sympathetic to him. He doesn't enjoy my advantages of supervision; he just has vision. He's also simple-minded. He thinks that if something happens to him, it's forever; but I know better." This extraordinary conception of an alter ego, different from himself and yet exposing the author's attitudes, came to Berryman in the middle fifties, after two years of experiment. As we spoke, Berryman claimed to have abandoned Henry, but on the table next to him was yet another Dream Song, scribbled in pencil and dedicated "To Bernard Bowron." He explained, "Well, mostly I'm through with Henry; but the minute I say that, pains course through me. I can't bear to be rid of that admirable outlet, that marvelous way of making your mind known to many other people."

It is an unlikely but perhaps significant fact that Berryman and Ralph Ellison, whose eminence as a novelist equals Berryman's as a poet, were both born in Oklahoma in 1914, two years after statehood, Ellison on March 1 in Oklahoma City and Berryman on October 25 in McAlester, 125 miles to the southwest. Berryman's natural father, John Allyn Smith, was a banker from Vermont, who claimed descent from Ethan Allen; his mother, born Martha Little, was a schoolteacher from the South. They met in a rooming house and married, their son suspects, "as the only two literate people in that part of the state. My mother had a good instinct for things. She read Steinbeck and Faulkner before anyone else, but Dad preferred magazines." The Smiths lived in Sasakwa at the time of the poet's birth (McAlester having the nearest large hospital); and the family later moved to Anadarko, also in Oklahoma. A second son was born in 1919.

In 1925, they went to Tampa, Florida. "As a boy I liked Florida very much. Tampa had a wonderful stamp dealer; and since my father made a lot of money in the real estate boom, I had a fantastic allowance each week—something like twenty-five dollars which I got on Thursday and spent on Friday." However, his father committed suicide the following year, and his mother subsequently married John Angus McAlpin Berryman, whose surname both sons took. This Berryman family moved to New York, where young John attended public school at South Kent. Graduating from prep school earlier than expected, he entered Columbia College in 1932. By this time he had departed from the Catholic Church, into which he was born; and today he has no doubts about his youthful waywardness. "I'm not sure that God exists, and I'm very hostile to the worship of the Virgin. In New York, half the time I vaguely feel Jewish."

His first year at Columbia was spent largely in student politics, as he lost an election for class vice-presidency, and in student sports, as he ran the quarter-mile and half-mile and joined the freshman wrestling team. "I wasn't good enough for any varsity sport," he mused. Instinctively attentive to good-looking women, accomplished as a social dancer, he had a busy social life, mostly with undergraduates from Smith alumna, then a university dean, who, standing apart from her husband, spoke warmly of dating Berryman some forty years before. As a sophomore, he switched undergraduate circles by joining the more literary crowd, contributing regularly to the *Columbia Review*. He also began to write a poem every day, even publishing a few of them in national magazines; and he wrote occasional book reviews for *The Nation*. His primary mentor at the time was Mark Van Doren, then professor of English at Columbia and now a co-dedicatee of Berryman's most recent book. "He lent me books, advised me on various things. I like his poetry, particularly his last book, which is his best; but there was no stylistic indebtedness—Yeats being my first and last major influence. If not for Van Doren, I must not have become a poet."

It was Van Doren who urged Berryman to apply for the coveted Kellett Fellowship to study in England, and the young man won it, entering Clare College, Cambridge the following fall. "I drew in my horns. I realized my stuff was no good." Instead, he concentrated on reading English literature, developing that fantastic literacy that impressed literate acquaintances a generation ago, and becoming the first American to win the Charles Oldham Shakespeare Scholarship (after four three-hour exams). Berryman also befriended Dylan Thomas, who had come to Cambridge to give a reading. "We drank as long as the pubs were open—no hard liquor then, just beer, for hard liquor came much later. Thomas was exactly one day older than me—October 24, 1914; and he used to make a lot of that, much to my annoyance. (In fact, however, Thomas, born on October 27, 1914, was two days younger than Berryman!) The young American abroad also took high tea with William Butler Yeats in 1936; and although not much more important was said, Berryman vividly remembers offering his master a cigarette, which

Yeats accepted, and then lighting it. Indeed, the incident is memorialized in number 215 of his Dream Songs.

Returning to America in 1938, he spent his first year at his mother's Manhattan apartment, "doing nothing but writing" and the next teaching at Wayne State University in Detroit. He also became in 1939, for one year, poetry editor of *The Nation*—a position that put him in correspondence, if not personal touch, with both established figures and aspiring poets of his generation, such as Delmore Schwartz, Randall Jarrell, and Karl Shapiro. "I always wanted to be much older than I was," Berryman reminisced between cigarette puffs, "and from an early age I took to advising my seniors." The composer Milton Babbitt remembers that in the forties, "John had the most magnificent capacity to improvise elegant and very literary speech," and Robert Lowell recently wrote, "As soon as he began to publish, one heard of his huge library . . . his endless ability to quote poetry, and his work on a conclusive text of *King Lear*." Unfit for the military, because of a mental breakdown several years before, he did not go to war.

In 1940, he was offered a teaching job at Harvard, partially thanks to Schwartz's recommendation; and three years later the poet-critic Richard P. Blackmur invited Berryman to Princeton to teach for two years in the Creative Arts Program. It was there that Berryman taught his best-known former students, all of them born around 1925—the poet-translator W. S. Merwin, the novelist Frederick Buechner, and the translator-classicist William Arrowsmith. Between 1945 and 1954, when he came to Minnesota, Berryman was an academic vagabond, winning several major fellowships, and taking short-term teaching appointments and lecture-tours around the country. To the novelist Edward Hoagland, who studied with Berryman at Harvard during the summer of 1954, "He taught by exemplitude. He talked mostly about books he had loved with a fervor that amounted to a kind of courage. He hated stupidity and was harsher to lazy students than any teacher I've ever known, but he was also affectionate toward promising writers." During this rather rootless period, he also published several important critical essays, drawn mostly from projected books that are still unfinished, and a few short stories, one of which, "The Imaginary Jew" (1945), has been frequently reprinted. In 1950 he published a commissioned biography of Stephen Crane, which belongs among the best literary monographs ever produced on these shores—lushly written, elaborately researched, continually perceptive.

Beside Berryman's living room chair was a spread-eagled copy of Baldassare Castiglione's sixteenth-century *Book of the Courtier*, which he planned to teach the following afternoon in his only course, a twice-a-week survey for seventy-five or so undergraduates on "The European Heritage." This semester was devoted to the Renaissance and Reformation. "If poets teach, they ought not to teach poetry. That's too much like the main thing, poetry and criticism; it can be comforting and yet cheapening. A writer never does the same thing twice, but a teacher is bound to his routine. He can't change courses every year—the physical labor would be too great." He paused to sip his drink. "Writing is not routine. Each fresh experience means the possibility of absolute failure. You take your chances. Every day I open my mail to see what they are saying about me; but poetry students, unlike the public audience, can't, or don't, get up and leave. It's better to teach the classics or the history of ideas."

Berryman's closest friends in life are and were the poets of his own generation, most of whom he has not seen too often. "In America, it is very difficult to keep in touch with your friends, because of geography; they are always elsewhere. In general, I like people, and poets, my own age better." Also some of them have died in the past few years—Theodore Roethke, Randall Jarrell, Richard P. Blackmur, and Delmore Schwartz (to whose "sacred memory" the last book is also dedicated); and remarks about each of them infiltrate both Berryman's poetry and conversation. (Indeed, at times in his poetry, the fortunes of these few people are rather pretentiously portrayed as a measure of the world's civility.)

"Delmore was extremely beautiful and miraculously brilliant, if not one of the best talkers I ever heard in my life; but he became too well-known too soon and came to count on fame. He began to plan his career, but a literary life is not to be planned that way." Though productive and successful as a young man, Schwartz in his later years became extremely erratic, if not psychotic; and Berryman painfully remembers bailing Schwartz, "acting like a maniac," out of a police station in Washington, DC. Earlier in the evening Schwartz had been trying to make long-distance calls on a telephone he had just pulled out of its socket.

"Roethke? A marvelous poet. We had a long session one time in Rome. He wanted me to read his recent poems, and I wanted him to read *Mistress Bradstreet*. However, he didn't work to keep his part of the bargain. He no more cared about my work than a hole in the head. Yes, Ted." Again a puff. "It was impossible not to like him, but difficult to make him a real friend, in both cases because he was so childish. He was interested in love and money; and if he found a combination of them in something else, he would have dedicated himself to it instead of poetry." Berryman first met Robert Lowell in 1944, under the aegis of Allen Tate, who a few years before had picked them both, as well as Jarrell and Schwartz, as the promising talents of the generation then under thirty; and Berryman proudly remembers proposing some persuasive changes for Lowell's most famous early poem, "The Quaker Graveyard at Nantucket" (1946).

From the beginning of his career, then, Berryman felt part of an insurgent poetic generation that knew each had professionally to help the others constantly, or they would *all* lose. "I still do," he added, though all four figures have very much succeeded as poets. "In the thirties, we hated the *New York Times Book Review*, and most of the existing magazines. All the places where one would have wanted to publish, like *The Dial* or *Symposium* or *Hound and Horn*, were interdicted, had died. There was a need for serious magazines, and most of the new journals, like *Partisan* and *Kenyon*, came into existence around 1935. Actually, you're setting your sights against the whole of American society, which is a dangerous business. Various diseases await you—women, homosexuality, silence." Was fear of risk among them, I suggested. "Yes, fear of risk. Some people hang onto their tiny reputation, sniping at everybody else; and you know where that takes you—straight to hell."

Inevitably, Berryman is haunted by the personal wreckage of this poetic generation—the high incidence of mental hospitalization, heavy drinking, broken marriages, and premature death; and after evading the equally inevitable question of why, he offered some explanations, both individual and social, none of them quite satisfactory to either him or me. "You asked why my generation seems so screwed up? But I really don't know why. They just seem to be very unhappy." His temper changed once he took another gulp: his voice grew louder.

"It seems they have every right to be disturbed. The current American society would drive anybody out of his skull, anyone who is at all responsive; it is almost unbearable. It doesn't treat poets very well; that's a difficulty. President Johnson invited me to the White House by ordinary mail, but the letter reached me in Ireland, a few weeks after the ceremony. From public officials we expect lies, and we get them in profusion. American society is running the most disgusting war in history in Vietnam, and it elects disgusting public officials like Nixon, who makes you want to vomit. Don't you agree? And it puts up [Hubert H.] Humphrey, who is barely more respectable. I wanted to see [Eugene] McCarthy and [Nelson] Rockefeller; and though a lifelong Democrat, I probably would have voted for Rockefeller." His voice became even louder and more raucous. "The protests are going to get worse and worse and worse and worse for years. Perhaps Sylvia Plath did the necessary thing by putting her head into the oven, not having to live with those lies."

Halfway through the afternoon, Berryman's daughter, six-year-old Martha (called "Twissy-Pitts," among other nicknames), let herself in the door (a son Paul by a second marriage lives with his mother in Westchester); and a short while later, Kate Berryman entered with school books under her arm. A tall, thirtyish, attractive brunette, with short curly hair, she had just returned from classes in elementary education; and not only does her constant sober cheerfulness contrast with her husband's decidedly volatile temperament, but her presence seemed, perhaps unintentionally, to dampen her husband's speech and activities.

II.

You liked him to live in another city.
—Robert Lowell, in a memorial memoir (1972)

Berryman's earliest poetry, that written back in the 1930s, came largely out of Yeats's influence, perhaps with a bit of Auden added—short, lyrical, rather formal, rhythmically intricate, and stylistically derivative. "A Point of Age," written in 1940, opens with this stanza: [Reproduces the first four lines of "A Point of Age"; see *Collected Poems 1937–1971*, p. 7] Some twenty early poems were collected in Berryman's section of *Five Young American Poets*, which New Directions published in 1940 (the other poets in debut included Randall Jarrell); and more short pieces went into *Poems* that was issued in 1942 by the same firm. Scarcely anyone outside of previous friends took notice of either book. Of his poetic aspirations during the middle forties, Berryman wrote in retrospect, "I wanted something that would be both very neat, contained, and at the same time thoroughly mysterious." His next collection, *The Dispossessed* (1948), attracted slightly more attention; but not until the fifties did Berryman's work begin to infiltrate the established anthologies. Obstacles arose when he tried to publish as a single book his poems of fifty-seven eight-line stanzas, *Homage to Mistress Bradstreet* that had originally appeared in *Partisan Review* in 1953. The publisher to whom he was contracted dallied so long that Berryman took the manuscript to Farrar, Straus and Cudahy, as it was then known, where a Columbia College friend, Robert Giroux, had just become an editor; and the book appeared in 1956, with illustrations by Ben Shahn, who was then less prominent than he is now. The years between 1953 and 1956 Berryman now regards as the low point of his life—the prolonged breakup of his first marriage, the premature death of his friend Dylan Thomas, the lack of permanent jobs; but Harvard and Iowa rescued him with short-term appointments, and then Minnesota offered his first permanent position.

The poet divides his total work into four distinct parts: (1) short poems, "to which I don't pay very much attention, though some are very good"; (2) *Berryman's Sonnets* (1967), which were largely written during and about an affair with an unnamed married lady in the late forties, but not published until recently; (3) *Homage to Mistress Bradstreet*, in which, as he puts it, "The 'I' of the twentieth-century poet modulates into her voice"; and (4) Dream Songs, which, though currently collected into two volumes, are formally divided into seven separate but untitled "books," each introduced by a Roman numeral. "All the way through my work is a tendency to regard the individual soul under stress," he explained. "The soul is not oneself, but the personal 'I,' me with a social security number and a bank account, never gets into the poems; they are all about a third person. I'm a follower of Pascal in the sense that I don't know what the issue is, or how it is to be resolved— the issue of our common human life, yours, mine, your lady's, everybody's; but I do think that one way in which we can approach it, by the means of art, coming out of Homer and Virgil and down through Yeats and Eliot, is by investigating the individual human soul, or human mind, whichever you prefer—I couldn't care less. I have tried, therefore, to study two souls in my long poems.

"The point of the Bradstreet poem," he continued, in his most sustained exposition of the afternoon, "was to take a woman unbelievably conventional and give her every possible trial and possibility of error and so on, and wind her up in a crazy love affair, and then get her out of it—better, get her out of it in ways that will allow her forgetting of it after a long period of time. The affair in the whole middle part of the poem is not historical but purely imaginary. The title is a pun—homage to *Mistress* Bradstreet, namely the poet's mistress in the twentieth century; he works from himself into her through the two of them, back into her, out of her, to the end of the poem, which ends in the twentieth century." Berryman took a hefty gulp from his glass.

"The point in Henry was to investigate a man with many opportunities, far more than those allowed to the lover in the Bradstreet poems—many chances to observe and to see what people of various nations are like, and what they do and are, and so on. Now Henry is a man with God knows, many faults, but among them is not self-understanding. He believes in his enterprise. He is suffering and suffering heavily and has to. This can't be helped. And he has a friend, Mr. Bones, but the friend is some friend. He's like Job's Comforter. Remember the three people in the poem of Job who pretend to be his friends. They sit down and lament with him, and give him the traditional Jewish jazz—namely, you suffer, therefore you are guilty. You remember that. Well, Henry's friend sits down and gives him the same business.

"I could have studied other things, for example, adultery, which is a big problem in the United States—people always sleeping with other people's wives. We don't use the word 'adultery' very much, but occasionally it even appears in the papers. It's not in *The Dream Songs*, and I don't know exactly why. The whole *Sonnets* sequence is about adultery, so I felt relieved of the problem, or that it wasn't my problem anymore. Let somebody else handle it from a new point of view. Also Henry is so troubled and bothered by his many problems that he never actually comes up with solutions, and from that point of view the poem is a failure. Another problem is limitations in the narrator. I couldn't let him use fancy language. That was out. It didn't go with the blackface business. The diction is very limited. He doesn't have the language to discuss, for example, Heisenberg's theory of indeterminacy, or scholarly questions, or modern painting."

Though common themes and concerns run through Berryman's poetry, the Dream Songs represent a distinct break from the earlier work, almost as if the preciously literary poet suffered rebirth as a sotted sensibility, speaking in a radically different style whose abrupt shifts in both cadence and syntax suggest as well as reflect incoherent drunkenness; for Berryman's forms are now looser, the diction less formal, the general impression sloppier, the frame of reference more contemporary, and, most important, the poetic voice instantly recognizable as his: [Recites lines 7–8 of "Dream Song 18: A Strut for Roethke"; see *The Dream Songs*, p. 20]

"After having done one thing," he explained, "you want to do something as different as possible. I wanted a completely modern poem, *Bradstreet* having been an essentially seventeenth-century poem with twentieth-century interpolations. I think my later work less stupid than my earlier work." In reviewing the second volume of Dream Songs, the critic Jascha Kessler was awed by Berryman's "increasing ability to project a writing voice as well as a voice speaking at many levels of both volume and diction, ranging from a kind of Gullah shorthand through breezy locker-room jocularity to meditative song, elegiac laments, and vision, sometimes running that entire diapason within the eighteen lines of one poem." A paradox peculiar to Berryman's own development is that as his speech became less elegant, less literary, and less coherent, his poetry became better, almost as if alcohol replaced literature as a primary oil of his poetic inspiration.

"I try to be coherent when I talk to another person, but one is sometimes incoherent regarding the sounds pushed at him by the progenitor. I feel further that we need a poetry that gives up everything—all kinds of traditional forms—and yet remains rich." He paused to draw from his cigarette. "What is wrong with poetry now is that poets won't take on observation, dealing with what is sent to individuals from the universe. It would seem to be that the job of the poet, if I may speak of such a ridiculous thing, is to handle the signs, to field them as in baseball." Why then, I asked, was he currently writing, as he put it, "a poem about heaven laid in ancient China?" ["Scholars at the Orchid Pavilion"] "Why not?"

The Dream Songs are not as difficult as they might seem at first; for once the reader accepts their logic as closer to the waywardness of dreams and of inebriated stupor than to discursive prose—in Robert Lowell's phrase, "not real dreams but a walking hallucination"—the relation among the parts often becomes more credible, if not coherent. "Both the writer and the reader of long poems need gall, the outrageous, the intolerable," he declared upon receiving the National Book Award, "and they need it again and again. The prospect of ignominious failure must haunt them continually." The central figure, Henry, who speaks, in Jonathan Cott's phrase, in "the singing brawl of a declamatory sot," concerns himself with a multitude of matters; and in the entire work, now stretched to 385 published songs (which their author regards *not* as individual poems but as parts of a whole), is a cumulative impact. Berryman has declared that the first collection of these songs "concerns the turbulence of the modern world, and memory, and wants," but to Cott the theme of the entire work is "nothing less than the decline and fall of the contemporary West."

Though quite unlike anything else in poetry, the Dream Songs nonetheless reveal Berryman's continuing debt to the modern masters. "From Pound," judges Lowell, "he learned the all-inclusive style, the high spirits, the flitting from subject to subject, irreverence and humor. I feel the presence of Stevens, in sonorous, suggestive, nuance-like, often not quite clear lines; in cloudy anecdote about fanciful figures, such as Quo, or in the sections on Clitus and Alexander the Great . . . The resemblance to Cummings is in the human, verbal contortion, the pathos. There is also Joyce." Those critics who write regularly on poetry have by and large preferred this later work to the earlier Berryman; but perhaps because the Dream Songs are so idiosyncratic, representing a style valid and relevant only to their author, their visible impact on contemporary poetry has so far been negligible.

Kate Berryman invited me to stay for dinner, which she made from a Chinese recipe; and at first the poet paid more attention to a beautiful, but politely unresponsive, young woman who had come to join us. Over a dessert of cheesecake he chanted a Bessie Smith blues, authentically reproducing the original subtle rhythms and intonations, and then brilliantly declaimed selected passages from his favorite younger poets—James Wright, W. D. Snodgrass, Adrienne Rich—as well as from his own Dream Songs, including the great one, number 18, subtitled "A Strut for Roethke."

Indicatively, though he speaks of abandoning traditional forms, he prefers the more conservative fortyish poets to the radicals, and confesses to not reading/knowing/appreciating any American poets under the age of thirty-five. "I don't keep up with contemporary writing, except my friends. I don't read much. I sit and think. Reading is for young people." After getting up from the dinner table, he settled down with another glass of Gluckenheimer with water, which he consumed quickly. "It's rather useful for poets, relaxing after their labors." Why about psychotropic drugs? "Know nothing about them." Kate chimed, "I don't know anyone who uses alcohol to such good advantage as you do, John." He smiled, evidently proud of his wife, and extended his glass, "Make me another drink." [Reproduces lines 1–2, 6 of "Dream Song 75"; see *The Dream Songs*, p. 82]

P.S. (1990) A year later he joined Alcoholics Anonymous; three years later he jumped off a Minneapolis bridge to his death.

As I reread this portrait two decades later, I realize how deeply Berryman came to represent in my own mind the kind of poet/person I didn't want to be.

Note

1. Bernard R. Bowron Jr., scholar and author of *Henry B. Fuller of Chicago: The Ordeal of a Genteel Realist in Ungenteel America* (Westport, Conn.: Greenwood Press, 1974).

People Individuals with Values: Poet John B. Talks about Life, War, Death

Pat Murphy / 1969

From *Lansing State Journal*, May 11, 1969, E-9

[From John Haffenden's biography, *The Life of John Berryman*: "As more and more newspapers and journals urged him for interviews during his reading visits, he took readily to the vulgar role of pundit, passing opinions not only about artistic values but also, as to Pat Murphy of the *Lansing State Journal*, about public issues like the Vietnam War" (Haffenden 1982, 354–55).—Ed.]

In a world calloused to human misery and indifferent to personal sorrow, the poet's role is to remain sensitive to human needs and to champion individual value.

This seems to be the way John Berryman—the Pulitzer Prize–winning poet who appeared recently at Michigan State University—viewed the function of poets in a mechanized world.

Berryman didn't directly outline his philosophy, but alluded to it and implied its concepts during a two-part interview before his appearance at MSU.

At that appearance, an overflow crowd of about 350 jammed the Kellogg auditorium for a reading of *77 Dream Songs* and other poems. *77 Dream Songs* won Berryman the Pulitzer in 1965.

In the "make-a-dollar" world, poets see people as individuals with hopes, fears and personal values.

It is this concern for the individual—and the ability to perceive and relate beauty—that separates the poet from the plumber, journalist, or policeman.

Humanities Prof

Berryman is a humanities professor at the University of Minnesota, a post that keeps him in contact with students both as a teacher and as a personal counselor.

"They come to me with their problems," Berryman said.

"After they've been failed by their parents, priests, and psychologists, they turn to me."

To illustrate, the Oklahoma-born poet cited a young man who wanted to be a policeman despite the objections of his family, his fiancée, and friends.

"He wanted reassurance," Berryman summarized, "reassurance that he wouldn't be wasting his life. So I advised him to try that profession."

"I have a great respect for policeman; they have a difficult job in a difficult period."

War Concern

"The most common concern among students and young people is the Vietnam War," Berryman said. "Many students come to me before running to Canada to avoid the draft."

The basic problem plaguing students, according to Berryman, is the same one that bothers people generally—the dehumanization of society.

Within this context, the Vietnam War is "totally wrong" because it dehumanizes civilians and the military alike, Berryman believes.

"In this war, it's Americans killing Asians," he emphasized. "We should have no part of it."

However, Berryman was also critical of North Vietnam for apparently not offering the United States an honorable way out—via a negotiated peace.

He also realized the problems stemming from commitments to allies and political face-saving.

"It's a difficult problem," he said. "I'm glad I don't have to make the decision as to how to get the United States out."

The first part of the interview was conducted in Berryman's room at the Kellogg Center. The second part was held in a local bar.

There, sipping a bourbon with water, Berryman discussed what he termed society's preoccupation with sex.

Sex Preoccupation

Berryman's approach parallels that of D. H. Lawrence—both see sex as a response to industrialism.

Berryman refrains from terms like "sin" but looks at sex as a human response.

"If I wasn't certain of society's preoccupation with sex before," Berryman said, "the last two books I've read confirm that suspicion."

He listed two best-sellers that deal with adultery and related sexual activity.

A Memoir and an Interview

William Heyen / 1970

Interview conducted October 7, 1970. Published in *Ohio Review* 15, no. 2 (Winter 1974): 46–65. Reprinted by permission.

[In his lengthy memoir that introduces the interview, William Heyen provides the reader with ample historical and emotional context for a televised interview with Berryman for local television, a harrowing tale of drunkenness, confused schedules, missed flights, embarrassments, disappearances, and infidelity, a painfully evocative portrait of a man suffering greatly from the advanced stages of alcoholism.—Ed.]

In 1964 I was teaching at SUNY College at Cortland. One of my colleagues was Jerome Mazzaro. One day Jerry came back from somewhere with a copy of *77 Dream Songs*, which had just appeared. I remember thinking the dust jacket very striking. I borrowed the book and read it, or tried to. It was difficult going. I hadn't read Berryman before this, but soon looked up *Homage to Mistress Bradstreet*, which I studied. Now that, I felt until a couple of years ago, was a language to envy.

It was about this time that Jerry and I drove to Syracuse University to hear a reading by W. D. Snodgrass, who began by reciting several of the *77 Dream Songs* of the man who had been his teacher. Snodgrass's high-pitched voice carried Berryman's voices through their levels of irony and pain and humor perfectly. From that time on, although I never felt able to write anything on Berryman (except for a brief review for *Southern Review* of *Berryman's Sonnets* when it appeared in 1967), few days went by when I did not read at least a little while from one of his books. I became convinced that he was one of the great ones that he was so determined to be.

Against my real will and better judgment, I became director of the Writers Forum at SUNY College at Brockport in 1970. My first thought was to write to John Berryman. I was to take over the Forum beginning that

September, but I wrote Berryman in late April or early May. I don't have my letter, or subsequent ones, but I have his. The first note from him is postmarked May 9, 1970: "Dear Mr. Heyen" it goes, "How do you get to Brockport, from Kennedy airport? I travel a good deal but hate it. Could somebody pick me up? The first Wednesday in November would be best for me." I must have written back, and very happily, simply to tell him either to fly into Buffalo, just an hour's drove away, or into Rochester, just twenty minutes away, where I could pick him up. Kennedy is a seven-hour drive from Brockport. His next note is dated June 6: "I've been in hospital five weeks & I'm afraid my doctors have forbidden anything until next Spring. Perhaps we can arrange something later." I'm not sure whether or not I answered right away. I know that his next note came as a surprise. No doubt, he'd forgotten he'd just written me. This note is dated June 18, 1970: "I'm just home after a long spell in hospital & my doctors advise against any more trips this year. Could your attractive invitation be extended to some time next Spring?" That was fine with me, certainly. I must have written him back to tell him I would hold onto the one thousand dollars of our budget that I'd offered him until he could appear for a spring reading and television interview.

A surprise note dated August 19, 1970 arrived: "I'll be at Loyola College in Montreal from mid-Sept. to mid-Dec, more convenient to you than here. If you want to propose a date or dates, do. Peter Stitt wd. be fine for the interview." I'd thought of flying Peter Stitt in from Vermont for the interview—I felt it best, when possible, to ask one of the poet's friends to co-interview: Allen DeLoach helped me interview Allen Ginsberg, and Jerry Mazzaro helped make James Wright comfortable—but Stitt's visit didn't work out. In any case, I wrote back to Berryman and proposed some dates. His next note makes it clear that he still expected to be in residence at Loyola in the fall: "Oct 7th sounds all right, if Loyola schedules me Mon-Tues as I suggested—but this is tentative: you haven't stated a fee yet ever, have you? My soc. sec. no. is [number], and I'll look out a photograph." His next note is from September 7, 1970: "I'm on Mohawk flight #196 arriving (fr. Buffalo) at Rochester 5:52 p.m. Wed. Oct 8th. That gives time for dinner—anyway, can't anyone who wants to meet me do so at a party somewhere (or just at a coffee shop or bar) after the reading?"

The problem here was that Wednesday was October 7, not 8. I wasn't sure what day he was arriving, and needed to know for television studio and room, program, and dinner arrangements. I wrote him. No answer. I had to call, and dreaded it. I hated the phone, and I hated to bother him. My memory blurs. I had to talk to him two or three times. It was incredible and baffling, but one of our conversations ended when he hung up immediately after saying he would fly into Kennedy. Another one left me with the feeling that he'd be flying to Pittsburgh (perhaps mistaking our Forum for the International Poetry Forum). But I never ascribed any of these confusions to his drinking. I felt that a man as brilliant and sensitive as Berryman ought to be distracted. I felt sure that if I had not been so awed and flustered and embarrassed on the phone, I could have made things clear.

Somehow things became settled. October 7 it would be. Worrying about JB's visit, I hadn't slept well in weeks. I was particularly worried about the television tape, and hoped he would be easy to interview. The morning arrived. Around noon, my wife got a call from Berryman from the Minneapolis airport. I got back from school and he called again. He was drunk, and had missed his plane, and would try to charter one, etc., etc. I said that if he could get to Brockport, even too late for the reading, we could schedule him for the next day. He was relieved. He said fine, because he hated to miss an engagement, and he'd see what he could do. We talked on the phone three or four times. Then he didn't call. At eight in the evening, still hoping that he would descend on us like a miracle, I drove over to the college and announced to a couple of hundred people that the poet had not arrived. I invited lots of friends over to my house for drinks and consolation. We sat around. Some of us played poker. Our hopes were dwindling when JB called to say he was in Buffalo. I was elated and told him to sit tight, that Jerry Mazzaro would be there to pick him up within a half hour. I called Jerry, who was standing by at his house in Buffalo. I began drinking in earnest and losing at poker and didn't care. All of us waiting for the man. At about the time I hoped Jerry would be pulling into my driveway, a call came through from Berryman from the airport. He'd seen Mazzaro, but Mazzaro, it seems, had left him! I told him to sit tight, that Jerry must only have gone to the bathroom. I was afraid Berryman and Mazzaro had had an argument. Somehow, I began winning at poker. At one in the morning I heard a crash outside. Jerry had hit a boulder that edges my driveway. Yes, I saw a silhouette on the other side of the front seat. Berryman had made it to Brockport.

The two days of his visit remain central to my life in ways I can only hope to suggest. It was not just that Berryman's visit, at mid-week, had all the qualities of the proverbial lost weekend. This had something to do, once and for all for me, with the reality of poetry in this life. This had something to do with Berryman's presence as a presence committed to the life of poetry. I kept feeling that Berryman was spending for vast returns, was driving himself toward the next poem in a necessary frenzy, and that he had been born to do this. He was always noting lines, sounding out lines, pulling one of his new short poems from one of his pockets. His moods were mercurial, and he always wrenched me with him. Lawrence Lieberman has described Berryman's voice as a "superarticulate mental wail." He was brilliant, dazzling, this man who had met Yeats and had written *Homage*, the *Sonnets*, and *The Dream Songs*. I still feel that he was the only genius I've ever met. (In the Emersonian sense, Genius as opposed to Talent, inspired form as opposed to the somewhat pedestrian ability to make meters and rhymes.) It is my feeling that he came to this Genius at the end of his life in *Love & Fame* (1970) and *Delusions, Etc.* (1972), that we will find this out, and that this will take a long time.

In his essay on Whitman, Randall Jarrell quotes some lines and says that either someone with a tin ear and no art at all wrote those lines, or someone with an incredibly sensitive ear. We know the truth by now. In the same way, I feel that those poems of *Love & Fame* and *Delusions, Etc.*, received with general suspicion and dislike, need us to catch up to them. Their sounds are odd. We will have to tune up to them, and it will take some doing. As Berryman wrote of Stephen Crane's poems, "They are not like literary compositions. They are like things just seen and said, *said for use.*" Those late Berryman poems are deceptively excellent. He was making a violent break, and wanted to trust himself (that constant protesting "Isn't that good?" "Isn't that good?"), but was at the same time caught up in a horror of suspicion that his alcoholism had already destroyed his ability to function without delusion. He was shedding the self in these poems, dealing directly with his life in order to get away from it. He wanted to be of use. And he began to find God, even in "a motor hotel in Wallace Stevens' town," as he said in "The Facts & Issues."

We were up all the night that Berryman arrived in Brockport. We made the television tape the next morning, had lunch at the college and dinner at my house that day, and Berryman read that evening. We were up all night long again and he left by plane that morning. As his plane took off, I cried. Exhaustion and relief. I'd never been through anything like that before. I know that I felt, after he left Brockport, that he would not live for long, and I began to write out some impressions and memories of his visit. I felt a sense of history in his presence. Some of these notes are now embarrassing or naive or otherwise silly. For better or worse, here is what I wrote:

> He said at dinner that when he left a town everyone went to sleep and he checked into a hospital. We laughed. How long could he last? For two days, 48 sleepless

hours, I wondered about his heart, miraculous machine: kept him going through fifty-six years, his chain-smoking, alcoholism, insomnia, rages and crying jags and a memory that would not let the dead die. His heart. Hard as a fist. Himself seeming to be all bone. What it must be like to live inside his head. Dream as the panorama of the whole mental life: in one of his four or five calls from the Minneapolis and Buffalo airports on Wed. as he was missing his reading here he spoke of the latest dream: a snake curled in a gold box that was half of his mother-in-law's French door. "What do you think it means," he asked me. I said, could you get to Syracuse? Sunday morning: his wife just called saying she does not know where he is, she is trying to retrace his steps. I told her I put him on a plane Friday morning at 9:00 to New York where he was going to meet Robert Giroux and have lunch, and spend the afternoon with friends, and fly back to Minneapolis at night, because he could not miss a talk he had to give in St. Paul on Saturday morning. Kate said she would call again. She said he did call her Friday night but she did not know where he was calling from. My wife just emptied out one of his ashtrays of Herbert Tareyton butts. His lips would snap the cigarette with each drag, forced, hurried, driven. He left one of his shirts here with, like his others, cigarette burns and holes along its left side. Too absent-minded now to drive he said, and too absorbed ever to use an ashtray. Sugar that my daughter spilled and his ashes now to vacuum from our shag rugs. All of this, the sleeplessness, an effort to murder time. His marriage is what he had to have it, a storm, he said. He kept telling me that he had one very fine piece of advice for me: to focus on my wife, write about her, but to see her from someone else's perspective, his, perhaps. This was the key. Wms. must have been much the same in both ways: incredible physical stamina and need to talk and write, living the 24 hr. day; to focus on his wife through 3 novels and many poems culminating in "Of Asphodel." I wanted, Friday morning to send him to Minneapolis and not New York: he replied: "No. I will negotiate from a position of strength, not weakness." The last time he had called her (5 in the morning) her line was busy. He believed she had taken it off the hook. He screamed, even to himself when I left him alone in the living room for a minute: "She'll get out of the house. Out. I will not live with her." "She hates me." "She cannot bear my fame." "She is waiting for me to die." He kept telling me he could not convince her that he loved her. He arrived, finally, from Buffalo with Jerry Mazzaro, at midnight on Wednesday. Fifteen or 20 of us at my house. He took over. Wanted, at first, only to talk to my wife and Sis Rock. Shut the rest of us out. I played cards with Bill Rock, Ned Grade, Allen DeLoach, Mirko. Won $125. Kept going into the living room to talk to him. He did not see the rest of us. Did not look like the pictures on *His Toy, His Dream, His Rest*. Beard trimmed, hair not as wild, or high. Glasses on. More professorial, academic. Charming, disputatious, dominating, brilliant. What it must be like to live in his head, to walk drunk into a living room filled with strangers halfway across the country, and to talk. Magnificent conceit. We were awed. "I won that round" after destroying someone trying to be friendly. He had a bad foot, pinched or displaced nerve. Went shoeless. Raged as we were going down steps into the television studio, saying he had not contracted to go up and down steps. Disdained a hand or shoulder to lean on. . . . He disliked Jerry though Jerry tried to be kind, flattered him, showing him his rare *The Dispossessed* bought with money from a poetry prize which Jerry spent on those books important to him. Shrug. He liked me, did not even hear me when I said I would have knocked his block off had he insulted and attacked me the way he did a student at the Thursday night party. Said the student had condescended to him. Egads. Sunday morning: I just called Mrs. Berryman to find out whether she has found him yet. She said he was in Minneapolis all the time. I was stupid enough to say I was glad things were all right. She said, well, things weren't all right: he had to go to the hospital again. But, at least, he was safe. There were people talking in the background, friends, no doubt, who got hold of him and checked him in. In my easy chair Friday morning, stretched out straight, he seemed unreal, his clothes much too big for him, or so it seemed, as though there were nothing under his clothes. And when before the reading he came out of the bathroom shirtless, all bone, I thought of Ezra Pound as I'd seen him in photos. He was cute. The last thing my wife said to him at the airport was: Mr. Berryman, your pants are open. And he laughed and zipped his fly. He cried twice: early Thursday morning, over Dylan Thomas; Thursday afternoon over R. P. Blackmur and Auschwitz & Belsen & Dachau. The reading Thursday night: incredible, powerful, he said later he hadn't done so well in a long time, that he had people in the audience he liked and wanted to read to. He went on past where he usually quits, he said. The six Dream Songs he read knocked me over. He's better than Thomas. Imagine, to have written *The Dream Songs*, and *Homage*. He asked me, Wed. night-Thurs. morning, where I lived. I said do you mean here, in my house, or spiritually. Yes, he nodded. I said someday I hope to write a poem as fine as *Homage*. He said: "I want you to." I said that stanza beginning "It is Spring's New England . . ." choked me up. He said it was the best in the poem. Yes. He was "hot as a pistol" these days, writing like hell. Explained the Dickinson origin of his new style, the unrhymed quatrains he's been writing w. a short 4th line. I realize as I write this he is in the hospital, probably in a dead sleep. What it must be like to live in his head. He stuck the $1000 check in his jacket pocket without opening the envelope. Dream Song 282 was his current favorite. He said God must have spoken to him when he wrote that one. Yes. He liked Dickey. Jerry told him, on their drive from Buffalo, that Dickey didn't know what to do with detail. He disliked Jerry. Told me on the phone, when he'd wandered away from Jerry, that he couldn't imagine Mazzaro wd. write another book on Lowell. His love-hate for Lowell always apparent. Screwed up all my plans for the tape. I threw away my notes as soon as we started or, rather, didn't get to use them. Read, to begin, "The Song of the Tortured Girl." Best single reading of any poem I've ever heard. Impossible to interview. Sometimes 15 second pauses and then continuing, interrupting our next question; once saying we'd have to ask him a question. His obliviousness: to cigarette ashes; to being in one back-straight position at the party for 6 hrs; to traffic as we crossed streets; to anything but poems. When he 1st got here he gripped my hand long & hard. The "strain" and "torsion" in his work is the man. We did get him to eat: a cup of chicken soup Wed. night; a ham & cheese sandwich Th. noon; a decent dinner Thurs. night. Constant bourbon, water, no ice. "Mr. Heyen, I'm an alcoholic. I'd like another drink." I'd say sure. Betrayer, I suppose. He wrote my wife a poem out, which we'll frame: "After you went to bed, / Your tall sweet husband and I talked all night, / until there was no more to be said." Jerry went to bed in Kristen's room around 6 Thurs. morning. J. B. gripped my wrist hard, told me what I had to do to join the great ones: focus on my wife, write sonnets, suffer. Told me I was a late starter. Said he read my book and didn't like it. I don't think he read it—he talked as though he'd read something by a beat. We talked in the car as I tried to drop him off at the motel, about Wilbur. Wilbur said one of his new poems was "low voltage." He respected Wilbur. "No one" had done the perfect the way Wilbur had. "Walking to Sleep" a very great poem, he said. I asked him how Henry was: O.K.—hard to leave him behind. . . . When he sat down he did not want to move. He wanted to talk and drink. He was content talking for hours. His rage at the television taping was not that he was to be interviewed, but that they didn't start quickly enough for him and that he would be cued, told when to begin. This he couldn't bear, but once we did begin he would have been content to sit and talk and say poems for ten hours. This is no exaggeration. Swore on the phone to kiss my wife's left ear when he saw her, and he hadn't done this, he said, since 1940. It was too powerful. Angry at his own body— the brilliant mind having to be borne by the dying animal, the clumsy partner. Now, I'm a famous man, was his usual preface to a story. Now it is three days after he left and I can't get over him. Told me he had been unfaithful only once in his nine years of marriage, but that Kate didn't trust him, hated him, envied him, wanted him dead. In the same breath admitted he was a masochist, and smiled. Tortured himself into poems. Had to stay hot as a pistol. "I haven't finished my coffee. Sit down." Late to everything but lucky to get anywhere. And a little child shall lead them as Kristen led him to dinner. Mr. Berryman talks silly, she said. He has a daughter my son's age. Billy was very quiet. . . . When he broke into an imitation of Maurice Chevalier, Kristen said: "Mr. Berryman, are you talking or singing?" Han remembers that he cried a third time: Wed. night when he called up an Yvonne, read his new poem to her, and, apparently, she didn't like it. About 6:30 Thurs. morning I drove him to the motel, had to come back for his suitcase, drove him there again, drove him back to my house again when he found there was no phone in his room. He told the woman: "Know that your accommodations are totally unsatisfactory." She winked at me as we left. / Two weeks later I travel to Rochester to hear John Logan read: before dinner, over drinks, Anthony Hecht says that he heard a great Berryman story from Bill Merwin: it seems that a couple of weeks before, Berryman was at the Minneapolis airport and couldn't remember whether he was supposed to go to Pittsburgh or Buffalo and. . . . Nov. 5: I travel to Buffalo to hear Robert Bly read. Later, at a party, Allen DeLoach says that Merwin and someone else *were* waiting in Pittsburgh for Berryman. A postcard arrives from Berryman in the hospital: he seems happy, has written 12 or 15 poems, promises to send *Love and Fame* when copies are available, remembers Patti Hancock "beautiful and serene," sends us all his love. I have written all this out of love.

I kept in loose touch with him after his visit, but never saw him again, except on the television tape we made. I sent him books and programs of his reading to sign. I have a letter from August 21, 1971, that ends: "I hope you both, & the kids, are flourishing. I am." And there's a postscript: "Reading in Rotterdam *1st* wk. in June, back for new baby due *2nd* wk. June. So it goes." I thought he was healthy and happy again and I was glad.

By September of 1971 I was walking the streets and woodpaths of a suburb of Hanover, Germany, where I'd gone for a year as a Fulbright lecturer. I was with my family, but I felt lost, gloomy. A whole year stretched darkly in front of me. I wrote to JB and asked him to write out a poem. A card arrived dated October 16, 1971: "You think *you-all* are lonely. Listen to this poor guy I invented in Wisconsin & NYC & back here last Dec." He wrote out "Old Man Goes South Again Alone" which would appear posthumously in *Delusions, Etc.* (1972). Even though he is heading for the beaches of exotic Trinidad, the old man of the poem is sad "without the one // I would bring with me. . . ." Berryman knew that his own solitary trips tore him apart. He was telling me that I had enough not to be lonely. The *you-all* was emphatic. It was the same message he'd given me that night when he told me to focus on Han, study her, write about her, lose myself in her—love was the only way out of the lonely reaches of the ego.

The high ones die. He chose the frozen Mississippi. I received this telegram from Al Poulin Jr. Han and I knew what it meant. I walked for miles through the woods that day, trying to will him back to life, playing mental tricks, trying to wake up earlier in the day than the telegram had arrived, often fighting back tears and losing, trying to believe his death. Over the next days, clippings came from friends.

This death struck/strikes us hard. We are still hurt. We cannot *understand* why he died. His suicide has deepened every question I have asked myself about poetry. W. D. Snodgrass once said to me that he would rather be happy than write great poems. I suspect that Berryman would not have said this, that he felt, although in the Brockport interview he denies this, that intense suffering led to the greatest poetry, and, certainly, he wanted nothing less than to write masterpieces. His horrible admission in the *Paris Review* interview that perhaps he needed something like cancer to get on with his writing, confirms this. "I hope to be nearly crucified," he says. I say *No* to this. *No*.

And now we have *Recovery* (1973), a powerful reading experience, certainly, for those who knew him. It lays bare the terrible dimensions of the battle Berryman fought against the forces that finally killed him. That he could not, or *would not* (I have to say this: if it is a delusion, it is a necessary one) cure himself and finish the book—this says something chilling about the death of art, and about where several other poets a decade younger than Berryman was when he died are now headed. Berryman's suicide, for me, has cast a pall over much of his work, the darkest and most painful of it. It may be true, as Lionel Trilling said of Robert Frost, that it takes a poet who terrifies us to satisfy us. But, I would think, there exists a line between truth-telling and morbidity. For Roethke, finally, the dead seemed to help.

I have come to feel that as magnificent as *The Dream Songs* is, it is a great death-flower, held in full bloom by Berryman's elegiac genius. I read the songs saying to myself, "Yes, yes, but poetry does not have to be what this is. It can be, but it does not have to be." I turn for comfort to Stevens and Wilbur: Stevens, who wrote at the end of his life about the "planet's encouragement," and Wilbur, to whom Sylvia Plath's "brilliant negative" is, finally, "unjust." I have come to feel that I have to find my own life in Stevens and Wilbur. There are lives of obsession and frenzy, and there are lives of gentleness and grace and control. And it may be that our lives are can sometimes be what we wish and will them to be. Stevens, Wilbur, William Stafford. This is one of Stafford's "Stories to Live in the World With" [reproduces poem in its entirety].

In the *Paris Review* interview, Berryman says that he has absolutely no observation of nature. Observation of nature, he says, "makes possible a world of moral observation for Frost, or Hopkins." Nature as the measure, and comfort, whether or not it ought to be, whatever the truth of the matter. All those burdens from earlier years never left Berryman. I have to try to believe that this is more than a matter of chemistry, that he could have turned his back and gone about a different business. In "Dream Song 265" he says "next time it will be nature & Thoreau." Henry admits to loving "the spare, the hit-or-miss, / the mad." Robinson Jeffers would have told Berryman, as he wrote to the American Humanist Association, "most of our time and energy are necessarily spent on human affairs; that can't be prevented, though I think it should be minimized; but for philosophy, which is an endless research of truth, and for contemplation, which can be a sort of worship, I would suggest that the immense beauty of the earth and the outer universe, the divine 'nature of things,' is a more rewarding object. Certainly it is more ennobling. It is a source of strength; the other of distraction." It may be that this goes too far. It may be, in fact, that Jeffers himself so loved and was so concerned with man that, in Hyatt H. Waggoner's words, Jeffers's single real theme was "his desperate effort to teach the heart not to love." I do not mean to oversimplify a very complex matter of balance. I mean to say that during the many years while he was writing the Dream Songs, Berryman did not dwell on those things that could have been sources of strength for him.

Many people were much closer to John Berryman than I was. But, as someone said, we can love even a stranger known for only a few moments, and grieve at his death, because the soul does not keep time. I loved/love him, and cherish him, and will always count it among the privileges of my life that I met him. But I realize, also, that I am often afraid of him, that the bad angels also hovered around him, that the God he turned to at the end did not rescue this rare man from his despair. Unless, and I will keep trying to find out, this is exactly what happened.

II.

For a while, as we got ready to begin the hour-long television interview at the Brockport studio, I was afraid that Berryman would not go through with it. I'd made the mistake of thinking we could walk, since it was a nice morning, the block or so up to the college's center mall to the studio. But Berryman's foot began to hurt him, and his complains reached a crescendo by the time we went up one flight of stairs and then down two to the studio. Phil

Gerber was with us and helped to soothe him. Jerry Mazzaro and I were settling some last-minute questions, and Frank Filardo, the director of the tape, was trying to brief Berryman when the poet began bellowing about how no "young shit" was going to tell him what to do. He would begin, he said, when he wanted to. He would not be cued. Frank took all the insults graciously and went back into the control room. The two students manning the cameras in front of us were petrified. So were Jerry and I. I told Berryman that this was his show, that Jerry and I would be happy if he would lead the discussion into the areas he wanted to, that we'd be content just to listen. Frank informed me over the intercom that the tape was rolling, and I informed Berryman, gently, that we could begin. My notes for the tape remind me that I hoped to get him to begin by reading "1 September 1939," an early poem about which I had several questions that would lead to others. But, out of the blue, Berryman began reading another poem that I couldn't immediately place. I groped for a question and came up with a wonderful goof.

Others tried to edit the tape before me and gave up on it. Berryman's voice very often hovers between the murky and the unintelligible. To make this transcript, I listened to an audio dub of the videotape many times over a period of several months. Sometimes I finally was able to hear what Berryman was saying after replaying a passage dozens of times. I've used brackets to note difficulties, and italics to shout where Berryman shouts the loudest. The whole tape is punctuated by Berryman's incessant movement, the squeaking of his chair, the tapping of his foot.

■　■　■

John Berryman: I'll read you a poem I wrote during the Second World War. I was living in Boston. It's called "The Song of the Tortured Girl." And it's about a heroine of the French Resistance captured by the Gestapo, and tortured, in various ways, to death, *without giving up any names.* [Recites "The Song of the Tortured Girl"; see *Collected Poems 1937–1971*, p. 52]

William Heyen: Mr. Berryman, the poem you just read, "The Song of the Tortured Girl," it's a powerful and rending poem, I think. Later on Yeats would write the "Crazy Jane" poems . . .

Berryman: No, before.

Heyen: This was before your poem? Yes.

Berryman: See any connection?

Heyen: Yes, but tell me about it.

Berryman: Well, I thought those poems were *marvelous*. But do you think I picked up something years later from them in this poem? I don't think so.

Jerome Mazzaro: I don't think so.

Berryman: I don't think so. They are refrain poems. Now, this last winter I wrote a refrain poem, but this is not a refrain poem. There is just one repetition here. It's not like the end of each stanza.

Mazzaro: It's more like the songs of Auden, the early Auden. Not that it resembles Auden either. It really comes alive in terms of voice. But Auden has some songs, or what he calls songs, in his first book, his first books actually, which take up that idea of a, an almost music sort of lyric.

Berryman: Yes, well, there are several ways of approaching the only problem, which is that of the expression of emotion in action. With data. That's all poetry is about, eh?

One time I was feeling very depressed, and was having a conversation with Robert Lowell, my old pal, and I said to him *very gloomy*, "Now what about this business that we have devoted our lives to?" He said, "John, I don't know any more about it than you do, but perhaps it has something to do with passion?" ’

Mazzaro: What made you decide to go into the business of poetry?

Berryman: Well, I always planned to be a writer, and I manifested my sincerity by writing half a science fiction novel at the age of twelve. And this was published by a rather tall girl named Helen Justice, and she thought I was wonderful. And I liked her very much, but she was too tall! Besides I was in love with Charlotte Coquet. But anyway, she had a marvelous Spenserian handwriting, and she took my manuscript, and put half inside a brown paper towel, with the title of the book, which I forget—it was about a trip to Neptune. Then my name, volume one. Then she did the same thing with the second part of the manuscript. Too bad we don't have them—bring a lot of money *these* days!

Heyen: You said, back in *those* days, that of course Yeats was your spiritual father, and of course you were very impressed already with "the brilliant young Englishman W. H Auden." And you felt that Eliot's influence would have been disastrous for what you wanted to do.

Berryman: It took me a *long* time to catch on to Eliot. I now *love* him, and have for a long time. But I had to get there through a *forest* of objections. I hated all of his *opinions*. [long pause]

Heyen: "The Literary Dictatorship"? "The Literary Dictatorship of T. S. Eliot," as your friend Delmore Schwartz called it?

Berryman: Yes, well, I don't know what there is. The Reverend George Gilfillan—I bet you never heard of him . . .

Heyen: No.

Berryman: I have forty-eight volumes edited by him! He was a Scot, and was literate and [unintelligible word]. Most people [unintelligible phrase]— they can't wait to hear it. So if somebody is prepared to tell them—godly like the Reverend Gilfillan, or softly with many reservations like Mr. Eliot, they receive the word, and pass it on.

Mazzaro: Your first collection was in one of the New Directions anthologies, wasn't it? A sort of group of . . .

Berryman: You mean my own stuff?

Heyen: Yes, *Five Young American Poets.*

Berryman: One of the few sensible things that I've ever done. I had begun to publish in the national magazines as an undergraduate at Columbia, and I went abroad for two years, and I knew my stuff was viable, and so forth, but, but it was *no good*, so I decided not to print anything for two years. And didn't. Then Robert Penn Warren, who was running the *Southern Review*, did a group of four poems, and *Partisan* did some—Delmore took them—and Mr. Ransom had started up the Kenyon [the *Kenyon Review*], and he wrote and asked me for stuff. So I was in business!

Mazzaro: Some of your early poems, surprisingly enough, have to do with Detroit. You taught there.

Berryman: I taught there for a year, yes. When I came back from England, I couldn't get a job—I lived in New York for a year—and then Columbia offered me a job. But then Detroit offered me a much better job, and my best friend, a young poet named Bhain Campbell—he was three years older than me but I was very much ahead of him—and his wife, we set up housekeeping, we shared an apartment. Then Harvard asked me to come and that Thanksgiving I flew out to Detroit to see Campbell. He had about ten days to live. And he was completely irrational, grinned at me all the time, looking like his own corpse, and told me not to worry, everything would be all right. As a TB patient, he would die of cancer. And it wiped him out, in about three months.

Many years later—after his death his poems were collected and published. Nobody paid any attention to them except Donald Stauffer at Princeton, who reviewed them for the *New York Times*. Maybe it sold eight copies. Many years later I had a letter from a completely unknown character named *James Dickey!*—who I think is one of our best writers. He knew I had known Campbell, and wanted to talk about him. He said, "I'm an advertising man." [long pause] You may ask me a question. Otherwise, I'll ramble!

Heyen: I don't think it would ever be rambling, really, but I do have a lot of questions. In the early forties you wrote a sequence of sonnets, 115 or so—I don't know whether you got rid of some finally. Working in this, moving into this terribly tight form, did this, was this the kind of apprenticeship that you think was necessary for you, if not necessary in general for young poets? What did working in this form do for you, do you think?

Berryman: Well, as I told you about a quarter-past-four last night, I believe in apprenticeship. Suppose I wanted to be a composer and write piano concertos. I don't buy some music paper and sit down. I don't know what an oboe can do! Isn't that so? Okay. We serve an apprenticeship.

Heyen: Only one of those poems was published, I think, before they finally did come out as *Berryman's Sonnets*.

Berryman: Yes.

Heyen: Why is it that you didn't publish them at the time?

Berryman: Well, the subject was unedifying, since the girl was married! So was I.

Heyen: Is "unedifying" the word?

Berryman: Well, I sat on them, and people heard about them, and I was offered to combine them and publish them. But on the whole I didn't. I was reading one of Jean Malaquais's books—it's about the relation between evil and art, that *close* relation—and he decided, after tossing it around for forty or fifty pages, that we have to suspend judgment, we are at the mercy of (I forget the French) the advanced man, namely the artist, a [unintelligible word] homosexual crook, like Jean Genet. So, that settles it. I'm not a homosexual crook. I'm a heterosexual maniac!

Mazzaro: But do you believe in the advanced man, the artist? So many of your central characters are poets, are creative people. Including yourself in your poetry.

Berryman: Well, I know more about them. But the advanced man, the idea—it's not a quotation from Maritain [sic], I made it up, five minutes ago—the advanced man comes to us as a statesman, or graphic artist. [unintelligible name] ruined French drawing. He taught them a formula. Thereafter women bowed their heads in certain ways. Research within the biological or natural sciences. It comes out of some new writer's head.

Heyen: Why were so many of the advanced men of your generation so unhappy?

Berryman: Our society, with all its vices and weaknesses, marvelous as it is, is really very unfavorable to higher talent. Somebody pointed out recently that out of our Nobel Prize winners in literature—six—four [William Faulkner, Ernest Hemingway, Sinclair Lewis, Eugene O'Neill] were alcoholics, and a fifth, Steinbeck, a very heavy drinker. And then you think of people like Poe and Fitzgerald. Vachel Lindsay killed himself. Hart Crane killed himself.

Heyen: We always hear America destroys its artists. To your mind, what does this mean, that America destroys its artists? [long pause] Is it something as mundane as American foreign policy? Is it the violence with which our land was settled? Is it the crassness of our general population? What does that mean?

Berryman: Well, when I think of Hart Crane walking down the ship, and jumping off the back; he did not give a *shit* about the foundation of the country and so on, and American foreign policy was not in his mind. Art is created out of ordeal and crisis. The greatest poem ever written was made by a fanatic who had to live in exile. The *Commedia.* There's a terrible passage somewhere in the *Paradiso* about the unpleasantness of *walking up and down somebody else's stairs.* Okay, life is hard on *everybody,* but especially so on the artist. I don't know. Anyway, he has to record it, most people don't. So he equips himself, and he's vulnerable, and in our society he gets no support.

Heyen: I think also he remembers for a long time. I think you've carried losses with you—I think of Bhain Campbell again—almost your whole life. You can't put it aside. There's a phrase in one of your early poems: "the epistemology of loss." And there's a sense in which that has always been your theme. You talk in the Dream Songs about Henry's "irreversible loss."

Berryman: Yes, well, I don't like to generalize, but isn't it true that the three of us sitting here, began with a great loss, from the controlled environment of the womb? After my son was born, I wrote him a little poem ["A Sympathy, a Welcome" (1958)] that started: "Feel for your bad fall how could I fail, / poor Paul, who had it so good." I have many objections to Freud's findings, but he was right about the importance of the womb. Years after the Second World War, a guy was discovered in Brooklyn, a draft evader. He and his mother—he was *very* fond of his mother—they had constructed a living place for him between floors in this apartment house, so there would be no record of him. So, he got in there, lived, and she sent him food by the dumb-waiter, also known as the umbilical cord. And when he came out a few years later, he could neither read nor write. He had regressed, until he was just about back there, where everything is warm and moist! And you're not threatened! Isn't that incredible!

Mazzaro: Mr. Lowell talks about needing pain to create art, that somehow art is the balance of pain, it's both the price and what keeps you going despite the pain. I think you are trying to say about the same thing, that pain is the price.

Berryman: Hold on. I don't feel happy with that. I don't know what Lowell's talking about, but there are some writers who are able to use what the psychologists call "the deposit of emotion" as a basis for production. And this I think goes back a fairly long way. The great paintings at Lascaux, and elsewhere, *unmatched*, were done out of reverence, and love, for the buffalo, and the bear. In our century, and in our place here, the picture that you quote from Lowell is more like a betrayal.

Mazzaro: Our great painting is *Guernica*, which is a very painful canvas.

Berryman: Yes.

Heyen: Theodore Roethke was dying to count himself "among the happy poets," and I think of the end of Auden's "September 1, 1939," in which he yearns to "show an affirming flame." I hate to talk about the responsibility of the artist, but does art in the end mean some kind of human affirmation? Does it have to? Is that part and parcel of it?

Berryman: Well, I don't know. I am *incredibly doubtful*. All you have to do is to think about Samuel Beckett: a mind so dark that it makes you wonder *if the Renaissance really took place!* You know, the incredible outbursts that we have in Cervantes and Shakespeare, people in the North, and the Italians. It's very doubtful.

Mazzaro: You managed in *Homage to Mistress Bradstreet* and subsequent to that, a wonderfully alive syntax and diction. How did you come about creating the language of that poem? It's just such a superb language.

Berryman: Thank you very much. I'm delighted. Everything is an experiment, I think. And so I was taking chances at the time of my poem. I had to get a language that was not hers, but not mine, but would *not be pastiche*, like Ben Jonson's projection of Spenser. He writ to language. I did not want to hear that. I think there's no doubt that sometimes I certainly succeeded. For example, I'll tell you a line I think is very good. It was about—she had children, the lady in the poem . . .

Well, I was staying with Robert and Sally Fitzgerald, in Connecticut. I had set a ration for myself of one stanza a day, and no more. And I had a glassine business, and I would put the draft of the stanza, based on five years of notes, behind the glassine, so I couldn't make notes on it. And study it. And Sally would be making dinner and I would come into the house and Robert would come back from teaching, and then we'd go over the stanza. And I couldn't get one line right. And I drafted and drafted, and I would take the new version of the line—it's about one of the children's teeth—and I couldn't get it right. I would take it out to Sally in the kitchen, bending over the refrigerator or stove, and read her the new version of the line. The second in the stanza. Anyway, dissatisfied. So I'd go back into the living room and sweat some more. At last, she was satisfied, and the result is so simple. It's not her seventeenth-century language. It goes like this: "if it's that loose, / let me wiggle it out. / You'll get a bigger one there, & bite." Isn't that good? But I was incredibly lucky! Sally kept on objecting! So, I don't know. I think all these problems in art are really problems. There exist solutions. I have no idea whether that is the correct or best solution. But it's one.

Mazzaro: That's the poem, too, with which you began your mastery of the pronoun, the shifting pronoun, which came to greatness, I think, in the Dream Songs where you change persons.

Berryman: Yes, I'm very good at pronouns.

Heyen: You're one of the few poets who has driven himself into a long poem. Sometimes in the Dream Songs Henry speaks for you, maybe not most of the time but sometimes anyway, and at one point he says that everyone in the world is happy except the guy who has to write a long poem. We had indications as early as the sonnet sequence, although it's not one poem. Then *Homage to Mistress Bradstreet* and then the eleven years of the Dream Songs. Have you asked yourself why you felt driven toward the long poem?

Berryman: Well . . .

Heyen: You're coming back to short poems now.

Berryman: Now I write short poems, yes.

Heyen: But why that terrific impulse for what Poe was trying to tell you was impossible?

Berryman: Well, my foot is killing me. I'll take off my shoe.

Heyen: They will censor us, probably.

Berryman: Well, Whitman agreed with Poe. He says he had often thought that same thing, but Poe summed it up. Namely, that long poems are impossible. They cannot exist. "Song of Myself" is *sixty pages*! He did not think of it as a work of literature.

Heyen: He thought of it as a man.

Berryman: Yes.

Heyen: The body.

Berryman: Yes.

Heyen: The living thing.

Berryman: Yes.

Mazzaro: What is the relation between your Dream Songs as a sequence, a sonnet sequence, which you also wrote, and something like Ezra Pound's *Cantos*, which is a sequence?

Berryman: Well, as you put the question I can't answer it. I don't know what the relation is between the sonnets and the Dream Songs. As for Pound's *Cantos*, I am on record as approving of the effort. But in general, I think Pound has been wasting his time for forty years. Canto 13 is a great masterpiece, and there are wonderful things in the other early Cantos. Then for many, many years we have *junk*. Then we get to the *Pisan Cantos*. Then for many, many years we get junk.

Mazzaro: One of the Dream Songs is based upon the same idea of the relationship between John Adams and Thomas Jefferson, which Pound talks about in one of his *Cantos*—the fact that they both died on the fourth of July in the same year.

Berryman: Yes, well, I didn't have to read Pound to find that out. It is known to any student of history. It's like quoting Professor So-and-so from some university about Hitler having died in 1945.

Mazzaro: No, I just wondered because . . .

Berryman: I make a point of it because people are so incredibly ignorant that they think I took some fact which they can find in the *Encyclopedia Britannica*, from some piece of shit somewhere, just because they don't know. It's like citing authority for my impression that both men and women possess arms and legs! I believe in citing authority, and in my lectures and in my writings. I am a scholar. I name my sources. When they are different from the *Encyclopedia Britannica*. But I don't cite authority for the *rising of the sun in the morning*, and its *going down at night*. I could cite the Egyptian *Book of the Dead* in Wallis Budge's translation, page 408, volume 1: "The sun rises, and sets."

Heyen: You said that with *Homage to Mistress Bradstreet* you didn't choose the subject, but that it chose you. Did that sort of thing happen when Henry came about? Can you tell us, generally, where Henry came from, where he had his beginnings?

Berryman: Aah, yes, many people have asked me about the name. That's simple. My second wife and I once were walking down Hennepin Avenue in Minneapolis one evening, in the direction of a bar, and we decided that the names that we disliked most were, feminine, Mabel, and masculine, Henry. So, in an affectionate and sweet way we began that I would call her Mabel and she would call me Henry. That's where the name started.

About the character. Somebody quoted me as saying there's a fiendish resemblance between Henry and me. But of course it's not me. I wish that here the three of us had some persistent plan. Most of this is wedding of what we may be, later on this afternoon, next week, what we were on September 12, what you are in relation to your little boy. Okay. Out of these possibilities of which I have given a new identity to, Henry, I let some flower. Don't you agree? Answer your question?

Heyen: Yes.

Berryman: Glad to have got that straight. That's a better account than I've given in a glance so far.

Heyen: Read us one of your Dream Songs, will you?

Berryman: Yes, sure.

Heyen: Do you have one that you particularly like, or I'll name one, but I'd rather you picked one.

Berryman: Well, there are various ones that I like. Here is a *beauty*! If this is no good, I don't know. It won't matter. [Recites "Dream Song 282"; see *The Dream Songs*, p. 304]

Surely, if I was ever touched by inspiration . . . What do you think about that one, Mr. Mazzaro?

Mazzaro: I like it very much. What you've been able to make, because you feel it so deeply and so well, are great poems out of your friendships, with both men and women, but in particular with—I assume the Richard is R. P. Blackmur . . .

Berryman: Yes.

Mazzaro: And Delmore Schwartz . . .

Heyen: And Randall Jarrell, of course. And there are so many elegies, the elegiac voice is so strong as the Dream Songs move along, that they contribute to a sense of an overwhelming burden on Henry. It's a wonder that the world . . .

Berryman: . . . "can bear and be." Well, it's a sad bit. Anybody that lives past thirty-five or forty must expect to have his friends drop dead. But I think I don't go around with my flag up saying "self-pity." But I think I've been unusually unlucky. My friends have wiped themselves out in large numbers. Thomas died in an alcoholic shock. Ted and Delmore died of heart attacks, but they were both alcoholics.

Mazzaro: Mental illness also seems to have hit the generation.

Berryman: Yes. That's so. To find anything resembling it, you have to look at two generations, at least that I think of offhand: the English poets of the nineteenth century—Beddoes, Darley, and so on—and the Soviet poets just after the Revolution—Mayakovsky and Yesenin. And now! Well, I don't know. I don't know. Some people certainly feel that it's the price you pay for an overdeveloped sensibility. Namely, you know, the door sticks, as I try to open it, it sticks. Okay, so I have a nervous breakdown. The guy at the corner of Fifth and Hennepin, the door sticks, shit, he fixes it and he opens it.

No sweat! I've been in hospital for six months! There is an overdevelopment of sensibility, okay, otherwise we couldn't draw, just as a really good carpenter or cabinet maker has a sensitivity, feels different about wood from the rest of us. It's the price we pay. So, every now and then we wind up in the hospital, where they find us completely untreatable, and pretty soon they let us go. And we're loose on the body of society again.

Mazzaro: Your new book is going to be called *Love & Fame.*

Berryman: Yes.

Mazzaro: We've talked mainly about your writing. But the love part. You've written a great deal about love, too.

Berryman: Well, there are people who get along without it. It's given me a lot of trouble. And I find, looking at people in love, visiting people in love . . . So, for example, you fall in love with somebody. And pretty soon you say, "Will you marry me," and she says, "yes," so you marry her! That's part of your bio. I married three women. I've screwed infinite numbers of them, and had maybe even seven or eight *very* serious affairs.

Mazzaro: The latter is the kind of love that runs through the love sonnets, and occasionally through Henry, but Henry is also very affectionate toward his children.

Berryman: He's very keen on his kids, yes. Aren't we all?

Heyen: What is the relationship between love and fame? An impossible question, but fame—what does fame do to love?

Berryman: Well, the poems are autobiographical, but they also represent part of an inquiry. Located in time and space in New York City, in the middle thirties. But a general inquiry between two overmatched *grabs* in an ambitious young man: one for girls, one for poetry. And it fights itself out. Sometimes one is on top, sometimes the other.

Heyen: That's the "Perfection of the life, or of the work" debate, I suppose.

Berryman: Yes. "The intellect of man is forced to choose." I tell you, like you I admire that poem ["The Choice" by William Butler Yeats]. It's wonderful. But it's full of shit. Because the results are not right, or if they are, the next poem will correct them. I thought, as I got older, that this interest in women would diminish, or leave me. Still waiting. In the *Phaedrus* the host asked some question about Sophocles (who not only wrote much better than me, but was much older, about eighty). This guy asked him how he felt, you know, about the loss of sexual passion. And you remember what he said: "Praise the gods that I am rid of all this madness." Yes, but I'm only fifty-five. He was eighty. Another twenty-five years of this stuff? I wouldn't trust myself alone with your wife last night. She's too attractive.

Heyen: Well, I don't trust you. But I trust my wife.

Berryman: I'm absolutely sure that you can. You can also trust me, because now I wouldn't go behind your back.

Heyen: Jerry, thank you very much for being with us. Mr. Berryman, it has indeed been a pleasure. Thank you very much for being with us today. I'm afraid our time is over.

Berryman: Thank you, sir.

The Art of Poetry: An Interview with John Berryman

Peter Stitt / 1970

Conducted October 27 and 29, 1970. Published in *Paris Review* 53 (1972): 177–207. Reprinted in *Berryman's Understanding: Reflections on the Poetry of John Berryman*, edited by Harry Thomas (Boston: Northeastern University Press, 1988), 18–44. Reprinted by permission.

Peter Stitt's introduction: On a Sunday afternoon in late July 1970, John Berryman gave a reading of his poems in a small "people's park" in Minneapolis near the west bank campus of the University of Minnesota. Following the reading, I reintroduced myself—we hadn't seen each other since I was his student, eight years earlier—and we spent the afternoon in conversation at his house. He had had a very bad winter, he explained, and had spent much of the spring in the extended-care ward at St. Mary's Hospital. I asked him about doing an interview. He agreed, and we set up an appointment for late October.

Berryman spent a week in Mexico at the end of the summer and had "a marvelous time." A trip to upstate New York for a reading followed, and by early October he was back at St. Mary's. It was there that the interview was conducted, during visiting hours on the twenty-seventh and twenty-ninth of October.

He looked much better than he had during the summer, was heavier and more steady on his feet. He again smoked and drank coffee almost continually. The room was spacious, and Berryman was quite at home in it. In addition to the single bed, it contained a tray table that extended over the bed, a chair, and two nightstands, one of which held a large AM-FM radio and the usual hospital accoutrements. Books and papers covered the other nightstand, the table, and the broad windowsill.

Berryman was usually slow to get going on an answer, as he made false starts looking for just the right words. Once he started talking, he would continue until he had exhausted the subject—thus, some of his answers are very long. This method left unasked questions, and the most important of these were mailed to him later for written answers. In contrast to the taped answers, the written answers turned out to be brief, flat, and even dull. (These have been discarded.) By way of apology, he explained that he was again devoting his energies almost entirely to writing poetry.

An edited typescript of the interview was sent him in January 1971. He returned it in March, having made very few changes. He did supply some annotations, and these have been left as he put them.

One notices Berryman's fascination with the term delusion. It occurs, like a liturgical refrain . . . in his last volume of poems, in his annotations to his Paris Review interview, and in dozens of places throughout Recovery. *It is the Gloria Patri of the drunk in treatment.*
—Roger Forseth, "Spirits and Spirituality," 250

Interviewer: Mr. Berryman, recognition came to you late in comparison with writers like Robert Lowell and Delmore Schwartz. What effect do you think fame has on a poet? Can this sort of success ruin a writer?

John Berryman: I don't think there are any generalizations at all. If a writer gets hot early, then his work ought to become known early. If it doesn't, he is in danger of feeling neglected. We take it that all young writers overestimate their work. It's impossible not to—I mean if you recognized what shit you were writing, you wouldn't write it. You have to believe in your stuff—every day has to be the new day on which the new poem may be *it*. Well, fame supports that feeling. It gives self-confidence, it gives a sense of an actual, contemporary audience, and so on. On the other hand, unless it is sustained, it can cause trouble—and it is very seldom sustained. If your first book is a smash, your second book gets kicked in the face, and your third book, and lots of people, like Delmore, can't survive that disappointment. From that point of view, early fame is very dangerous indeed, and my situation, which was so painful to me for many years, was really in a way beneficial.

I overestimated myself, as it turned out, and felt bitter, bitterly neglected; but I had certain admirers, certain high judges on my side from the beginning, so that I had a certain amount of support. Moreover, I had a kind of indifference on my side—much as Joseph Conrad did. A reporter asked him once about reviews, and he said, "I don't read my reviews. I measure them." Now, until I was about thirty-five years old, I not only didn't read my reviews, I didn't measure them, I never even looked at them. That is so peculiar that close friends of mine wouldn't believe me when I told them. I thought that was indifference, but now I'm convinced that it was just that I had no skin on—you know, I was afraid of being killed by some remark. Oversensitivity. But there was an *element* of indifference in it, and so the public indifference to my work was countered with a certain amount of genuine indifference on my part, which has been very helpful since I became a celebrity. Auden once said that the best situation for a poet is to be taken up early and held for a considerable time and then dropped after he has reached the level of indifference.

Something else is in my head; a remark of Father Hopkins to Bridges. Two completely unknown poets in their thirties—fully mature—Hopkins, one of the great poets of the century, and Bridges, awfully good. Hopkins with no audience and Bridges with thirty readers. He says, "Fame in itself is nothing. The only thing that matters is virtue. Jesus Christ is the only true literary critic. But," he said, "from any lesser level or standard than that, we must recognize that fame is the true and appointed setting of men of genius." That seems to me appropriate. This business about geniuses in neglected garrets is for the birds. The idea that a man is somehow no good just because he becomes very popular, like Frost, is nonsense, also. There are exceptions—Chatterton, Hopkins, of course, Rimbaud, you can think of various cases—but on the whole, men of genius were judged by their contemporaries very much as posterity judges them. So if I were talking to a young writer, I would recommend the cultivation of extreme indifference to both praise and blame because praise will lead you to vanity, and blame will lead you to self-pity, and both are bad for writers.

Interviewer: What is your reaction to such comments as: "If Berryman is not America's finest living poet, then he is surely running a close second to Lowell"?

Berryman: Well, I don't know. I don't get any frisson of excitement back here, and my bank account remains the same, and my view of my work remains the same, and in general I can say that everything is much the same after that is over.

Interviewer: It seems that you, along with Frost and several other American writers, were appreciated earlier in England than in America.

Berryman: That's true. More in Frost's case. Stephen Crane is another.

Interviewer: Why do you think this is true?

Berryman: I wonder. The literary cultures are still very different. Right this minute, for example, the two best reviewers of poetry in English, and perhaps the only two to whom I have paid the slightest attention, are both Englishmen—Kermode and Alvarez. Of course, that's just a special case—ten years ago it was different, but our people have died or stopped practicing criticism. We couldn't put out a thing like the *Times Literary Supplement.* We just don't have it. Education at the elite level is better in England, humanistic education—never mind technical education, where we are superior or at least equal—but Cambridge, Oxford, London, and now the red-brick universities provide a much higher percentage of intelligent readers in the population—the kind of people who listen to the Third Programme and read the *Times Literary Supplement.* They are rather compact and form a body of opinion from which the reviewers, both good and mediocre, don't have to stand out very far. In our culture, we also, of course, have good readers, but not as high a percentage—and they are incredibly dispersed geographically. It makes a big difference.

Interviewer: You, along with Lowell, Sylvia Plath, and several others, have been called a confessional poet. How do you react to that label?

Berryman: With rage and contempt! Next question.

Interviewer: Are the sonnets "confessional"?

Berryman: Well, they're about her and me. I don't know. The word doesn't mean anything. I understand the confessional to be a place where you go and talk with a priest. I personally haven't been to confession since I was twelve years old.

Interviewer: You once said: "I masquerade as a writer. Actually I am a scholar." At another time you pointed out that your passport gives your occupation as "Author" and not "Teacher." How do your roles as teacher and scholar affect your role as poet?

Berryman: Very, very hard question. Housman is one of my heroes and always has been. He was a detestable and miserable man. Arrogant, unspeakably lonely, cruel, and so on, but an absolutely marvelous minor poet, I think, and a great scholar. And I'm about *equally* interested in those two activities. In him they are perfectly distinct. You are dealing with an absolute schizophrenic. In me they seem closer together, but I just don't know. Schwartz once asked me why it was that all my Shakespearean study had never showed up anywhere in my poetry, and I couldn't answer the question. It was a piercing question because his early poems are really very much influenced by Shakespeare's early plays. I seem to have been sort of untouched by Shakespeare, although I have had him in my mind since I was twenty years old.

Interviewer: I don't agree with that. One of the Dream Songs, one of those written to the memory of Delmore Schwartz—let me see if I can find it. Here, number 147. These lines [recites the first four lines from "Dream Song 147"; see *The Dream Songs*, p. 166]. That sounds very Shakespearean to me.

Berryman: That sounds like *Troilus and Cressida*, doesn't it? One of my very favorite plays. I would call that Shakespearian. Not to praise it, though, only in description. I was half-hysterical writing that song. It just burst onto the page. It took only as long to compose as it takes to write it down.

Interviewer: Well, that covers scholarship. How about teaching? Does teaching only get in the way of your work as a poet?

Berryman: It depends on the kind of teaching you do. If you teach creative writing, you get absolutely nothing out of it. Or English—what are you teaching? People you read twenty years ago. Maybe you pick up a little if you keep on preparing, but very few people keep on preparing. Everybody is lazy, and poets, in addition to being lazy, have another activity which is very demanding, so they tend to slight their teaching. But I give courses in the history of civilization, and when I first began teaching here I nearly went crazy. I was teaching Christian origins and the Middle Ages, and I had certain weak spots. I was okay with the *Divine Comedy* and certain other things, but I had an awful time of it. I worked it out once, and it took me nine hours to prepare a fifty-minute lecture. I have learned much more from giving these lecture courses than I ever learned at Columbia or Cambridge. It has forced me out into areas where I wouldn't otherwise have been, and, since I am a scholar, these things are connected. I make myself acquainted with the scholarship. Suppose I'm lecturing on Augustine. My Latin is very rusty, but I'll pay a certain amount of attention to the Latin text in the Loeb edition, with the English across the page. Then I'll visit the library and consult five or six old and recent works on St. Augustine, who is a particular interest of mine anyway. Now all that becomes part of your equipment for poetry, even for lyric poetry. The Bradstreet poem is a very learned poem. There is a lot of the theology in it, there is a lot of theology in *The Dream Songs*. Anything is useful to a poet. Take observation of nature, of which I have absolutely none. It makes possible a world of moral observation for Frost, or Hopkins. So scholarship and teaching are directly useful to my activity as a writer.

Interviewer: But not the teaching of creative writing. You don't think there is any value in that for you as a poet.

Berryman: I enjoy it. Sometimes your kids prove awfully good. Snodgrass is well known now, and Bill Merwin—my students—and others, and it's delightful to be of service to somebody. But most of them have very little talent, and you can't overencourage them; that's impossible. Many of my friends teach creative writing. I'm not putting it down, and it certainly is an honest way of earning a living, but I wouldn't recommend it to a poet. It is better to teach history or classics or philosophy of the kind of work I do here in humanities.

Interviewer: You have given Yeats and Auden as early influences on your poetry. What did you learn from them?

Berryman: Practically everything I could then manipulate. On the other hand, they didn't take me very far, because by the time I was writing really well, in 1948—that's the beginning of the Bradstreet poem and the last poems in the collection called *The Dispossessed*—there was no Yeats around and no Auden. Some influences from Rilke, some influence from a poet whom I now consider very bad, Louis Aragon, in a book called *Crèvecoeur*—he conned me. He took all his best stuff from Apollinaire, whom I hadn't then read, and swept me off my feet. I wrote a poem called "Narcissus Moving," which is as much like Aragon as possible, and maybe it's just as bad. I don't know. Then the Bradstreet poem—it is not easy to see the literary ancestry of that poem. Who has been named? Hopkins. I don't see that. Of course there are certain verbal practices, but on the whole, not. The stanza has been supposed to be derived from the stanza of "The Wreck of the Deutschland." I don't see that. I have never read "The Wreck of the Deutschland," to tell you the truth, except the first stanza. Wonderful first stanza. But I really just couldn't get onto it. It's a set piece, and I don't like set pieces. I'll bet it's no good—well, you know, not comparable with the great short poems. Then Lowell has been named. I see the influence of *Lord Weary's Castle* in some of the later poems in *The Dispossessed*. There's no doubt about it. In the Bradstreet poem, as I seized inspiration from *Augie March*, I sort of seized inspiration, I think, from Lowell, rather than imitated him. I can't think, offhand—I haven't read it in many years—of a single passage in the Bradstreet poem which distinctly sounds like Lowell. However, I may be quite wrong about this, since people have named him. Other people, I don't think so.

Interviewer: How about Eliot? You must have had to reckon with Eliot in one way or another, positively or negatively.

Berryman: My relationship with Eliot was highly ambiguous. In the first place, I refused to meet him on three occasions in England, and I think I mentioned this in one of the poems I wrote last spring. I had to fight shy of Eliot. There was a certain amount of hostility in it, too. I only began to appreciate Eliot much later, after I was secure in my own style. I now rate him very high. I think he is one of the greatest poets who ever lived. Only sporadically good. What he would do—he would collect himself and write a masterpiece, then relax for several years writing prose, earning a living, and so forth; then he'd collect himself and write another masterpiece, very different from the first, and so on. He did this about five times, and after the *Four Quartets* he lived for twenty years. Wrote absolutely nothing. It's a very strange career. Very—a pure system of spasms. My career is like that. It is horribly like that. But I feel deep sympathy, admiration, and even love for Eliot over all the recent decades.

Interviewer: You knew Dylan Thomas pretty well, didn't you?

Berryman: Pretty well, pretty well. We weren't close friends.

Interviewer: Any influence there?

Berryman: No. And that's surprising, very surprising, because we used to knock around in Cambridge and London. We didn't discuss our poetry much. He was far ahead of me. Occasionally he'd show me a poem or I'd show him a poem. He was very fond of making suggestions. He didn't like a line in a poem of mine, later published by Robert Penn Warren in the *Southern Review*, called "Night and the City"—a very bad poem modeled on a poem by John Peale Bishop called "The Return." Well, Dylan didn't like one line, and so he proposed this line: "A bare octagonal ballet for penance." Now, my poem was rather incoherent, but couldn't contain—you know, in the military sense—it couldn't contain that! I was very fond of him. I loved him, and I thought he was a master. I was wrong about that. He was not a master; he became a master only much later on. What he was then is a great rhetorician. Terrific. But the really great poems only came towards the end of World War II, I think. There was no influence.

Interviewer: Do you think he had an impulse towards self-destruction?

Berryman: Oh, absolutely. He was doomed already when I first knew him. Everybody warned him for many years.

Interviewer: Can one generalize on that? So many of the poets of your generation have encountered at least personal tragedy—flirting with suicide, and so on.

Berryman: I don't know. The record is very bad. Vachel Lindsay killed himself. Hart Crane killed himself, more important. Sara Teasdale—quite a good poet at the end, killed herself. Then Miss Plath recently. Randall—it's not admitted, but apparently he did kill himself—and Roethke and Delmore might just as well have died of alcoholism. They died of heart attacks, but that's one of the main ways to die from alcoholism. And Dylan died in an alcoholic coma. Well, the actual cause of death was bronchitis. But he went into shock in the Chelsea, where I was staying also, and they got him to the hospital in an ambulance, where he was wrongly treated. They gave him morphine, which is contraindicated in cases of alcoholic shock. He wouldn't have lived anyway, but they killed him. He lay in a coma for five days.

Interviewer: You were there, weren't you?

Berryman: I was in the corridor, ten feet away.

Interviewer: What was it like to take high tea with William Butler Yeats?

Berryman: All I can say is that my mouth was dry and my heart was in my mouth. Thomas had very nearly succeeded in getting me drunk earlier in the day. He was full of scorn for Yeats, as he was for Eliot, Pound, Auden. He thought my admiration for Yeats was the funniest thing in that part of London. It wasn't until about three o'clock that I realized that he and I were drinking more than usual. I didn't drink much at the time; Thomas drank much more than I did. I had the sense to leave. I went back to my chambers, Cartwright Gardens, took a cold bath, and just made it for the appointment. I remember the taxi ride over. The taxi was left over from the First World War, and when we arrived in Pall Mall—we could see the Athenaeum—the driver said he didn't feel he could get in. Finally I decided to abandon ship and take off on my own. So I went in and asked for Mr. Yeats. Very much like asking, "Is Mr. Ben Jonson here?" And he came down. He was much taller than I expected, and haggard. Big though, big head, rather wonderful looking in a sort of blunt, patrician kind of way, but there was something shrunken also. He told me he was just recovering from an illness. He was very courteous, and we went in to tea. At a certain point, I had a cigarette, and I asked him if he would like one. To my great surprise he said yes. So I gave him a Craven-A and then lit it for him, and I thought, "Immorality is mine! From now on it's just a question of reaping the fruits of my effort." He did most of the talking. I asked him a few questions. He did not ask me any questions about myself, although he was extremely courteous and kind. At one point he said, "I have reached the age when my daughter can beat me at croquet," and I thought, "Hurrah, he's human!" I made notes on the interview afterwards, which I have probably lost. One comment in particular I remember. He said, "I never revise now"—you know how much he revised his stuff—"but in the interests of a more passionate syntax." Now that struck me as a very good remark. I have no idea what it meant, and I still don't know, but the longer I think about it, the better I like it. He recommended various books to me, by his friend, the liar, Gogarty,[1] and I forget who else. The main thing was just the presence and existence of my hero.

Interviewer: William Faulkner once ventured to rate himself among contemporary novelists. He rated Thomas Wolfe first, himself second, Dos Passos third, Hemingway fourth, and Steinbeck fifth.

Berryman: Oh, no! Really? That's deluded! The list is abominable. I think what must have happened is this. There are two ways to rank writers: in terms of gift and in terms of achievement. He was ranking Wolfe in terms of gift. Wolfe had a colossal gift. His achievement, though—to rank him first and Hemingway fourth is openly grotesque.

Interviewer: Would you be interested in doing this, in ranking yourself among contemporary American poets?

Berryman: I don't think I could do it. I'll tell you why. First, most of these characters are personal friends of mine, and you just don't sit around ranking your friends. After I published *The Dispossessed* in '48, I quit reviewing poetry. By that time I knew most of the people writing verse, and how can you deliver a fair judgment of the man you had dinner with the night before? Preposterous! It's supposed to be easy, but actually it's impossible. My love of such poets as Schwartz, *In Dreams Begin Responsibilities*, Roethke, and Lowell, *Lord Weary's Castle*, is very great. I would love to be in their company, and I feel convinced that I am, but I don't want to do any ranking. It's just not a sweat.

Interviewer: In *The Dream Songs* there is a passage about assistant professors becoming associate professors by working on your poems. How do you feel about being cannon fodder for aspiring young critics and graduate students?

Berryman: As for the graduate students, some of the work they do is damned interesting. A woman somewhere in the South did an eighty-page thesis investigating the three little epigraphs to the *77 Dream Songs* and their bearing on the first three books of the poem. I must say that her study was exhaustive—very little left to be found out on that subject! But it's good, careful work. I take a pleased interest in these things, though there is ineptness and naiveté, and they get all kinds of things wrong and impute to me amazing motives. Another woman thought I was influenced by Hebrew elegiac meter. Now, my Hebrew is primitive, and I don't even know what Hebrew elegiac meter is—and, moreover, neither does she. It's a harmless industry. It gets people degrees. I don't feel against it and I don't feel for it. I sympathize with the students.

The professional critics, those who know what the literary, historical, philosophical, and theological score is, have not really gone to work yet, and may not do so for a long time yet. I did have a letter once from a guy who said: "Dear Mr. Berryman, Frankly I hope to be promoted from assistant professor to associate professor by writing a book about you. Are you willing to join me in this unworthy endeavor?" So I joined him. I answered all his questions. I practically flew out to pour out his drinks while he typed.

Interviewer: I would like to change the subject now and talk about your work. Let's start with *The Dream Songs*. As you know, there is some controversy over the structure of the work—why it was first published in two volumes, why it consists of seven sections of varying lengths, and so on. What structural notion did you have in mind in writing it?

Berryman: Several people have written books about *The Dream Songs*, not published, and one of them, a woman, sees it as a series of three odysseys, psychological and moral, on the part of Henry, corresponding vaguely to Freud's differentiation of the personality into superego or conscience, ego or façade or self, and id or unconscious. Each has a starting point and a terminus and so forth. I don't know whether she is right or not, but if so, I did not begin with that full-fledged conception when I wrote the first dream song.

I don't know what I had in mind. In *Homage to Mistress Bradstreet* my model was *The Waste Land*, and *Homage to Mistress Bradstreet* is as unlike *The Waste Land* as it is possible for me to be. I think the model in *The Dream Songs* was the other greatest American poem—I am very ambitious—"Song of Myself"—a very long poem, about sixty pages. It also has a hero, a personality, himself. Henry is accused of being me and I am accused of being Henry and I deny it and nobody believes me. Various other things entered into it, but that is where I started.

The narrative such as it is developed as I went along, partly out of my gropings into and around Henry and his environment and associates, partly out of my readings in theology and that sort of thing, taking place during thirteen years—awful long time—and third, out of certain partly preconceived and partly developing as I went along, sometimes rigid and sometimes plastic, structural notions. That is why the work is divided into seven books, each book of which is rather well unified, as a matter of fact. Finally, I left the poem open to the circumstances of my personal life. For example, obviously if I hadn't got a Guggenheim and decided to spend it in Dublin, most of book VII wouldn't exist. I have a personality and a plan, a metrical plan—which is original, as in *Homage to Mistress Bradstreet*. I don't use other people as metrical models. I don't put down people who do—I just don't feel satisfied with them.

I had a personality and a plan and all kinds of philosophical and theological notions. The woman thinks the basic philosophical notion is Hegelian, and it's true that at one time I was deeply interested in Hegel. She also thinks, and so do some other people, that the work is influenced by the later work of Freud, especially *Civilization and Its Discontents*, and that is very likely.

For years I lectured on the book every year here at Minnesota, so I am very, very familiar with it—almost know it word by word. But at the same time I was what you might call open-ended. That is to say, Henry to some extent was in the situation that we all are in in actual life—namely, he didn't know and I didn't know what the bloody fucking hell was going to happen next. Whatever it was he had to confront it and get through. For example, he dies in book IV and is dead throughout the book, but at the end of the poem he is still alive, and in fairly good condition, after having died himself *again*.

The poem does not go as far as "Song of Myself." What I mean by that is this: Whitman denies that "Song of Myself" is a long poem. He has a passage saying that he had long thought that there was no such thing as a long poem and that when he read Poe he found that Poe summed up the problem for him. But here it is, sixty pages. What's the notion? He doesn't regard it as a literary work at all, in my opinion—he doesn't quite say so. It proposes a new religion—it is what is called in Old Testament criticism a wisdom work, a work on the meaning of life and how to conduct it. Now, I don't go that far—*The Dream Songs* is a literary composition, it's a long poem—but I buy a little of it. I think Whitman is right with regard to "Song of Myself." I'm prepared to submit to his opinion. He was crazy, and I don't contradict madmen. When William Blake says something, I say thank you, even though he has uttered the most hopeless fallacy that you can imagine. I'm willing to be their loving audience. I'm just hoping to hear something marvelous from time to time, marvelous and true. Of course *The Dream Songs* does not propose a new system; that is not the point. In that way it is unlike "Song of Myself." It remains a literary work.

Interviewer: Christopher Ricks has called *The Dream Songs* a theodicy. Did you have any such intention in writing the poem?

Berryman: It's a tough question. The idea of theodicy has been in my mind at least since 1938. There is a passage in Delmore's first book, *In Dreams Begin Responsibilities*, which goes: "The theodicy I wrote in my high school days / Restored all life from infancy." Beautiful! He is the most underrated poet of the twentieth century. His later work is *absolutely* no good, but his first book is a masterpiece. It will come back—no problem. So that notion's always been with me. I can't answer the question. I simply don't know. I put my stuff, in as good condition as I can make it, on the table, and if people want to form opinions, good, I'm interested in the opinions. I don't set up as a critic of my own work. And I'm not kidding about that.

Interviewer: You once said that, among other things, a long poem demands "the construction of a world rather than the reliance upon one already existent." Does the world of *The Dream Songs* differ from the existent world?

Berryman: This is connected with your previous question. Is said that *The Dream Songs* in my opinion—only in my opinion—does not propose a new system, like Whitman. But as to the creation of a world: it's a hard question to answer. Suppose I take this business of the relation of Henry to me, which has interested so many people, and which is categorically denied by me in one of the forewords. Henry both is and is not me, obviously. We touch at certain points. But I am an actual human being; he is nothing but a series of conceptions—my conceptions. I brush my teeth; unless I say so somewhere in the poem—I forget whether or not I do or not—he doesn't brush his teeth. He only does what I make him do. If I have succeeded in making him believable, he performs all kinds of other actions besides those named in the poem, but the reader has to make them up. That's the world. But it's not a religious or philosophical system.

Interviewer: Where did you get the name "Henry"?

Berryman: Ah, big sweat about that too. Did I get it from *The Red Badge of Courage* or *A Farewell to Arms* or what? O.K., I'll tell you where it came from. My second wife, Ann, and I were walking down Hennepin Avenue one momentous night. Everything seemed quiet as usual, but it was going to puzzle literary critics on two continents many years later. Anyway, we were joking on our way to a bar to have a beer, and I decided that I hated the name Mabel more than any other female name, though I could mention half a dozen others that I didn't like either. We had passed from names we liked to names we disliked, and she decided that Henry was the name that she found completely unbearable. So from then on, for a long time, in the most cozy and affectionate lover kind of talk—we hadn't been married very long at this time—she was Mabel and I was Henry in our scene. So I started the poem. The poem began with a song that I killed. I've never printed it. It set the prosodic pattern, but for various reasons I killed it. It had not only a hero but a heroine. It was mostly about Henry, but it also had Mabel in it. It began:

> The jolly old man is a silly old dumb
> with a mean face, humped, who kills dead.
> There is a tall who loves only him.
> She has sworn "Blue to you forever,
> grey to the little rat, go to bed."
> —I fink it's bad all over.

It winds up:

> Henry and Mabel ought to but can't.
> Childness let's have us honey—

Then, for reasons which I don't remember, I wiped Mabel out and never printed that song. For a long time after that, every now and then Ann would complain that Mabel didn't seem to be taking any part in the poem, but I couldn't find myself able to put her back in the poem, so it has no heroine. There are groups of heroines, but no individual heroine. By that way, the first song sounds quite good. Maybe I ought to pull it out.

Interviewer: You once said in speaking of *Homage to Mistress Bradstreet* that you started out thinking you would write a fifty-line poem and ended up with fifty-seven stanzas. When you started *The Dream Songs*, did you know how long it was going to be or how far you were going to go?

Berryman: No, I didn't. But I was aware that I was embarked on an epic. In the case of the Bradstreet poem, I didn't know. The situation with the poem was this. I invented the stanza in '48 and wrote the first stanza and the first three lines of the second stanza, and then I stuck. I had in mind a poem roughly the same length as another of mine, "The Statue"—about seven or eight stanzas of eight lines each. Then I stuck. I read and read and read and thought and collected notes and sketched for five years, until, although I was still in the second stanza, I had a mountain of notes and draftings—no whole stanzas, but passages as long as five lines. The whole poem was written in about two months, after which I was a ruin for two years. When I finally got going, I had this incredible mass of stuff and a very good idea of the shape of the poem with the exception of one crucial point, which was this. I'll tell you in a minute why and how I got going. The great exception was this; it did not occur to me to have a dialogue between them—to insert bodily Henry into the poem . . . *Me*, to insert me, in my own person, John Berryman, *I*, into the poem . . .

Interviewer: Was that a Freudian slip?

Berryman: I don't know. Probably. Nothing is accidental, except physics. Modern physics is entirely accidental. I did not have the idea of putting him in as a demon lover. How he emerged was this. The idea was not to take Anne Bradstreet as a poetess—I was not interested in that. I was interested in her as a pioneer heroine, a sort of mother to the artists and intellectuals who would follow her and play a large role in the development of the nation. People like Jefferson, Poe, and me.[2]

Well, her life was very hard in many, many ways. The idea was to make it even harder than it had been in history. There is a lot of history in the poem. It is a historical poem, but a lot of it is invented too. I decided to tempt her. She was unbelievably devoted to her husband. Her few really touching passages, both in verse and in prose, are about her love for her husband, who was indeed a remarkable man—and she was a remarkable woman, and she loved him, with a passion that can hardly be described, through their whole life together, from the age of sixteen on. I decided to tempt her. I could only do this in fantasy—the problem was to make the fantasy believable, and some people think I have completely failed with that. It is not for me to judge. I am deeply satisfied. I only do the best I can—I think I succeeded and some other people do too.

So, with the exception of the dialogue in the middle—that's the middle third of the poem—all the rest was one whole plan, but it took a series of shocks to get it going. What happened? My wife and I were living in Princeton, had been for a year. She was in the hospital in New York for an operation, what they call an operation, a kind of parody of childbirth. Both she and I were feeling very bitter about this since we very much wanted a child and had not had one. So I had very, very strong emotions and solitude. Second, at this point Saul Bellow had almost finished *Augie March*, his first important novel and one of the great American novels, I think. His later novels are far more important still, but *Augie March* is a landmark. He had almost finished that and wanted me to see it. We didn't know each other very well—since then he has become perhaps my best friend—but he was living just a few blocks away. I remember sitting in my chair, drinking as usual, reading the typescript. It was very long, about nine hundred pages. I was amazed. The word "breakthrough" has become kind of a cliché. Every two minutes somebody in *Life*, *Time*, or *Fortune* has a breakthrough. But the term does describe something that actually happens. A renaissance. Suddenly, where there was pure stasis, the place is exploding. For example, the twelfth century—suddenly Europe was blazing with intelligence and power and insight, fresh authority, all the things that had been missing for centuries. I recognized in *Augie March* a breakthrough—namely, the wiping out of the negative personality that had created and inhabited his earlier work. Some critics like those novels, but in my opinion they're shit. They're well written, and if you look closely you can see a genius coming, but the genius is absolutely not there—he is in a straightjacket. In *Augie* he's there.

My plans for the Bradstreet poem had got very ambitious by that time. I no longer had any idea of a fifty-line poem. That was five years before. My idea was now very ambitious. The Bradstreet poem is just as ambitious as *The Dream Songs*. Saul once said to me that it is the equivalent of a five-hundred-page psychological novel. That is exactly my opinion, also—in spite of the fact that it is short, the poem is highly concentrated. So I was exhilarated. One of my pals had made a major attempt. You know, these things don't happen very often. Most even very fine artists don't try to put up the Parthenon, you know, and most of those who do turn out to be imposters. Merely grandiose, like Benjamin Haydon, Keats's friend. A very good, very minor painter who thought he was Michelangelo, then killed himself. It's hard to take the risk of joining that terrible, frightful company. Contemptible, pathetic, they move your heart but they draw you to scorn. Saul had decided to make a big attempt, so my idea of my poem improved.

And the third thing was that I had recently reread, for the first time in many years, *Anna Karenina*, which I think is the best portrait of a woman in world literature. You just can't mention any other attempt at a woman, except perhaps *Madame Bovary*. I recently reread it for a seminar I am giving, and I have a very high regard for it. It's a beauty. It deserves its reputation, which is saying a lot. But *Anna Karenina* is even greater. The only woman in American literature is Hester Prynne, and she is very good. I have great respect for her and the book, but *Mistress Bradstreet* is much more ambitious. It is very unlikely that it is better, but it attempts more.[3] So again my notion of my poem expanded. The fourth thing that got me going was this. I had been in group therapy. The analyst who had been treating me individually for several years set up a group. There were two lawyers, a chemist, an alcoholic housewife, a psychiatric social worker, and me. I tried to run the group, of course, and they all killed me. I would leave, and come back, and so on, but it was a shattering business—I mean emotionally shattering—much more so than individual therapy had been. That had been kind of cozy. Well, I got fed up and left the group forever, and this left me blazing with hostility and feelings of gigantism, defeated gigantism. So these four things—the deep wound of Eileen's tragic operation, Saul's wonderful daring, Tolstoy's commanding achievement, and the emotional shock of my experience with the group—swung me into action, and suddenly I was on fire every second.

Interviewer: What was your method of composition on that poem? You must have worked very hard to finish it in two months.

Berryman: I started out writing three stanzas a day, but that was too much, so I developed a more orderly method. I got one of those things that have a piece of glassine over a piece of paper, and you can put something in between and see it but not touch it. I would draft my stanza and put it in there. Then I would sit and study it. I would make notes, but I wouldn't touch the manuscript until I thought I was in business—usually not for hours. Then I'd take it out, make the corrections, pull it back in, and study it some more. When I was finally satisfied, I'd take it out and type it. At that point I was done—I never touched any stanza afterward. I limited myself to one a day. If I finished at eleven in the morning, I still did not look at the stanza until the next morning. I had a terrible time filling the hours—whiskey was helpful, but it was hard.

Interviewer: Do you consider your latest book, *Love & Fame*, a long poem?

Berryman: *Love & Fame* is very shapely and thematically unified, and in that it resembles a long poem. But it is absolutely and utterly not a long poem at all; it's a collection of lyrics. The last eleven all happen to be prayers, but even there each poem is on its own. This is even more true in the earlier sections. It is unified through style and because most of the poems are autobiographical, based on the historical personality of the poet. By historical I mean existing in time and space, occupying quanta.

Interviewer: How does the composition of *Love & Fame* compare with that of your earlier work? Did you write these poems more quickly than the long poems?

Berryman: The composition was like that of the Bradstreet poem, and to some extent like that of the Dream Songs, many of which were also written in volcanic bursts. Not all. I worked daily over a period of years, but sometimes I would write fifty in a burst and then not write any for months. The Bradstreet poem as I say, took two months. *Love & Fame* took about three months.

Interviewer: What made you turn your back to the short form after having written two long poems?

Berryman: When I finished *The Dream Songs*, two years ago, I was very tired. I didn't know whether I would ever write any more poems. As I told you, it took me two years to get over the Bradstreet poems before I started the Dream Songs. Your idea of yourself and your relation to your art has a great deal to do with what actually happens. What happened in this case was something that contradicted my ideas, as follows. I saw myself only as an epic poet. The idea of writing any more short poems hadn't been in my mind for many years. The question after *The Dream Songs* was whether I would ever again attempt a long poem, and I thought it improbably, so I didn't expect to write any more verse.

But suddenly one day last winter I wrote down a line "I fell in love with a girl." I looked at it, and I couldn't find anything wrong with it. I thought, "God damn it, that is a *fact*." I felt, as a friend of mine says: "I feel comfortable with that." And I looked at it until I thought of a second line, and then a third line, and then a fourth line, and that was a stanza. Un-rhymed. And the more I looked at it, the better I liked it, so I wrote a second stanza. And then I wrote some more stanzas, and you know what? I had a lyric poem, and a very good one. I didn't know I had it in me! Well, the next day I knocked out a stanza, changed various lines, this and that, but pretty soon it looked classical. As classical as one of the *Rubáiyát* poems—without the necessities of rhyme and meter, but with its own necessities. I thought it was as good as any of my early poems, and some of them are quite good; most of them are not, but some are. Moreover, it didn't resemble any verse I had ever written in my entire life, and moreover the subject was entirely new, solely and simply myself. Nothing else. A subject on which I am an expert. Nobody can contradict me.[4] I believe strongly in the authority of learning. The reason Milton is the greatest English poet except for Shakespeare is because of the authority of his learning. I am a scholar in certain fields, but the subject on which I am a real authority is me, so I wiped out all the disguises and went to work. In about five or six weeks I had what was obviously a book called *Love & Fame*.

I had forty-two poems and was ready to print them, but they were so weird, so unlike all my previous work, that I was a little worried. I had encouragement from one or two friends, but still I didn't know what to do. I had previously sent the first poem to Arthur Crook at the *Times Literary Supplement*. He was delighted with it and sent me proof. I in turn was delighted that he liked the poem, so I corrected the proof and sent him five more—I didn't want the poem to appear alone. So he printed the six, which made up a whole page—very nice typographically—and this was further encouragement. But still I wasn't sure. Meanwhile, I was in hospital. I was a nervous wreck. I had lost nineteen pounds in five weeks and had been drinking heavily—a quart a day. So I had my publisher in New York, Giroux, Xerox a dozen copies, which I sent out to friends of mine around the country for opinions. It is a weird thing to do—I've never heard of anybody else doing it—but I did it, looking for reassurance, confirmation, wanting criticism and so on, and I got some very good criticism. Dick Wilbur took "Shirley & Auden," one of the most important lyrics in Part I—some of the poems are quite slight and others are very ambitious—and gave it hell. And I agreed—I adopted almost every suggestion.

I also got some confirmation and reassurance, but there were other opinions as well. Edmund Wilson, for whose opinion I have a high regard, found the book hopeless. He said there were some fine lines and striking passages. How do you like that? It is like saying to a beautiful woman, "I like your left small toenail that's very nice indeed," while she's standing there stark naked looking like Venus. I was deeply hurt by that letter. And then other responses were very strange. Mark Van Doren, my teacher, an old, old friend and a wonderful judge of poetry, also wrote. I forget exactly what he said, but he was very heavy on it. He said things like "original," and "will be influential," and "will be popular," and so on, but also "will be feared and hated." What a surprising letter! It took me days to get used to it, and it took me days even to see what he meant. But now I see what he means. Some of the poems are threatening, very threatening to some readers, no doubt about it. Just as some people find me threatening—to be in a room with me drives them crazy. And then there is a good deal of obscenity in the poems, too. And there is a grave piety in the last poems, which is going to trouble a lot of people. You know, the country is full of atheists, and they really are going to find themselves threatened by those poems. The *Saturday Review* printed five of them, and I had a lot of mail about them—again expressing a wide variety of opinion. Some people were just purely grateful for my having told them how to put what they'd felt for years. Then there are others who detest them—they don't call them insincere, but they just can't believe it.

Interviewer: There has always been a religious element in your poems, but why did you turn so directly to religious subject matter in these poems?

Berryman: They are the result of a religious conversion which took place on my second Tuesday in treatment here last spring. I lost my faith several years ago, but I came back—by force, by necessity, because of a rescue action—into the notion of a God who, at certain moments, definitely and personally intervenes in individual lives, one of which is mine. The poems grow out of that sense, which not all Christians share.

Interviewer: Could you say something more about this rescue action? Just what happened?

Berryman: Yes. This happened during the strike which hit campus last May, after the Cambodian invasion and the events at Kent State. I was teaching a large class—seventy-five students—Tuesday and Thursday afternoons, commuting from the hospital, and I was supposed to lecture on the Fourth Gospel. My kids were in a state of crisis—only twenty-five had shown up the previous Thursday, campus was in chaos, there were no guidelines from the administration—and besides lecturing, I felt I had to calm them, tell them what to do. The whole thing would have taken no more than two hours—taxi over, lecture, taxi back. I had been given permission to go by my psychiatrist. But at the beginning of group therapy that morning at ten, my counselor, who is an Episcopalian priest, told me that he had talked with my psychiatrist, and that the permission to leave had been rescinded. Well, I was shocked and defiant.

I said, "You and Dr. So and So have no authority over me. I will call a cab and go over and teach my class. My students need me."

He made various remarks, such as "You're shaking."

I replied, "I don't shake when I lecture."

He said, "Well, you can't walk and we are afraid you will fall down."

I said, "I can walk," and I could. You see I had had physical permission from my physician the day before.

Then the whole group hit me, including a high official of the university, who was also in treatment here. I appealed to him, and even he advised me to submit. Well, it went on for almost two hours, and at last I submitted—at around eleven-thirty. Then I was in real despair. I couldn't just ring up the secretary and have her dismiss my class—it would be grotesque. Here it was, eleven-thirty, and class met at one-fifteen. I didn't even know if I could get my chairman on the phone to find somebody to meet them. And even if I could, who could he have found that would have been qualified? We have no divinity school here. Well, all kinds of consolations and suggestions came from the group, and suddenly my counselor said, "Well, I'm trained in divinity. I'll give your lecture for you."

And I said, "You're kidding!" He and I had some very sharp exchanges. I called him sarcastic, arrogant, tyrannical, incompetent, theatrical, judgmental, and so on.

He said, "Yes, I'll teach it if I have to teach it in Greek!"

I said, "I can't believe it. Are you serious?"

He said, "Yes, I'm serious."

And I said, "I could kiss you."

He said, "Do." There was only one man between us, so I leaned over and we embraced. Then I briefed him and gave him my notes, and he went over and gave the lecture. Well, when I thought it over in the afternoon, I suddenly recalled what has been for many years one of my favorite conceptions. I got it from Augustine and Pascal. It's found in many other people too, but especially in those heroes of mine. Namely, the idea of a God of rescue. He saves men from their situations, off and on during life's pilgrimage, and in the end. I completely bought it, and that's been my position ever since.

Interviewer: What about the role of religion in your earlier works? I remember that when the *Sonnets* came out, one critic, writing in the *New York Review of Books*, spoke of "the absence of thematic substance" in your poems generally. Another critic, writing in the *Minnesota Review*, picked this up and disagreed with it, pointing out what he felt was a firm religious basis in the sonnets—the question of guilt and atonement, etc. What would you say about the role of religion generally in your poetry?

Berryman: It's awfully hard for me to judge. I had a strict Catholic training. I went to a Catholic school and I adored my priest, Father Boniface. I began serving Mass under him at the age of five and I used to serve six days a week. Often there would be nobody in the church except him and me. Then all that went to pieces at my father's death, when I was twelve. Later, I went to a High Church Episcopalian school in Connecticut, called South Kent, and I was very fond of the chaplain there. His name was Father Kemmis, and, although I didn't feel about him as I had about Father Boniface as a child, I still felt very keen, and was a rapt Episcopalian for several years. Then, when I went to Columbia, all that sort of dropped out. I never lost the sense of God in the two roles of creator and sustainer—of the mind of man and all its operations, as a source of inspiration to great scientists, great artists, saints, great statesmen. But my experience last spring gave me a third sense, a sense of a God of rescue, and I've been operating with that since. Now the point is, I have been interested not only in religion but in theology all my life. I don't know how much these personal beliefs, together with the interest in theology and the history of the church, enter into particular works up to those addresses to the Lord in *Love & Fame*. I really think it is up to others—critics, scholars—to answer your question.

By the way, those addresses to the Lord are not Christian poems. I am deeply interested in Christ, but I never pray to him.[5] I don't know whether he is in any special sense the son of God, and I think it is quite impossible to know.[6] He certainly was the most remarkable *man* who ever lived. But I don't consider myself a Christian. I do consider myself a Catholic, but I'd just as soon go to an Episcopalian church as a Catholic church. I do go to mass every Sunday.

Interviewer: Let's turn to new directions. What has happened to the poem about heaven set in China, titled "Scholars at the Orchid Pavilion," which you were working on a couple of years ago? Are you still working on that?

Berryman: I intended that to be a rather long poem. As with the Bradstreet poem, I invented the stanza—it's a very beautiful, sort of hovering, seven-line stanza, unrhymed—and wrote the first stanza and stuck. I then accumulated notes on Chinese art history in most of the major forms. Chinese art is much more complicated than ours—they have many forms. I have a whole library on Chinese art and early Chinese philosophy, Chinese history. Chinese folk tales, ghost stories, all kinds of Chinese stuff. I even tried to learn classical Chinese one time, but I decided after a few days that it was not for me.

Anyway, I finally decided that I was nowhere, that all this accumulation of knowledge was fascinating and valuable to me, but that I was personally not destined to write a Chinese epic. So at that point I felt fine, and I wrote a second stanza, and a third stanza, and a fourth stanza. They're not as good as the first stanza, but they are all pretty good. And then I put some asterisk and that's what I'll publish sooner or later. I may say, "Scholars at the Orchid Pavilion: A Fragment."

Interviewer: Where do you go from here?

Berryman: I have written another book of poetry, called *Delusions.* It won't be out for some time yet, however. We're doing a volume of my prose, probably spring of fall of '72. After that—I am very much interested in the question, or will be when I get my breath back from the composition of the last nine months. I've written over a hundred poems in the last six months. I'm a complete wreck. I'm hopelessly underweight, and the despair of about four competent doctors. When I get my breath back—it may be next spring—maybe I'll begin to think. I don't know whether I'll ever write any more verse at all. The main question is whether I will ever again undertake a long poem, and I just can form no idea.

There are certain subjects that have interested me for a long time, but nothing commanding and obsessive, as both the Bradstreet poem and Dream Songs were. What is involved in the composition of a long poem, at least by my experience, is five to ten years. I don't know how long I'll live. Probably I wouldn't be able to begin it for—well, it took me two years to get over the Bradstreet poem. I finished *The Dream Songs* only two years ago, and I've written two more books since, besides a lot of other literary work. I've been working on a play, an anthology, and revising the volume of my criticism. I probably wouldn't get to it for at least three to five years. That makes me getting on to sixty. Taking on a new long poem at the age of sixty is really something. I have no idea whether I would still have the vigor and ambition, need, that sort of thing, to do it.

I have a tiny little secret hope that, after a decent period of silence and prose, I will find myself in some almost impossible life situation and will respond to this with outcries of rage, rage and love, such as the world has never heard before. Like Yeats's great outburst at the end of his life. This comes out of a feeling that endowment is a very small part of achievement. I would rate it about 15 or 20 percent. Then you have historical luck, personal luck, health, things like that, then you have hard work, sweat. And you have ambition. The incredible difference between the achievement of A and the achievement of B is that B *wanted* it, so he made all kinds of sacrifices. A could have had it, but he didn't give a damn. The idea that everybody wants to be president of the United States or have a million dollars is simply not the case. Most people want to go down to the corner and have a glass of beer. They're very happy. In *Henderson the Rain King*, the hero keeps on saying, "I want. I want." Well, I'm that kind of character. I don't know whether that is exhausted in me or not, I can't tell.

But what I was going on to say is that I do strongly feel that among the greatest pieces of luck for high achievement is ordeal. Certain great artists can make out without it, Titian and others, but mostly you need ordeal. My idea is this: the artist is extremely lucky who is presented with the worst possible ordeal which will not actually kill him. At that point, he's in business. Beethoven's deafness, Goya's deafness, Milton's blindness, that kind of thing. And I think that what happens in my poetic work in the future will probably largely depend not on my sitting calmly on my ass as I think, "Hmm, hmm, a long poem again? Hmm," but on being knocked in the face, and thrown flat, and given cancer, and all kinds of other things short of senile dementia. At that point, I'm out, but short of that, I don't know. I hope to be nearly crucified.

Interviewer: You're not knocking on wood.

Berryman: I'm scared, but I'm willing. I'm sure this is a preposterous attitude, but I'm not ashamed of it.

Notes

1. Oliver St. John Gogarty, poet, author, otolaryngologist, politician, athlete, and the model for Buck Mulligan in James Joyce's *Ulysses*.

2. Get the delusion (JB, March 1971).

3. Delusion (JB, March 1971).

4. Delusion (JB, March 1971).

5. Situation altered, see "Ecce Homo," poem to be published in the *New Yorker* (JB, March 1971).

6. Delusion (JB, March 1971).

A Truly Gentle Man Tightens and Paces: An Interview with John Berryman

Martin Berg / 1971

From *Minnesota Daily Literary Supplement*, January 20, 1971, 9, 10, 14, 15, 17. Reprinted by permission.

[In his interview with Martin Berg, which appeared in a weekly literary supplement included with the Wednesday edition of the *Minnesota Daily Literary Supplement*, Berryman primarily discusses *Love & Fame*, in particular its mixed reception, and, pointedly, his next work, yet another departure. By now, Berryman has joined Alcoholics Anonymous and is in and out of recovery.—Ed.]

[Reproduces lines 20–25 of Berryman's "Antithesis"; see *Collected Poems 1937–1971*, p. 202]

Thirty-three Arthur Avenue is a box-like, two-story house with white asbestos siding and black trim. In the living room, the complete or collected works of major poets line the walls. Other books fill the coffee table and scatter onto the floor.

Among the books and pictures is occasional evidence of Mr. Berryman's eight-year-old daughter, Martha. During the interview, lively Martha, a white miniature of her mother, sat reading, or at one point, obediently followed her father's instruction for a stomach ache cure.

The rocking-chair is dark blue. With a cigarette in one hand and a ginger ale in the other, Mr. Berryman sat there, and talked.

"You'll find me very agreeable Mr. Berg, because I've just had a very fine letter from my old friend Robert Lowell. The last section of my new book is a series of prayers; there are eleven of them. He thinks they're all one poem, which is wrong, and says that it is one of the great poems of the age. I hope he's right. I'm feeling quite peaceful.

"My friend Edmund Wilson writes his own interviews. He asks himself pointed questions, for example, 'What do you consider your greatest contribution?' And then he answers the questions at great length and with absolute relish. He's terribly resistant. More resistant than I am. I used to be very hard to interview, but lately, I've relaxed."

Martin Berg: Do you consider *Love & Fame* a continuation of what you were doing in the Dream Songs?

John Berryman: Well, just some relaxation.

It's the next business. As for continuation, I don't know. The poem came to an end. The dancer song and Henry's visit to his father's grave and the song about his daughter, that's the end. I've written some more since. In the next edition, I'm going to kill some of the songs and replace them. But this new work is entirely different. The poet speaks in his own person; they're not dramatic, they're lyric.

Berg: Auden has recently said that major poets are the ones who show continual improvement. How do you feel about that?

Berryman: These reformations of material and address and technique are only found in ambitious writers. That is correct. Most poets are not effective for very long. But in some poets, for example de la Mare, who is a minor poet, a very fine one, there is really no change or improvement from beginning to end. Auden did a selection of de la Mare's work which I am going through right now. It seems to me astonishing. Also, Frost at all periods was capable of astonishing poems. Of course, Frost wrote four or five different kinds of poems, de la Mare only wrote one.

Berg: What do you think of Lawrance Thompson's biography of Frost?[1]

Berryman: I haven't seen it.

According to Mrs. [Helen] Vendler, it's absolute horse shit. It's honest, but it has the honesty of a guinea pig. No guinea pig has ever told a lie. But of course he's never told the truth either. It simply doesn't come out.

I used to know Thompson at Princeton. He's a nice guy. But, he knows nothing about poetry and he knows nothing about life. You would have to be familiar with both topics to write about Frost.

Frost was a cross-grained, unbelievable grandiose and cruel, a tyrannical, and in general, an awful man. He made life absolute hell for everyone around him for fifty years. The problem with Frost is how work of great moral depth and passion, beauty, came out in a life so inappropriate.

Incidentally, Frost was the most incredible talker I've ever heard. Thompson talked to Frost off and on for many years. Or rather Frost talked to him. Nobody ever talked to Frost. Frost talked to them, a monologist.

But apparently, Thompson didn't write any of this down. So the books don't have Frost's conversation in them. That's a very great fault. Anybody who listened to Frost for an hour could write, I could write six pages. Frost told stories so very well that you remembered them almost verbatim.

Berg: What do you think about the critical reaction to your books?

Berryman: I don't pay as much attention to it as you might think. First, there's a lot of built in indifference. I never read reviews of any of my books until I was about forty years old. Allen Tate, for instance, asked me what I thought of some review one time at Princeton. And I said I hadn't read it; I didn't read reviews. He didn't really believe me, it's so unusual. I don't take the slightest credit for it, it just happens to be there.

I've written hundreds of book reviews myself, and read reviews of books by friends of mine a lot. There's very seldom anything in them that you get anything out of.

You might get hurt, if somebody kicks you in the face. Or you might be pleased if somebody says you're just slightly better than Sophocles. But on the whole there isn't much in it. You have to consider the source of the remarks. The three best reviewers of poetry at the moment are all English.

Conrad said to somebody once that he didn't read reviews, he measured them. The only review of *Love & Fame* that has appeared was before the book was published. A man named [Hayden] Carruth reviewed it for *The Nation*. And they printed it, which they shouldn't have done; my publisher protested.

It's six columns of unadulterated hostility. He's hated my work for many years, and now he figures he's got me. He's playing Berne's game called "now I've got you, you son of a bitch." Do you know that game? Nice little game.[2]

I could feel bad about that. But first, I haven't even got the slightest respect for Carruth, and second, what he's trying to do is knock me off a pedestal he himself created. He accused me of being no better than Lowell, Roethke, Miss Bishop, Randall Jarrell, Delmore Schwartz, all my old friends. Who cares. It's pleasant to be compared to them. As I said in a bitter letter to the editor, which to my surprise, they printed verbatim. I was very gentle with him. But I did force him to bring the patibulum and the cross bar to the upright and put it up. Then, I nailed him down on it, waited until he died, took him down, put him in the grave, filled the grave, and placed a nosegay on it.

So, I pay attention to some reviews.

Berg: Are you working on any new books?

Berryman: My next book is finished, more or less. I've been writing two or three poems a week for many months now. I don't know, I have four or five unfinished books now. I don't know what I'll be doing; if I keep on writing lyric poems, that's all I'll be doing. I'm going to run out sooner or later.

I wrote a poem yesterday and a poem today. Please, this is very unnatural; that's 365 poems a year.

In the ordinary way, if there is any ordinary way, maybe you write a poem a month. That's twelve poems a year, twenty-five poems in two years; publish a book. I've never heard of such a person, but it sounds reasonable. Anyway, one a day would put me right in my grave. Or back in the hospital.

Berg: Is the new book you spoke of similar to *Love & Fame*?

Berryman: The work in *Love & Fame* is not all the same by any means; there are very great differences. Also, some of the poems are awful beyond description, and are being killed in the second edition and in the British edition. I killed various poems in galleys, but not enough.

Berg: Which parts of *Love & Fame* do you like best?

Berryman: The third and fourth parts. The second half of the book is much better than the first half. The opening poem is quite good. The third poem is pretty good, though too long. Then there's hardly anything of interest for a long while. The third part is extremely various. Several of the political poems are ghastly. There's a thing called "Death Ballad." Which is good.

The only two rhymed poems in the book are "Death Ballad" and "Home Ballad." They're very different, one from another. I'm using rhyme now again. There's almost no rhyme in *Love & Fame*.

The poems at the end, I take a high view of at the moment because I published five of them in the *Saturday Review* and had a great deal of mail, and then this letter from Lowell that I told you about came this morning. He thinks, I don't want to quote him wrong, "Anyway, it's one of the great poems of the age. A puzzle and triumph for anyone who wants to write a personal devotional poem. Along with your posthumous poems, in my mind the crown of your work."

Lowell has from the beginning taken a very, very high view of the fourth book of *The Dream Songs*. And two of them certainly are beauties. That puts them above the Bradstreet poem, of which Lowell also thinks very highly. In print. I pay more attention to what people say in print than what they say across the cocktail table.

Berg: How do you decide when another book is ready for publication?

Berryman: I held off a long time on the first volume of the Dream Songs. Mostly, it's obvious when something is more or less done. With regard to short poems, when you have sixty or a hundred pages or so, if it seems to make a kind of design.

But I didn't write any short poems for twenty-two years until last spring one day I wrote the poem called "Her & It." It was originally called "Love & Fame" until I transferred the title to the whole book. I wrote that down one morning. I didn't see myself as a writer of short poems at all.

So the problem is really the long poems. And with a long poem, you publish it either when you can't stand it anymore, as with the Dream Songs, or when you don't feel you can improve it, as with the Bradstreet poem.

The Bradstreet poem is completely professional. It took me five years. I invented the stanza and wrote the first one on the 22nd of March 1948, and I changed the last word in the last stanza exactly five years later, on the 22nd of March 1953. A reading had already been arranged at Princeton, a public reading, and publication in *Partisan*. The poem was very well known long before it was finished. The money from that took me abroad for six months. Which didn't recover me from the poem. It took me two years. But I didn't blow my brains out either.

Berg: Do you have any readings planned?

Berryman: I was giving a tour this winter, a reading tour. But I gave a reading one night in Northfield, and then I gave four readings on four nights at four colleges in Wisconsin. And I was supposed to give five more. But I decided I was tired of exposing the secrets of my soul to all these strangers. So, I rang up all the people who arranged the damn tour and conned me into it. And said no.

Berg: What do you think of all the attention your poetry has brought you?

Berryman: It's a bore, a bore.

It ought to be pleasant, but frankly, it isn't.

Interviews are no great problem because you don't feel put in the position of an entertainer. But often you are. I gave a reading at Vassar last winter. They put me up in some University building in a suite of rooms. Then a faculty member turned up at the door with a lot of girls. And he said they wanted to meet me. I said sure.

So, they all trooped into my room, fifteen or twenty of them, mostly pretty, weirdly dressed. And draped themselves across the bed, the chairs, the floor, and the ceiling, and the walls. And looked at me. Well, what can you do? I picked out two nearby, pretty, and talked to them, found out their names, invited questions, and so on. It lasted half, three-quarters of an hour.

Exhausting, it's exhausting. Then the same thing happened later on down the line. Does that strike you as agreeable?

That's called lionization and there are people who get a charge out of it. And there are people who don't need that kind of gratification. It counts. I don't happen to need it, and I don't get a charge out of it any more. Maybe I used to.

Berg: Do you have any advice for young poets?

Berryman: Quit, quit.

They ought to write sonnets.

The only thing I have in common with Ezra Pound is that he told me once that he wrote a hundred sonnets. He never printed any of them. There the resemblance ends; I printed mine. I once wrote 115. I didn't print them for twenty years, but that was not for literary reasons. He wrote his when he was young; I wrote mine when I was fully developed.

I'll give you high authority here. Coleridge liked Tennyson's first book, the *Two Brothers*. He said to one of his friends, Coleridge then an old man, 'young Alfred Tennyson, pretty good.' Coleridge said he ought to write nothing but sonnets for two years, then resume his career. So the idea is not original. That's 150 years ago. Same advice.

Some of the best kind of writing is really transparent; you don't notice that you are reading an article. I'll show you what I mean. This is the most marvelous Madonna I have ever seen. And you get no impression of viewing art.

Berg: Can you give an example from literature that has this transparency?

Berryman: The *Odyssey*, the *Paradiso*. Mostly works of late age. Beethoven's late quartets, where the appearance of art disappears, everything becomes unbelievably simple. The artist just says what he thinks, or says how he feels. For example, instead of making a long speech, he says "I hurt," or he says to the reader, "are you hurting?"

Take a line from *The Tempest*. "Turfy mountains where live nibbling sheep." Now that is absolutely magnificent, but incredibly simple. The great power is done by placing. The elements are simple. And the effect is simple. The art comes just in placing, pure syntax.

Admittedly, "turfy" is good, and "nibbling" is good, and it's nicely held together. That's what happens, turf is what you nibble, if you're a sheep. But, it really is so powerful because "live" is so low keyed. You expect something bigger. The height at the front of the line, and another height at the end of the line, so you want something way low-keyed down the middle.

Berg: Can you think of any twentieth-century works that exhibit this transparency?

Berryman: *Four Quartets* by Eliot. At a certain point it occurs to him to say, "Humility is endless." How's that. In verse.

Berg: How did you happen to become a poet?

Berryman: After I got through the usual business of wanting to be a priest, an astronomer, and an archaeologist, those were the three main ones, I decided to be a writer. This was perhaps at the age of ten. Then I did in fact write a novel, a science fiction novel, when I was twelve. I didn't finish it. It was about a trip to Neptune, and the name of a Neptunian was Eeloro-a'ala. That's all I can remember about it. It's lost, thank God.

Then I went through a completely blank four years at a preparatory school in Connecticut and only got going again at Columbia. There, by pure accident, the people on the *Columbia Review*, the literary magazine at Columbia, asked me to review a new book of poems by one of my teachers, Mark Van Doren. It was called *A Winter Diary*, and it was the first book of poems I had ever read. And I felt nothing but contempt for poetry because of the way it had been taught to me at school. I had never read a passage of poetry that seems to have the slightest interest.

So I was amazed by this book, I thought it was magnificent. And wrote a review of it. Then I read other books by him. And then, I began to read like a maniac. In the course of ten months, I made my way through English and American poetry. A young man can read eighteen hours a day.

I met Allen Tate in the summer of '35. I had begun to write verse already. My first two poems were a free-verse poem which had the word "grey" in it, and a villanelle in which one of the rhyme words was "sere." I never use the word "grey" anymore, and I wouldn't be caught dead with the word "sere." Next I wrote four sonnets, and then I began to write poems: I wrote a whole book. All very bad. Some of those I published in the *Columbia Review*, and they were printed in the *Columbia Anthology*.

Then a fairly good, fairly short poem on E. A. Robinson ["Note on E.A. Robinson"], who had recently died. It was taken by *The Nation*. At this time I realized I was not up to scratch. So when I went abroad in the fall of '38, I decided not to publish anything for two years. By publish, I mean not send out any for publication. It was clear to me now that I could print things in magazines if I wanted to, but I didn't want to. I was devoted to my poems as I wrote them, one after another, but I also knew that they were no good. A complete double-think on the subject. So I protected myself: I destroyed them.

Until I had a bunch of stuff. Robert Penn Warren and Cleanth Brooks were then running the *Southern Review*, the best magazine in the country, and Warren was very much interested in my work. He had seen a long poem called "Ritual at Arlington," which he didn't publish, but which almost won a big prize they had set out. And he pushed for stuff. I waited until I had a batch of about twenty, and I sent some to him and some to Eliot for the *Criterion*, therefore he should have taken some of them. They were no good, but they were better than the stuff he was printing. But Warren published four. That was in '38 when I came back to New York. I was writing all the time by then.

Berg: Of what use do you think art is in the moral world?

Berryman: I don't know.

I really don't know.

It is absolutely certain that you can learn a great deal about life from the novels of Jane Austen. Or from the later novels of George Eliot, say *Middlemarch*. Or from the plays of Shakespeare; that's an example at the highest level. It's very clear that the conduct of someone who has really read the whole *Commedia* is likely to be altered.

At a much lesser level, take a poem like "Death of a Son" by Jon Silkin. This poem is now about fifteen years old. Silkin was quite young when he wrote it—I suppose now he must be forty. He had a son who was mentally defective. And lived for a year or so, and died. I don't know how the poem would affect conduct, but your feelings about this very important topic, death, I think are likely to be refined, and sort of exploded, by that poem if you read it.

It depends on what you take the end of life to be; whether it issues in conduct or feelings. Those two are very different areas.

Notes

1. *Robert Frost: The Early Years, 1874–1915* (New York: Holt, Rinehart and Winston, 1966) and *Robert Frost: The Years of Triumph, 1915–1938* (New York: Henry Holt & Company, 1970).

2. Eric Berne (May 10, 1910–July 15, 1970) was a Canadian psychiatrist who developed the theory of transactional analysis, which applied game theory to the field of psychiatry. Berne believed that, contrary to Freud's talk therapy, greater insight into a patient's psychology could be gleaned by instead studying their social interactions.

Who Killed Henry Pussy-cat? I Did, Says John Berryman with Love and a Poem and for Freedom

Joseph Haas / 1971

From *Chicago Daily News*, February 6, 1971, 4–5

[In late January 1971, Berryman delivered the William Vaughn Moody lecture at the University of Chicago, where his friend Saul Bellow was a professor for the Committee on Social Thought. Bellow discusses the lecture in his foreword to Berryman's unfinished novel *Recovery*:

> He had arrived during a sub-zero wave . . . High-shouldered in his thin coat and big Homburg, bearded, he coughed up phlegm. He looked decayed. He had been drinking and the reading was a disaster. His Princeton mutter, once an affectation, had become a vice. People strained to hear a word. Except when, following some arbitrary system of dynamics, he shouted loudly, we could hear nothing. We left a disappointed, bewildered, angry audience. Dignified, he entered a waiting car, sat down, and vomited. He passed out in his room at the Quadrangle Club and slept through the faculty party given in his honor. But in the morning he was full of innocent cheer. He was chirping. It had been a great evening. He recalled an immense success. His cab came, we hugged each other, and he was off for the airport under a frozen sun. (Berryman 1973, xiv, quoted in Haffenden 1982, 393)]

[Reproduces lines 1–6 of "Dream Song 16": see *The Dream Songs*, p. 18]

Henry Pussy-cat came to town and the visit was delightening. And yet, huffy Henry, unappeasable Henry, had the audacity to deny (eyes in an outrageous twinkle as if to say, Who knows if and when I mean what I say?) that he was, indeed, Henry Pussy-cat.

"I'm not Henry! How could I be, for Christ's sake?" poet John Berryman blares with the brass section of his sometimes-orchestrated voice. Then, calling on the woodwinds, he purrs, "How could he be me? I have a Social Security number, or I would have said so.

"I located him here and there, but I left out all kinds of fascinating places where I've been. So how could he be me? He's fiction! I made him up!"

Berryman ends this passage with a drum roll . . . and yet, it's not convincing. The resemblances between fictional Henry and living Berryman are so real that, for years to come, PhD candidates will be shuttling between their lines and lives, using one to illuminate the other.

Of course, Berryman is Henry Pussy-cat, huffy Henry, unappeasable Henry, Henry Hankovitch and Henry Donnybrook, just as he is Mr. Bones and Dr. Bones and Bones—and I, and you, and he. Berryman is every voice in a phenomenal production of poetry that has the critics debating today over which one, Berryman or Robert Lowell, is America's finest living poet.

For thirteen years, Berryman as Henry wrestled with their life and times and, Laocoön-like, with one another, and it was moot which of them was the serpent, and which would survive. The result was *77 Dream Songs* in 1964 and the concluding 308 songs, *His Toy, His Dream, His Rest*, in 1968, before Berryman rested, and Henry was laid to rest. (Or was he? At six-to-five, you can bet either way.)

Berryman's earlier work earned him acclaim and probably would have assured his reputation. There were his first volume of poetry, *The Dispossessed*, in 1948, and a biography, *Stephen Crane*, in 1950, and his first long poem, *Homage to Mistress Bradstreet*, in 1956. And now, there is a new volume of poems, *Love & Fame*.

But *The Dream Songs*, all 385 of them (so far) collected in one volume in 1969 by Berryman's publishers, Farrar, Straus & Giroux, lifted him to that plateau with Lowell. It simply knocked all of the poets and critics on their adjectives in attempts to find phrases to describe why this poetry was so great and, suddenly, Berryman was a celebrity, profiled in depth in national magazines, sought after on the campuses, and honored with every major literary prize and fellowship (the Pulitzer, the National Book Award, the Guggenheim, the Bollingen, the Academy of American Poets fellowship, etc., etc.) we can bestow upon our poets.

You cannot read *The Dream Songs* without recognizing that greatness. And it derives partly from the simple fact, dispute it as whimsically as he will, that Berryman is a unique everyman, and he is Henry. And so we have, in this poetic cycle, something very little poetry gives us: the full-bodied portrait of a hot-blooded, gloriously human, irascible, brilliant, complex, and simple man, so vital and yet brooding intensely upon his mortality, opinionated and indecisive, battling his enemies and mourning lost friends, loving and hating in Rabelaisian measure, gently and kindly, harsh and cruel, and a patriot in that misused word's best sense.

The poetry is conceived in a form and rhetoric that stretches, or compresses, our language to new limits of loveliness and meaning and cadence. In fact, Berryman handles English as if everything that was written before him was merely ore mined for his use, to shape as pleased him, to wield as no one had done before. There is a freshness to it.

Of the several people I have met who know Berryman, each has some wild tale to tell: of his boozing, his wenching, his unpredictability. And, time after time, in *The Dream Songs* and his new *Love & Fame*, he rails against the critics and the journalists who besiege him with pencils poised over tablets, tape recorders at the ready. So, I confess, I approached the opportunity to talk to John Berryman with some uneasiness.

If first impressions were always trustworthy, I would have spun on hell and left soon after I entered the dimly lit room in the Quadrangle Club at the University of Chicago where Berryman was staying. And it would have been a terrible mistake.

An attractive young woman answers the door. The poet, his once bushy, grizzled beard trimmed neatly now to van dyke proportions, lolls in an easy chair, his blue eyes hazy, his casual clothing and his brown hair disheveled, a half-full whisky bottle on the dressing table, a water glass in one hand with a deep amber drink in it and the first of a continuous chain of cigarettes in the other.

"What's the point of this, this interview?" he asks, brusquely, in a thick voice, and for the first few minutes, much of what he says is almost unintelligible. But then, he's smiling and, swiftly, he seems to recover full alertness to talk freely about his poetry.

I shall not get a chance to talk about his early life, however. Before we can get into that, he will reach across, turn off the tape recorder, and say "Let's knock this off"—not in an unfriendly way, but as if he's just weary of the formalities of question-and-answer. And so, for another hour, we shall just drink and chat, as he makes me feel like an old friend—no, a new one—and not just another journalist.

So I can write only this much about his life. He was born fifty-six years ago in McAlester, Oklahoma, the eldest of two sons of a banker and a former teacher. Both of his parents had emigrated from the East and they were drawn together, he has said, "because they were the only two people for miles around who could read."

Later the family moved to Florida where, when Berryman was twelve, his father shot and killed himself one morning outside his elder son's bedroom window. As several of Berryman's poems attest, this is a trauma from which he has never fully recovered and that he has not entirely assimilated.

He did not get interested in poetry until he became a student of Mark Van Doren at Columbia University when, he was told, he learned there could be more to it than "Abou Ben Adhem" and Sir Walter Scott. Then, as he said in a full-scale profile of him in *Life* magazine in 1967 when he was visiting Ireland on a Guggenheim fellowship, "Suddenly, I wanted to read . . . It took me three years to work my way through English and American literature and various foreign literatures."

After he was graduated Phi Beta Kappa from Columbia, he studied for a year at Heidelberg and then grew his first bear and spent a year at Clare College, Cambridge, on a fellowship. When he returned to the United States, he sought work as an advertising copywriter on Madison Avenue (and what an inconceivable image that summons, that wild man among the gray flannel manikins), but they wouldn't have him. And so he began to teach, and to write poetry, and to fall in and out of love affairs and marriages. In the last thirty years, he has taught from one end of the country to the other—hitting such universities as Harvard, Chicago, Princeton, Brown, and California along the way—with numerous jaunts abroad as a visiting lecturer. Currently, he is one of fourteen regents professors at the University of Minnesota where he teaches "what I want" (starting in March: Dante and Christian origins in the Middle Ages) under the title of humanities.

He lives in a solid old frame house in Minneapolis that he must love, judging from the pride with which he describes it in some of his poetry. He and his third wife, Kate, who is twenty-five years younger than he is, have a daughter, Martha, whom Berryman calls Twissy-Pits, Twiss for short ("What's wrong with that?" he says. "Don't ask me to account for it, why should I? My wife calls her Buttsy-Do. Isn't that weird?"), and Kate is expecting a second child in June. Berryman's son by his second marriage lives with his mother.

Slumped in his rumpled clothes (he has said of how he dresses, "You know how long it takes me to buy a shirt? Two minutes—I just go in and buy the first one I see"), he considers the question about that subtle relationship between Henry Pussy-cat and himself.

"Well, now, we could be very fancy about that. One of the best fictional portraits is *Madame Bovary* by Flaubert. I just recently reread it and it knocked me flat on my back. It's absolutely wonderful. Anyway, years after it was written, Flaubert said to somebody about it, 'Madame Bovary, c'est moi.' So, at my level, 'Henry, c'est moi' . . . but only in the context of the story. Hmm?

"Then people bug me about the name, 'Henry.' Does it come from *The Red Badge of Courage*? They know I wrote a book on Stephen Crane. Ah, does it come from *A Farewell to Arms*? I've written about Hemingway—like everybody else. It's ridiculous.

"I'll let you into a deep and boring secret. One time, my second wife and I were walking along Hennepin Avenue in Minneapolis on our way to a bar and we got to talking about names. We talked about names that we liked, then we talked about names that we didn't like. And she decided that Henry was the most awful name of all and I decided that Mabel was the woman's name we didn't want to hear again. So, we'd only been married a few months, and we were very cozy, and I became Henry and she became Mabel.

"So when I wrote the first 'Dream Song,' which I later killed in place of the one that is first now, Mabel was in it, and Henry. Well, Mabel was never mentioned again, but Henry survived, and later on my wife would complain about that. In fact, she complained about several things and the marriage only lasted two years."

Most of Berryman's poetry before *The Dream Songs* was collected a few years ago in a volume titled *Short Poems*, except for one long, lovely sonnet sequence he wrote in the early forties to chart the unhappy course of an adulterous love affair. That was only published a few years ago under the title *Berryman's Sonnets*.

If you read those early poems now and then you get right into *The Dream Songs*, you are struck with what a revolution occurred of his poetry. Everything changed—style, subject matter, language—from a rather traditional kind of poetry to the most radical invention.

"I like the way you put that," the poet says, and then wryly adds, "and maybe there's some truth to it. Anyway, like all young poets, I aimed to become 'Poet One!' Yeah, but at a certain point, I thought, fuck it! And I got interested in Anne Bradstreet (the wife of the colonial governor of Massachusetts in the seventeenth century who is considered America's first native poet) and her poems, and in *Homage to Mistress Bradstreet*, I served as a sort of agent provocateur, and I pronounced my blessings.

"And then I got interested in Henry, and this was a character with all kinds of problems, and he could really make you sweat! I spent thirteen years with him. But this doesn't explain the reason for it, though, which was completely self-obsession. It's all about me . . . and God . . . and . . . well, that's still going on."

Did he have any notion when he began the first Henry poem that he was locking himself into a form and a style?

"No, no. Oh, no! *Homage to Mistress Bradstreet* began, in 1948, as a poem of, I figured, about fifty lines. But I read and read and thought and accumulated and, really, only got going on it about five years later. Then I wrote the whole thing in two months and it's not very long, only about 450 lines, but that's different from fifty lines.

"So when I got into the Dream Songs, I had a double think, says Henry. I expected a fairly short poem, but it was open-ended, and then I didn't know how to end it and it took me thirteen years, and that's scary, and it's not healthy."

It was to be a short poem, then?

"Yeah. But I don't like the term 'short poem' because what is short? Robert Penn Warren has a wonderful definition of a short story, it goes like this: 'A short story is a story which is short, namely, shorter than some other stories.' Isn't that good? That's what a short poem is.

"I use the term 'scale poem.' Namely, a poem designed on a certain scale, whereby there's a geography which you don't have in a short poem, and there's an interpolation of various characters, which you don't have in a short poem, and there's a commitment over a long period of time, months or years. It's a working definition, don't you think?"

I mention that, when you read the Dream Songs in sequence, you get that feeling of building characterization that a good novel gives you. "Well, that's interesting, because my beloved friend and sort of hero, Saul Bellow, if a friend can be considered a hero, once said about the Bradstreet poem, which is only twenty pages, that it's the equivalent of a five hundred-page psychological novel—and that means psychological novel on his scale, which is heavily symbolic."

How did he dispose of Henry? "I wiped him out. Even though he won all of those awards, and the Pulitzer Prize, which is never given for hopelessly experimental work. Even though it became very agreeable with my bank account so that my banker is very friendly with me.

"But to this business of getting rid of Henry. I killed him in the first song of the fourth book, the thing I called *His Toy, His Dream, His Rest*, and I called that Opus posthumous No. 1 ("Op. posth. 1"), so nobody would think I was kidding, and so on up to Opus posthumous No. 14. He's dead for fourteen poems.

"The *Harvard Advocate* did an article on me several years ago and one of those bright boys asked me if, with these 'Opus posthumous' poems, I had in mind Odysseus's descent into the underworld, and I said," dramatic pause, "No . . . But that was one way of getting rid of Henry."

As the Henry poems developed, what was his intention for them? "It developed quite rapidly. The idea was, sort of, the way Whitman puts his idea about *Leaves of Grass*. The idea is to record a personality, to make him visible, put him through tests, see what the hell he's up to, and through him, the country—and to commit him to his country.

"We have an atrocious government, very bad, and yet this country is magnificent. My people have been here since before the Revolution, except for one great-great-grandmother. So while I agree that our record as a nation is atrocious, it makes you sweat, still you have to be committed to this idea and its possibilities. I don't blame the kids, though, for waking up sweating."

How does he feel about the youth revolution? "I don't like their life-style, but I feel very friendly toward them. I feel life is a revolution, you have to get in and sweat or else you're wasting your time, which is the only thing we have. So I like the kids; many of them work hard.

"But their life-style . . . well, rock is contemptible, and so on, and so on. And I don't like women dressing like men. When Brooks Brothers put in a woman's department—I'm an old fogey—I thought, 'This is the beginning of the end!' And I'm a male chauvinist to the extent that I feel women ought to perform the domestic functions."

With *The Dream Songs* gone, and an eighteen-month dry spell behind you, how did you get started again? "Well, one morning at the end of January, a year ago, I wrote one line. It said, 'I fell in love with a girl,' and then I wrote a second line, and a third and fourth, and it was unrhymed.

"I've been studying Emily Dickinson very closely recently, for no reason whatever, and I was fascinated with what can be done with unrhymed verse, though I use longer lines than she does. Then I wrote another line, and pretty soon I had a poem, and I was grateful, and I put it in the mail right away.

"I wrote another one in the afternoon, and the next day, and I wrote a whole goddamned book in about five weeks, not planning ever to write a short poem again. Much depends, you see, on how you see yourself. I saw myself as an epic poet. I hadn't written a short poem in twenty-two years, so I was bowled over by this happening."

It sounds as if you have little control over the pacing of your creativity? "That's an interesting word. Control? Not much, no. I see myself as a sort of medium. Things occur to you and you put them down."

Is there any more to the notion of himself as "medium"? "I interpret that as . . . well, I have always seen myself as . . . somebody trying to be useful to our effort here in this country, to the American effort.

"Yet, sometimes I shame this notion. In 1968, Congress voted me a ten-thousand-dollar grant as part of some federal arts program and a reporter called me to ask if I expected to get it. I said, 'Expected it? I never even heard of the goddamn thing!' And this was spread all over the country and some guy on the floor of the House said, 'Why do we give money to these jerks when they've never even heard of the program?' and pretty soon the agency was wiped out.

"Well, this means that some of my friends, and some of the younger people who need it, won't get a very useful ten thousand bucks. So I'm very ashamed of myself. That is, I hadn't adjusted to this notion of myself as a sounding board. Anybody lifted out of obscurity has to be goddamned careful what he says and there's no excuse for me because that was three years ago and I had been in a very special position for a number of years."

Does he feel the writing of poetry can be taught? "That's a problem. Let me say that you can be useful, there's no doubt about that. Two of my kids, one at Princeton and one at Iowa, W. S. Merwin and W. D. Snodgrass, are now valuable characters. I was of real service to Merwin. To Snodgrass? Well, he got a charge out of my admiration, and that helps.

"Snodgrass is a wonderful guy, a wild man. I'll tell you a story about him, off the record . . ." And he tells a story. A Few months ago, Snodgrass also had a wonderful story to tell about Berryman—also off the record.

Back, as always, to *The Dream Songs*. There seems to be a definite change of attitude and style between the *77 Dream Songs* and *His Toy, His Dream, His Rest*, or is that my imagination? "No, many people have remarked on the gain in the lucidity in the second volume. But it's not an unmixed gain. In general, I would say that it takes about three songs in books 5 and 6 and 7 to get done what I was doing in one in the first volume.

"So it's a gain and a loss. The loss is of conciseness. The whole point of writing today, it seems to me, is to be just the business of putting things short, just as short as possible. I could tell you many stories about that—I'll tell you one. Kipling was once asked by someone how he wrote a story. He said, 'I hold it up and let the wind blow through it and, if there's anything left, I publish it.' Isn't that good? That's the way I feel.

"I'm very busy now. I won't have any rest for three or four years. I've got about fifty poems done for my next book, *Delusions*, and that's a very good title. And we're doing a collection of my critical prose. And there are other poems. Well, they'll be bringing out about four volumes of my writings in the next couple of years."

And the final formal question I can ask before he tires of answering any more. At the end of *Love & Fame*, there is a cycle of moving poetry of worship and praise of God; does this mean he has recovered his faith?

"That's true. As a boy, after my father died, I lost my faith. But I never lost it in the sense, of . . . ah, I don't like the word 'God.' But I never thought he concerned himself with individual life, and that's the kind of belief I had as a child, before my father's death, and which all prayer is based on. I have recovered that sense.

"How did it happen? I underwent a conversion experience in the hospital about a year ago. I was there for alcoholism; it was a rescue operation. It happened in the morning, about a quarter to twelve. I was in a crisis, and a man came to my rescue, a mortal enemy, a Protestant clergyman, and in the afternoon I saw the messenger, and . . ."

Messenger? "I saw this man who rescued me as an agent," Berryman says, earnestly. "It's a long story, there's no way to put it shortly. My psychiatrist had given me permission to leave the hospital to do a lecture on the Holy Gospel and that permission was rescinded at the beginning of group therapy in the morning. And I was shocked, and rebellious. I said to the group leader, I can get in a taxi and go teach my course, and you the psychiatrist have no power to keep me here.

"But I wasn't peaceful with that, and I sweated over it. The nationwide student strike was on[1] and the university administration put everybody on their conscience about whether to conduct their classes or not, which is no way to run a university. I admire the [university] president very much, but in this case he was lacking.

"Well, I was saying to somebody, 'I don't know how I can go,' and then somebody, this clergyman, said, 'I'll take your course.' So it was quite plain to me that . . . well, this was some kind of intervention. And I recovered my faith in that sense of a personal God.

"But that's enough of that," he says, reaching over to turn off my tape recorder, sensing perhaps that I want to push further into this unusual recovery of faith. We drink and chat, and soon it is growing dark outside, nearing the time for him to read in the university's William Vaughn Moody lecture series.

It's time to leave. For my last words on this visit with the poet, the best thing seems to be to quote from "Dream Song 366":

These songs are not meant to be understood, you understand.
They are only meant to terrify & comfort.

Note

1. On April 3, 1970, President Richard M. Nixon announced the expansion of the Vietnam War into Cambodia, resulting in considerable student protests, including sit-ins, marches, and demonstrations, and the fatal demonstration at Kent State on May 2 wherein students burned down the ROTC building. Responding to the unrest, the National Guard opened fire on the demonstrators, which led to the death of four students.—Ed.

Appendix: A Recommended
Selected Berryman

Of the four *Selected Poems* published to date (John Berryman [1972], Kevin Young [2004], Michael Hofmann [2004], and Daniel Swift [2014, rev. ed. 2016]), all are problematic. Some provide editorial reasons for their selections—in the case of Swift's original edition, no Dream Songs were included as a separate, collected volume accompanied his selection's initial release; a revised edition of the selected with several Dream Songs appeared, almost apologetically, two years later. Berryman's selection, published posthumously in the United Kingdom by Faber & Faber in 1972, is also unsatisfactory in that, like Young's selection, it chooses many early poems and sonnets—of the latter, Young retains fifty-five or roughly half the sequence, far too many—and nothing post *The Dream Songs*.

While Berryman's and Swift's selections of the early work are more judicious, and exhibit admirable restraint, both occasionally leave out some of Berryman's best material. *Homage to Mistress Bradstreet* is, rightly I think, reprinted in its entirety in Berryman, Young, and Swift, and unforgivably truncated to seven sections by Hofmann, whose slight, ninety-two-page selection also includes a total of ten short poems early and late, twenty-one sonnets, and fifty-eight Dream Songs. Indeed, in all the selected volumes, the Dream Songs are woefully underrepresented while, conversely—particularly in Berryman's case—some of the least memorable early poems are overrepresented, almost as rescue. It should be the easiest thing in the world to include the dozen core Dream Songs (1, 4, 5, 15, 29, 46, 75, 89, 145, 366, 384, and 385). Young's selection of Songs is arguably the most representative of the best Songs, as it manages to exclude only 5 and 89. Hofmann's idiosyncratic selection leaves out 5, 15, and 384, and includes many less successful Songs, arguably those poems that best support the view of Berryman as *poète maudit* and hopeless alcoholic. Swift, for his part, manages, untenably, to overlook 5, 46, 75, 77, 89, 145, 366, and 384 of the Songs. Berryman is far too generous with his selection of later songs. This shouldn't be surprising, and is perhaps forgivable, given that most writers believe their best work to be their most recent. He also likely had other personal reasons for their inclusion.

Berryman's selection, made in 1969–70, intentionally omits any poems post–*Dream Songs*, as it was intended to be published simultaneously with the first UK edition of *Love & Fame*. As noted, Berryman's selection stops at 1968, while Young's and Swift's cannot seem to agree on which poems merit inclusion apart from an obvious handful. Young has the indefensible habit of truncating "Eleven Addresses to the Lord" and "Opus Dei," while Swift at least has the considerable merit of his reprinting in their entirety the two sequences. Both are completely absent in Hofmann.

Henry's Fate and Other Poems 1967–1972 is generally overlooked—the poems are not included in Charles Thornbury's *Collected Poems 1937–1971*, for example, and only Young sees fit to include any of them—largely because *Henry's Fate* is comprised almost entirely of published and previously unpublished Dream Songs and other uncollected poems and draft fragments, compiled by scholar and biographer John Haffenden.

Therefore, presumptuously, I offer my own *Selected Poems*, one that, with rare exception, requires reference to just four volumes: the *Collected Poems*, *The Dream Songs*, *Henry's Fate*, and Young's *Selected*. I have been perhaps too generous with my selection of Dream Songs and Berryman's late poems, and too restrictive with the early poems and sonnets, displaying my own preferences. My selection is admittedly inclusive, particularly by Hofmann's standards. As he notes, "any selection of Berryman has, to some extent, to oppose itself to the worst tendencies of the poet. There will always be a little denial in it, and a little false innocence" (Hofmann 2004, viv).

Here, then, is my small measure of denial and false innocence.

The Contents:

Early poems: Note on E. A. Robinson, Elegy: Hart Crane, To Bhain Campbell, Epilogue

The Dispossessed: Winter Landscape, The Traveller, The Ball Poem, Parting as Descent, The Animal Trainer (i and ii), The Moon and the Night and the Man, Canto Amor, The Song of the Demented Priest, A Professor's Song, The Song of the Tortured Girl, The Lightning, New Year's Eve, The Dispossessed

Berryman's Sonnets (or, as Thornbury presents them, *Sonnets to Chris*): 1, 7, 9, 10, 11, 12, 13, 22, 23, 25, 29, 32, 33, 36, 37, 43, 47, 65, 67, 71, 75, 77, 80, 97, 101, 106, 107, 109, 110, 114, and 115 as well as the Dream Song included as an introduction/epigraph

The Cage, Elegy, for Alun Lewis, From *The Black Book*: the will, waiting

Homage to Mistress Bradstreet in its entirety

Of Isaac Rosenfeld

His Thought Made Pockets & the Plane Buckt: Venice, 182—, The Black Book (i), The Black Book (iii), The Poet's Final Instructions, A Sympathy, a Welcome, Note to Wang Wei

77 Dream Songs: 1, 3 A Stimulant for an Old Beast, 4, 5, 6 A Capital at the Wells, 8, 11, 13, 14, 16, 17, 18 A Strut for Roethke, 19, 22, 23 The Lay of Ike, 24, 25, 26, 27, 28 Snow Line, 29, 31, 33, 34, 36, 37 Three around the Old Gentleman, 39, 40, 41, 42, 44, 45, 46, 48, 51, 52 Silent Song, 53, 54, 55, 56, 63, 67, 68, 69, 74, 75, 76 Henry's Confession, and 77

Formal Elegy

His Toy, His Dream, His Rest: 78–91 (the entirety of Opus Posthumous), 94, 95, 96, 97, 108, 119, 125, 126 A Thurn, 127, 129, 133, 136, 137, 142, 143, 145, 147, 150, 151, 153, 155, 156, 171, 177, 178, 179, 184, 190, 191, 192, 195, 197, 200, 202, 203, 204, 207, 219 So long? Stevens, 220, 225 Pereant qui ante nos nostra dixerunt, 233 Cantatrice, 235, 239, 242, 244, 256, 259, 260, 263, 264, 265, 266, 269, 274, 275, 279, 282, 283, 285, 287, 298, 303 Three in Heaven I Hope, 305, 308 An Instruction to Critics, 309, 310, 320, 325, 338, 341 The Dialogue, aet. 51, 342, 353, 354, 355 Slattery's, in Ballsbridge, 356, 359, 366, 368, 370, 372, 373, 374, 375 His Helplessness, 378, 379, 380 From the French Hospital in New York, 901, 383, 384, and 385

Love & Fame: Cadenza on Garnette, Freshman Blues, Images of Elspeth, Two Organs, Olympus, Nowhere, Recovery, Message, Have a Genuine American Horror & Mist on the Rocks, Damned, Of Suicide, Despair, The Hell Poem, Heaven, Eleven Addresses to the Lord

Delusions etc. of John Berryman: Opus Dei, Washington in Love, Beethoven Triumphant, Your Birthday in Wisconsin You are 140, Drugs Alcohol Little Sister, In Memoriam (1914–1953), Scholars at the Orchid Pavilion, Tampa Stomp, Old Man Goes South Again Alone, He Resigns, Henry's Understanding, Certainty Before Lunch, The Facts & Issues, King David Dances

Henry's Fate & Other Poems: An Afternoon Visit, Henry's Fate, Glistening, Henry freed himself from money, Phase Four

Works on John Berryman

Bibliography

Arpin, Gary Q. *John Berryman: A Reference Guide*. Boston, MA: G. K. Hall, 1976.

Kelly, Richard J., ed. *John Berryman: A Checklist*. New Jersey: Scarecrow Press, 1972.

Kelly, Richard J. *John Berryman's Personal Library: A Catalogue Biography*. New York: Peter Lang Publishing Inc., 1999.

Stefanik, Ernest C., Jr. *John Berryman: A Descriptive Bibliography*. Pittsburg, PA: University of Pittsburgh Press, 1974.

Biography

Bawer, Bruce. *The Middle Generation: The Lives and Poetry of Delmore Schwartz, Randall Jarrell, John Berryman and Robert Lowell*. New Haven, CT: Archon Books, 1986.

Haffenden, John. *The Life of John Berryman*. London: Routledge, 1982.

Halliday, E. M. *John Berryman and the Thirties: A Memoir*. Amherst: University of Massachusetts Press, 1988.

Mariani, Paul. *Dream Song: The Life of John Berryman*. New York: Paragon House, 1989.

Samway, Patrick. *John Berryman and Robert Giroux: A Publishing Friendship*. Notre Dame, IN: Nortre Dame University Press, 2020.

Simpson, Eileen. *Poets in Their Youth*. New York: Random House, 1982.

Selected Criticism

Arpin, Gary Q. *The Poetry of John Berryman*. Port Washington, NY: Kennikat Press, 1978.

Bloom, Harold, ed. *John Berryman (Bloom's Modern Critical Views)*. New York: Chelsea House, 1989.

Bloom, James D. *The Stock of Available Reality: R. P. Blackmur and John Berryman.* Lewisburg, PA: Bucknell University Press, 1984.

Coleman, Philip. *John Berryman's Public Vision: Relocating the scene of disorder.* Dublin: University College Dublin Press, 2014.

Coleman, Philip, and Peter Campion. *John Berryman: Centenary Essays.* New York: Peter Lang Publishers, 2017.

Coleman, Philip, and Philip McGowan, eds. *"After Thirty Falls": New Essays on John Berryman.* New York: Rodopi, 2007.

Connaroe, Joel. *John Berryman: An Introduction to the Poetry.* New York: Columbia University Press, 1977.

Cooper, Brendan. *Dark Airs: John Berryman and the Spiritual Politics of Cold War American Poetry.* New York: Peter Lang, 2009.

Dodson, Samuel Fisher. *Berryman's Henry: Living at the Intersection of Need and Art.* New York, NY: Rodopi, 2006.

Gustavsson, Bo. *Soul Under Stress: A Study of the Poetics of John Berryman's "Dream Songs."* Sweden: Academiae Ubsaliensis, 1984.

Haffenden, John. *John Berryman: A Critical Commentary.* London: Palgrave Macmillan, 1980.

Kelly, Richard J., and Alan Lathrop. *Recovering Berryman: Essays on a Poet.* Ann Arbor: University of Michigan Press, 1993.

Kirsch, Adam. *The Wounded Surgeon: Confession and Transformation in Six American Poets.* New York: W. W. Norton & Company, 2005.

Linebarger, J. M. *John Berryman (Twayne's United States Authors Series).* New York: Twayne Publishers, 1974.

Mancini, Joseph. *The Berryman Gestalt: Therapeutic Strategies in the Poetry of John Berryman.* New York: Garland, 1987.

Matteson, Stephen. *Berryman and Lowell: The Art of Losing.* London: Palgrave Macmillan, 1988.

Rogers, Tom. *God of Rescue: John Berryman and Christianity.* New York: Peter Lang, 2011.

Stefanik, Ernest C., Jr., and Cis Stefanik, eds. *Once in a Sycamore: A Garland for John Berryman.* Derry, PA: Rook Press, 1976.

Thomas, Harry, ed. *Berryman's Understanding: Reflections on the Poetry of John Berryman.* Boston, MA: Northeastern University Press, 1988.

Index

Whitman, Charles, 78
Whitman, Walt, xiii, xvi, 12, 101, 114,
    129, 130, 155; *Song of Myself*, xvi,
    114, 128, 129
Whittier, John Greenleaf, 12
Wilbur, Richard, 43, 104, 106, 135;
    "Walking to Sleep," 104
Williams, Flossie, 76
Williams, William Carlos, xviii, 12, 76,
    80n3, 102; *Of Asphodel, That
    Greeny Flower*, 102
Wilson, Edmund, 20, 24, 136, 142
Winters, Yvor, xviii, 79
Winthrop, John, 14
Wittke, Carl, xix; *Tambo and Bones: A
    History of the Minstrel Stage*, xix
Wolfe, Thomas, 126, 127
Wordsworth, William, 25

World War I, 126
World War II, 6, 7, 29, 37, 108, 112, 125
Wright, James, 94, 99

Yale University, 81
"Yankee Doodle," 54
Yeats, William Butler, xiii, xiv, xv, xxx,
    27, 28, 29, 30, 46, 49, 54, 55, 57,
    64, 72, 77, 86, 87, 90, 91, 101,
    108, 109, 117, 124, 126, 140; "The
    Choice," 117; the "Crazy Jane"
    poems, 108; "In Memory of
    Major Robert Gregory," 30, 77;
    Last Poems, xiv; "The Tower," 46;
    A Vision, 46; *Words for Music
    Perhaps and Other Poems*, 46
Yesenin, Sergei, 116
"Yvonne," 105

About the Editor

Photo by Robin Adorno

Eric Hoffman is the author of several books of poetry, most recently *This Thin Mean: New Selected Poems* (2019), *Presence of Life* (2018), and *Losses of Life* (2018). The revised and expanded edition of his biography of poet George Oppen, *Oppen: A Narrative*, was published in 2018. His translations of the haiku of Ozaki Hōsai have been published in *Otoliths*, *Frogpond*, and *Chrysanthemum*. He lives in Connecticut with his wife and son.

Printed in the United States
by Baker & Taylor Publisher Services